REVISE FOR
NEAB
MODULAR
science

NIGEL ENGLISH

HIGHER

Heinemann Educational Publishers
Halley Court, Jordan Hill, Oxford, OX2 8EJ
a division of Reed Educational & Professional Publishing Ltd

Heinemann is a registered trademark of Reed Educational & Professional Publishing Ltd.

OXFORD FLORENCE PRAGUE MADRID ATHENS
MELBOURNE · AUCKLAND KUALA LUMPUR SINGAPORE
TOKYO IBADAN NAIROBI KAMPALA JOHANNESBURG
GABORONE PORTSMOUTH NH (USA) CHICAGO
MEXICO CITY SAO PAULO

© Nigel English, 1997

Copyright notice
All rights reserved. No part of this publication may be reproduced, stored in a retrieval system, or transmitted in any form or by any means, electronic, mechanical, photocopying, recording, or otherwise without either the prior written permission of the Publishers or a licence permitting restricted copying in the United Kingdom issued by the Copyright Licensing Agency Ltd, 90 Tottenham Court Road, London W1P 9HE.

First published 1997

ISBN 0 435 10162 5

01 00 99 98
10 9 8 7 6 5 4 3

Edited on-screen by Sarah Ware

Designed and typeset by Ken Vail Graphic Design

Illustrated by Graeme Morris (Ken Vail Graphic Design)

Cover design by Keith Shaw, Threefold Design

Cover artwork by Stephen May

Printed and bound in the UK by Bath Press

Acknowledgements
The authors and publishers would like to thank the following for permission to use photographs:

p.1 Tony Stone Images/Tim Davis,
p.41 Sygma/Noboru Mashimoto,
p.85 Tony Stone Images/Steve Powell.

The publishers have made every effort to trace the copyright holders, but if they have inadvertently overlooked any, they will be pleased to make the necessary arrangements at the first opportunity.

Picture research by Natalie Stewart

From the author
I would particularly like to thank my family, Chris, Philip and Katharine, for their help and forbearance in writing this book.

Contents

How to use this book   iv

AT2 Life Processes and Living Things   1

    Humans as Organisms   2
       Questions   10

    Maintenance of Life   12
       Questions   20

    Environment*   22
       Questions   30

    Inheritance and Selection*   32
       Questions   40

AT3 Materials and their Properties   41

    Metals   42
       Questions   48

    Earth Materials   50
       Questions   62

    Patterns of Chemical Change*   64
       Questions   73

    Structures and Bonding*   74
       Questions   84

AT4 Physical Processes   85

    Energy   86
       Questions   94

    Electricity   96
       Questions   106

    Forces*   108
       Questions   119

    Waves and Radiation*   120
       Questions   132

Answers   134

    Module tests and terminal exam questions   134

    End of spread questions   147

* against a module denotes it is a module assessed only by terminal examination.

How to use this book

This revision guide contains the 12 modules which form the NEAB Modular Science scheme. They cover the Higher Tier of the syllabus.

You will need to learn and understand these six modules for module tests during the course:

AT2	**AT3**	**AT4**
Humans as Organisms	*Metals*	*Energy*
Maintenance of Life	*Earth Materials*	*Electricity*

You will need to learn and understand these six modules for the terminal exam:

AT2	**AT3**	**AT4**
Environment	*Patterns of Chemical Change*	*Forces*
Inheritance and Selection	*Structures and Bonding*	*Waves and Radiation*

You will also have to revise certain areas of the first group of six modules above for the terminal exam. These are very clearly marked by a vertical black line in the margin of the text, as shown here.

As you approach a module test or the terminal exam in your course, you can organise your work like this.

> Work through the module or modules you need. Pace yourself – do one double page spread at a time and look back at the notes you have made in class on this topic.

> Try the questions at the end of every double page spread to check that you really understand the topic.

> Check your answers under *Answers to end of spread questions* (page 147). Go back over anything you find difficult.

> Do the test style questions at the end of each module. These are in the same style as the questions you will have to do in the real end of module test or terminal exam, so they are very good practice.

> Check your answers against the *Answers to module tests and terminal exam questions* (page 134). In terminal exam style questions take care to cover all the points needed to get full marks. Go back over areas you find difficult.

When you are revising for the terminal exams you will also need to revise the material marked with a vertical black line in the other six modules. Revise these alongside modules in the same AT. For example, as you work through *Structures and Bonding* or *Patterns of Chemical Change* in AT3 it would be a good idea to revise the terminal exam material in *Metals* or *Earth Materials* at the same time.

The words in **bold** are all key words you need to know. A useful revision idea would be to build up your own glossary of these as you work through the book. For quick reference to a word or topic use the *Index* at the back of the book.

AT2

Life Processes and Living Things

Humans as Organisms

Maintenance of Life

Environment

Inheritance and Selection

Cells

Cells make up animals and plants. Most animal cells have:

- a nucleus that controls what the cell does
- cytoplasm in which the chemical reactions take place
- a cell membrane which controls the passage of substances in and out of the cell.

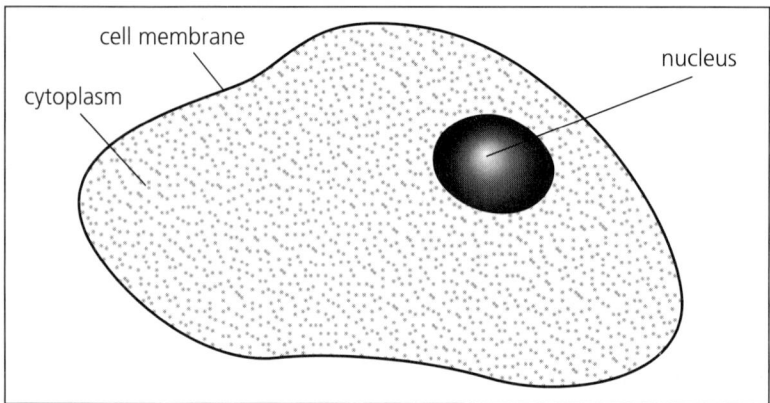

A typical animal cell

Specialised cells may group together to do a job (e.g. muscles and glands). These are called **tissues**.

Organs (e.g. the heart and liver) are made up from tissues. Organs combine to form **systems** (e.g. the circulatory system and the nervous system).

Eating and digestion

The human digestive system (often called the gut) includes the gullet, stomach, liver, pancreas, small intestine and large intestine. Its job is to turn food we eat into a form which can be used by the body cells. Its tissues include **muscles** to move food along and **glands** to make the enzymes which digest the food.

Much of the food we eat is insoluble (e.g. starches, proteins and fats). This food needs to be digested in the gut so that the large insoluble lumps are broken down into small soluble molecules which can be absorbed into and carried by the blood. This breakdown of larger molecules into smaller ones is speeded up (catalysed) by **enzymes**.

Enzymes break down starch (carbohydrates) to sugars; proteins to amino acids; and fats (lipids) to fatty acids and glycerol. The enzymes are produced at different points in the digestive system.

The soluble molecules are absorbed into the blood through the wall of the small intestine. Some food cannot be digested and this passes into the large intestine. Here, most of the water is absorbed from it. The remainder passes out of the body as faeces. Most of the faeces is indigestible food and it leaves the body by the anus.

 *Help*

The names of the enzymes are related to the food that they work on, so:

- carbohydrases break down carbohydrates
- proteases break down proteins
- lipases break down lipids (fats).

Humans as Organisms

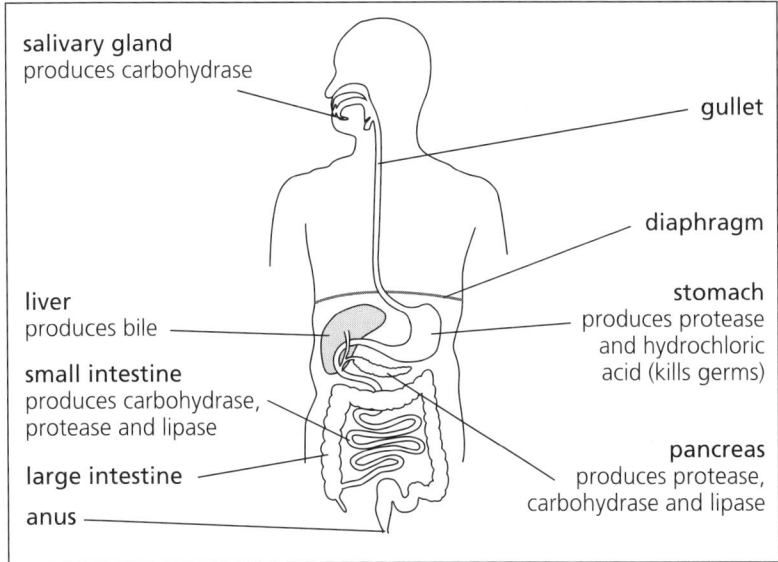

The human digestive system

Bile is produced in the liver and stored in the gall bladder. It has two functions.

- As food enters the small intestine bile neutralises the acid added to it in the stomach. It makes conditions in the small intestine alkaline, allowing the enzymes to work there more effectively.
- It breaks down large fat globules into smaller ones, resulting in a larger surface area for enzymes to work on. This is known as **emulsification**.

Diffusion

The soluble molecules in the small intestine pass into our bloodstream by **diffusion**. This is the movement of particles from a more concentrated solution to one of lower concentration. The blood circulating around the small intestine while a meal is being digested has a lower concentration of simple sugars, amino acids, mineral ions and water than the mixture flowing through the small intestine. The molecules therefore diffuse out through the walls of the small intestine.

This diffusion is helped by the structure of the small intestine walls. They are covered by millions of small, finger-like projections called **villi**. These help the food diffuse through the wall because they:

- slow down the passage of food through the small intestine
- provide a very large surface area for the absorption to take place.

 **Help**

Why is a large surface area important?
This speeds up the rate of absorption because molecules can cross the boundary into the bloodstream across a very wide area instead of a small one. Think of it as a crowd running across an open field instead of trying to crush through a gate!

 **Questions**

1. Make a table showing where the different enzymes are made and what they do.
2. The enzymes in the small intestine need alkaline conditions to work in. What conditions do the stomach enzymes need to work in?
3. Explain why emulsifying fat droplets helps the lipase enzymes to work on them.

Breathing and respiration

A 16 year-old has breathed in and out about 75 million times since birth. Why? The answer is to provide oxygen to release energy from food and to get rid of the carbon dioxide produced.

This process is called **aerobic respiration**. All living cells in the body respire. The food which is used in respiration is glucose, a type of sugar and one of the small molecules produced by the digestive system from the complex food that you eat. During aerobic respiration chemical reactions use the glucose and oxygen to release energy. The by-products (waste products) are carbon dioxide and water.

glucose + oxygen → carbon dioxide + water + energy

This energy is used:

- to allow body muscles to contract
- to keep body temperature constant
- to build large useful substances from the small digested ones, for use in the body
- for **active transport** of materials across boundaries.

How do we breathe in?

When we breathe in:

- the muscles between the ribs contract so that the ribs move up and out
- at the same time the muscles of the diaphragm contract and it flattens
- the space inside the thorax (chest) increases and the lungs get larger
- this causes a decrease in air pressure in the lungs
- atmospheric pressure outside is higher, so air rushes in.

... and to breathe out, the process happens in reverse.

Help

Active transport
This is the movement of certain particles from a dilute solution to a more concentrated one. This is opposite to the way substances normally diffuse, so energy is needed to make it happen. It is called *active transport* because substances have to be 'pushed' across cell boundaries against the normal flow.

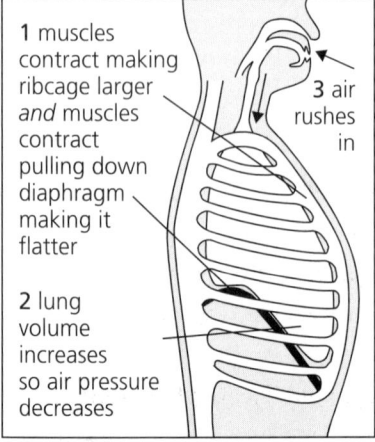

Breathing in

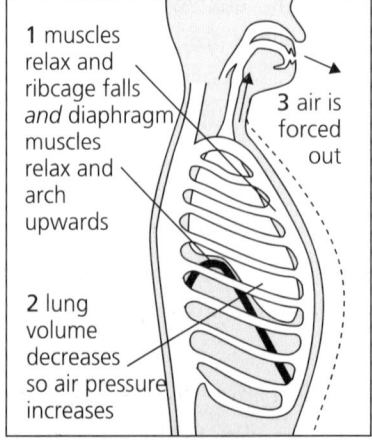

... and breathing out

How are gases exchanged with the blood?

The oxygen we breathe in diffuses into the air sacs (**alveoli**) of the lungs. It then diffuses through the walls of the alveoli into the surrounding blood capillaries. Carbon dioxide diffuses from the blood in the capillaries into the air sacs.

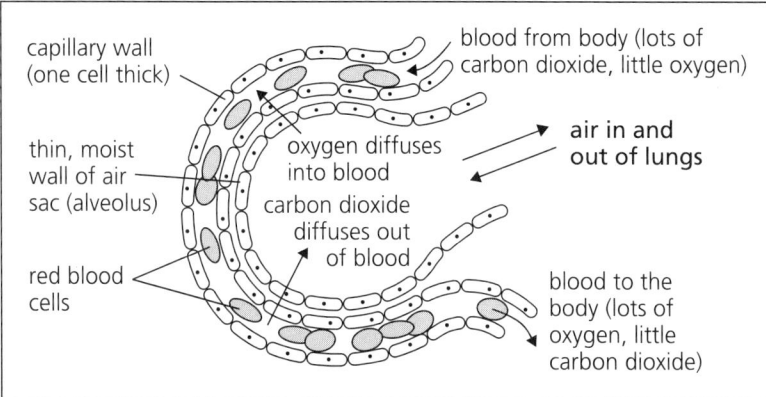

Gas exchange inside the lungs

The lungs have features which make them efficient at exchanging these gases:

- a very large, moist surface area
- a very good capillary blood supply.

Not enough oxygen?

If you run you get tired and your muscles stop contracting efficiently. If there is not enough oxygen for aerobic respiration it slows down and eventually stops.

Anaerobic respiration then takes over. This is respiration without using oxygen. Body cells break down sugar incompletely, into lactic acid, to produce just enough energy for them to work. Lactic acid causes muscle fatigue, so the body can't keep up anaerobic respiration for very long.

When you stop running you still breathe hard. This is because you need the oxygen to break down the lactic acid, releasing carbon dioxide and water. You have built up an **oxygen debt**.

 Questions

1. How does the body get the glucose and oxygen needed for respiration?
2. What happens to the carbon dioxide produced by cells during respiration?
3. Explain why the large surface area provided by the alveoli helps the diffusion of gases.
4. Explain why oxygen diffuses into the blood around the lungs and carbon dioxide diffuses out of it.
5. Write a brief description of what happens to the ribs, diaphragm and lungs when you breathe out.

The circulatory system

This contains **blood** which is made up of red cells, white cells and platelets carried in a fluid called plasma.

Plasma transports:
- carbon dioxide from all cells in the body's organs to the lungs
- digested food (mostly glucose) from the small intestine to organs
- urea from the liver to the kidneys.

The red cells transport:
- oxygen from the lungs to the cells (organs).

Parts of the blood

Red cells have no nucleus but lots of **haemoglobin**. As the blood passes the lungs the haemoglobin picks up the oxygen to form **oxy-haemoglobin**. The oxygen is released as the blood passes respiring cells.

White cells have a nucleus. They help defend the body against microbes (bacteria).

Platelets are small cell fragments. They don't have a nucleus and help to form clots (scabs over cuts).

Plasma is the liquid part of the blood.

The circulation system

There are two circulation systems:
- one to the lungs
- one to the rest of the body.

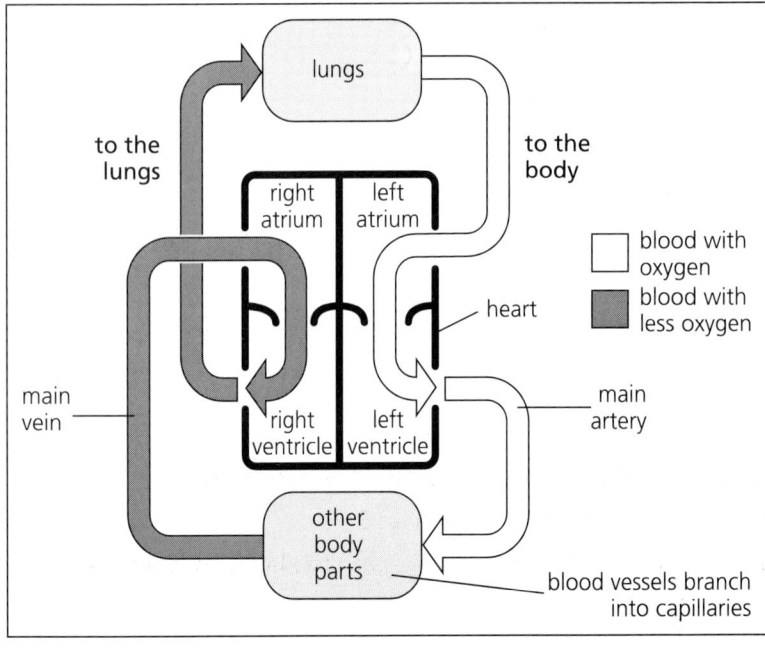

The two circulation systems

The blood enters the two atria of the heart. The muscles of the atria contract and force the blood into the ventricles. The muscles of the ventricles now contract and force the blood out of the heart. This happens on both sides of the heart at the same time.

The different blood vessels

Arteries take blood away from the heart under high pressure. They have thick, muscular, elastic walls so that they don't burst when the heart beats.

Veins bring blood back to the heart under low pressure. They have thinner walls and also have valves along their length to prevent backflow of blood. This is especially important when it is coming back from the feet!

Capillaries are very, very small. Their walls are only one cell thick to allow the exchange of substances with the cells. Oxygen diffuses from the red blood cells in the capillaries to the cells of the body. Carbon dioxide diffuses from these body cells into the blood. Glucose and other useful substances in the plasma diffuse out of the capillary to reach the cells.

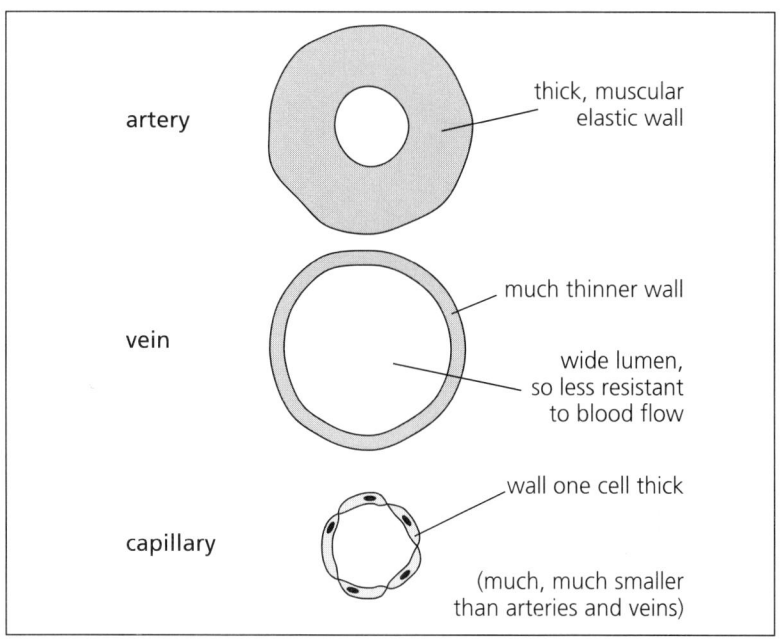

Types of blood vessel

Questions

1. What is transported in the plasma?
2. How is the structure of a vein different to that of an artery?
3. What substances are exchanged between the capillaries and the body cells?
4. What are the functions of white cells, red cells and platelets?
5. Trace the journey of a red cell from entering the left atrium of the heart to its arrival at the right atrium.

Disease

What causes disease? One of the main causes is when **microbes** (micro-organisms), such as certain **bacteria** and **viruses**, get into our body. These cause a whole range of illnesses, from the common cold to meningitis and AIDS.

Microbes

A bacterial cell has cytoplasm surrounded by a cell membrane. All of this is surrounded by a cell wall. It has no nucleus.

Usually the genes which allow a cell to reproduce and make copies of itself are in the nucleus. In bacteria the genes are in the cytoplasm.

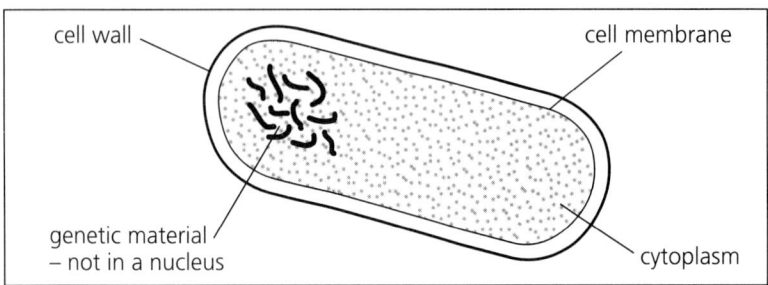

A bacterial cell

Viruses are much smaller than bacteria. They are very different to cells. They have a protein coat surrounding a few genes. They can only reproduce inside the living cells of other organisms.

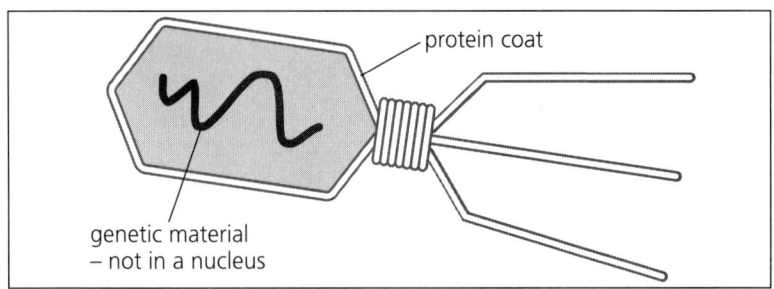

A virus cell

If large numbers of microbes (bacteria or viruses) enter your body then you may catch a disease. The microbes can reproduce very quickly inside your body so that there are soon millions of them. They may produce **toxins** (poisons) which make you feel ill.

If a virus reproduces inside one of your cells the cell will be damaged.

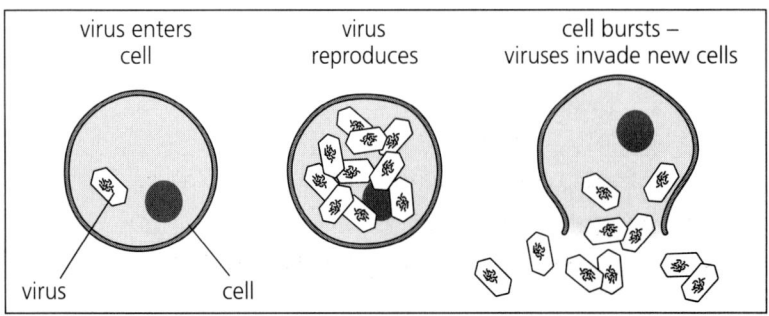

A virus reproducing

Humans as Organisms

Defence against disease

The best defence is to stop the bugs getting in! Your body does this in several ways.

- Your skin acts as protection. If you have a cut microbes can get straight into your blood.
- Blood clots to form a scab. This seals cuts in the skin and stops microbes getting in.
- Air passages in your nose and lungs have a thick, sticky mucus on their surface inside to trap microbes. When you blow your nose or cough you are getting rid of these trapped microbes.
- Your stomach contains acid which can kill most microbes.

If the microbes get into your body then the white cells take action. They:

- ingest (eat) the microbes
- produce **antibodies** which help destroy particular microbes
- produce **antitoxins** to neutralise (get rid of) the poisons.

Once white cells have produced antibodies against a particular microbe then the next time the microbe enters your body they can produce the right antibodies more quickly. Your body is said to be **immune** to the microbe.

Disease and lifestyle

How do you come into contact with harmful microbes? There are two main ways.

- When ill people cough or sneeze they release a fine spray which contains microbes. If you breathe these in you risk catching the same illness.
- If you eat food prepared in unhygienic conditions or drink unclean water then you may become ill. Unclean water is often found when large numbers of people are crowded into one place without proper sewage treatment systems. Dirty water can carry cholera which spreads very fast and is very dangerous.

Questions

1. How are viruses different to other cells?
2. What are toxins and how does the body get rid of them?
3. If microbes do get into the body and disease results, what does the body do about it?
4. How are microbes prevented from getting into the body?
5. Sometimes in dense populations disease is able to spread very fast. Why is this?

Module test questions

1. These sentences are about the blood system. Choose words from the list for each of the spaces **1–4** in the sentences.

   white cells   platelets
   plasma   red cells

   Oxygen is carried by ___1___ in the bloodstream. The liquid part of the blood is called ___2___. Normally the skin keeps microbes out but if the skin is cut, ___3___ help to form blood clots. If microbes do get into the blood, then ___4___ help defend the body.

2. These sentences are about how we breathe in. Choose words from the list for each of the spaces **1–4** in the sentences.

   decreases   increases
   flattens   contracts

   When we breathe in the diaphragm ___1___ as the muscle ___2___. The space inside the thorax ___3___ and the pressure therefore ___4___.

3. This table is about digestion and parts of the gut. Match words from the list with each of the numbers **1–4** in the table.

   large intestine   pancreas
   liver   stomach

	Function of the part
1	produces protease and hydrochloric acid
2	produces bile
3	absorbs much of the water
4	produces protease, carbohydrase and lipase

4. Which *two* of the following statements are correct?
   Bile is a liquid which:
   A breaks down fats to fatty acids and glycerol
   B neutralises stomach acid
   C breaks down fat droplets
   D is produced by the gall bladder
   E works in the large intestine

5. Which *two* of the following statements are correct?
   Arteries are blood vessels which:
   A take blood away from the heart at high pressure
   B have valves along their length
   C have thin, muscular walls
   D have thick, elastic walls
   E return blood to the heart under low pressure

6. This is a diagram of the gut.

   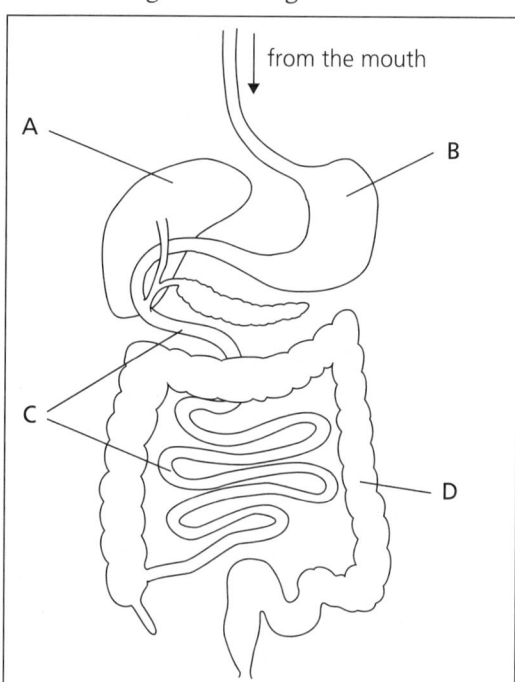

   1. In which part is bile produced?
      A B C D
   2. In which part does most absorption of water take place?
      A B C D
   3. In which part are the products of digestion mainly absorbed?
      A B C D
   4. In which part does fat digestion take place?
      A B C D

7   This is a diagram of the circulatory system.

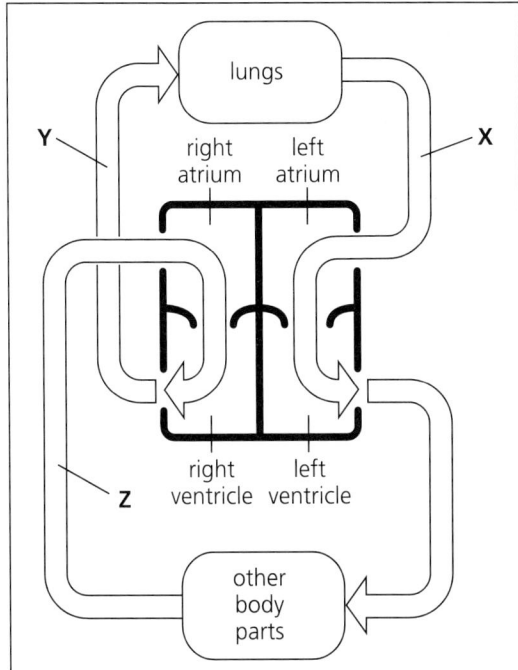

1. The blood vessel labelled X is:

A   an artery carrying oxygenated blood
B   a vein carrying oxygenated blood
C   an artery carrying deoxygenated blood
D   a vein carrying deoxygenated blood

2. The blood vessel labelled Y is:

A   an artery carrying oxygenated blood
B   a vein carrying oxygenated blood
C   an artery carrying deoxygenated blood
D   a vein carrying deoxygenated blood

3. The blood vessel labelled Z has the following features:

A   thick walls and no valves
B   elastic walls and no valves
C   valves and thin walls
D   muscular walls which are thin

4. In order to be efficient capillaries have:

A   valves
B   muscular walls
C   a large surface area
D   elastic tissue

8   These are diagrams of a bacterium and a virus.

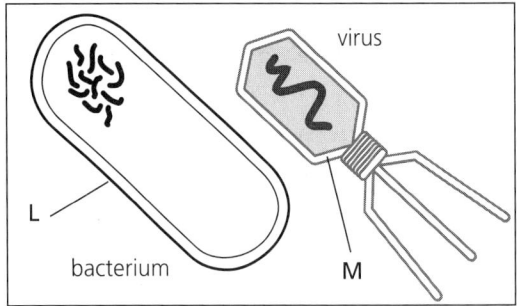

1. The part labelled L is:

A   a cell membrane
B   a protein coat
C   a nuclear membrane
D   a cell wall

2. The part labelled M is:

A   a cell wall
B   a protein coat
C   a cell membrane
D   the nuclear material

3. Which part of the blood helps to destroy microbes?

A   white cells
B   platelets
C   red cells
D   plasma

4. The function of antibodies is to:

A   attack microbes on their own
B   help the blood to clot
C   destroy poisons (toxins)
D   allow the white cells to attack certain microbes

Plant and animal cells

Like animals, plants are made up of cells. Plant and animal cells have the following parts:

- a **nucleus** controlling the cell
- **cytoplasm** where the chemical reactions take place
- a **cell membrane** allowing substances in and out.

Plant cells also have:

- a **cell wall** which maintains a rigid shape
- **chlorophyll** for photosynthesis (in **chloroplasts**)
- a **vacuole** containing cell sap.

Some cells are specialised to do certain work. Groups of cells with the same structure and function are called **tissues**. In plants, xylem cells make up **xylem** tissue which transports water. Different tissues make up an **organ** (e.g. a leaf).

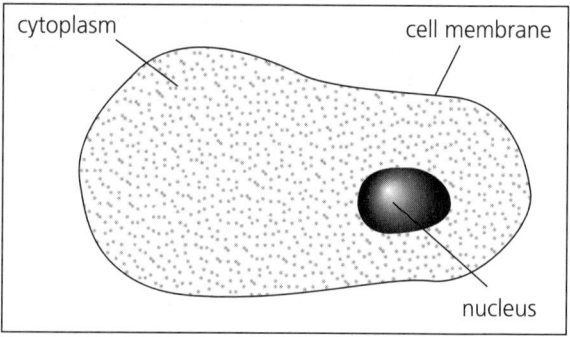
A typical animal cell

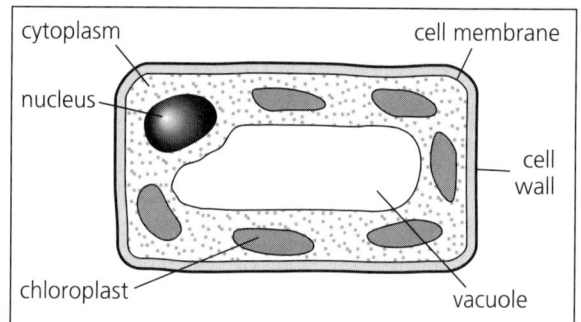
A typical plant cell

How do plants make their food?

Green plants make their food by **photosynthesis**. Light provides the energy for the process:

- green chlorophyll traps (absorbs) the light energy
- the energy is used to make glucose by combining carbon dioxide and water
- oxygen is released as a waste product

$$\text{carbon dioxide} + \text{water} \xrightarrow[\text{chlorophyll}]{\text{light energy}} \text{glucose} + \text{oxygen}$$

The rate of photosynthesis can be limited by:

- low temperature
- shortage of carbon dioxide
- too little light.

If you were growing lots of plants in a greenhouse it might be an idea to heat it. This would work as long as there was enough carbon dioxide and light getting into the greenhouse. If either light or carbon dioxide was in short supply you would be wasting your money because the plants couldn't photosynthesise any faster, no matter how much you heat the greenhouse.

Maintenance of Life

Carbon dioxide

Carbon dioxide enters the plant through holes in the surface of the leaves, called **stomata**. It moves into the leaf by diffusion. It diffuses from a higher concentration of carbon dioxide in the air to an area of lower concentration in the leaf. Inside the leaf it also moves to the cells by diffusion.

 **Help**

One stoma – many stomata.

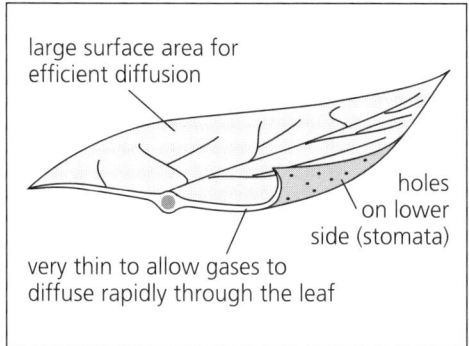

Structure of a leaf

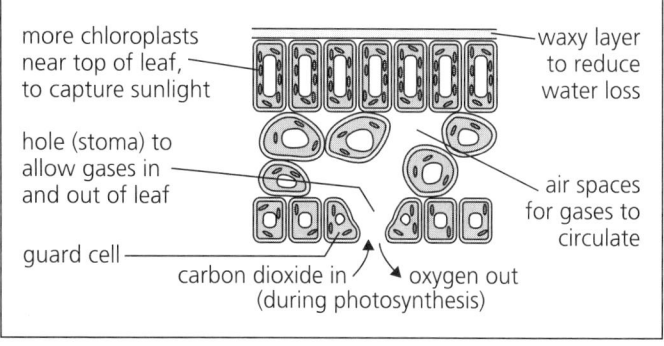

Section through a leaf

Respiration

The glucose produced during photosynthesis can be stored as insoluble starch or used to release energy in respiration.

This energy can be used to build smaller molecules (particles) into larger ones for growth. Energy is used to change:

- sugars (glucose) into **starch** for storage
- sugars into **cellulose** for cell walls
- sugars, nitrates and some other nutrients into **proteins** for growth.

For healthy growth plants also need mineral ions taken from the soil through their roots:

- **nitrate** – makes proteins for growth
- **potassium** – helps the enzymes controlling photosynthesis and respiration
- **phosphate** – important in photosynthesis and respiration.

If a plant lacks some of these nutrients (ions) then the symptoms are shown in the table.

Nutrient lacking	Symptoms
nitrate	stunted growth with yellow, older leaves
phosphate	poor root growth and purple younger leaves
potassium	yellow leaves with some dead areas

 **Questions**

1. Use a spider diagram to show all the parts a plant cell has that an animal cell does not have.
2. Why do lawns not need cutting in winter?
3. How does carbon dioxide get to the cells in a plant?
4. Give *three* uses for the sugars which plants produce.
5. A plant is not taking up enough phosphate. How could you tell by looking at it?
6. What is the equation for photosynthesis?

Transport in plants

Water

Plants take up water mostly through **root hair** cells on their roots. The root hairs provide a very large surface area for absorbing water.

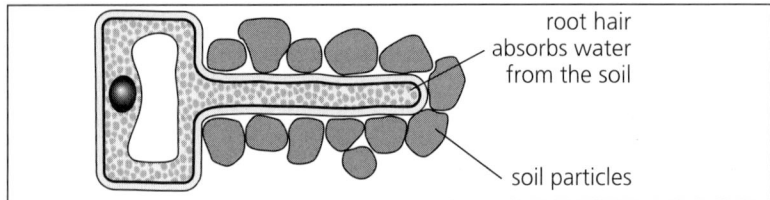

A root hair cell

Water is transported to all of the other cells in the plant. In flowering plants the **xylem** vessels transport water from the roots to the stem, leaves and other parts. **Phloem** vessels transport sugars from the leaves to all parts of the plant, but particularly to growing points and storage areas.

Osmosis

Water moves into the root hair cells by **osmosis**.

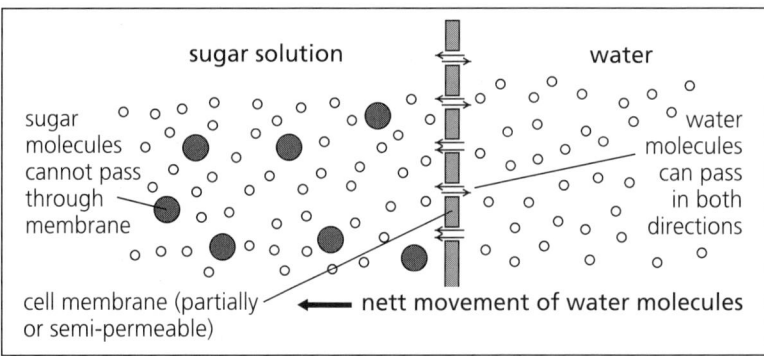

You can see from the diagram that there is a greater concentration of water molecules to the right of the cell membrane (the part which is only water). There is a lower concentration of water molecules in the sugar solution. There is therefore a **concentration gradient** between the two. Water molecules will move both ways in a random way. However, more will move from the water to the sugar solution than the other way. We say that there is a **nett movement** from the water to the sugar solution.

Water helps to keep a plant upright. It enters the cells and makes them swell, or become **turgid**. A small seedling cannot stand up on its own without enough water – it **wilts**. However, plants do not want to take up too much water so they store the sugar they produce as starch – starch is insoluble and has no effect on osmosis.

Keeping the water

Plants lose water by evaporation from the leaves (**transpiration**). Much of this takes place through the stomata. If a plant loses more water than it can take up, it will wilt.

Maintenance of Life

More water transpires on hot, dry, windy days.

Plants can reduce water loss by:

- closing the stomata – this is done by changing the shape of the guard cells which surround each stoma
- the waxy layer on the upper surface of plant leaves which stops too much water escaping. Plants which live in hot, dry conditions have a thicker waxy layer.

Active transport

Sometimes substances have to be absorbed into cells against a concentration gradient. For example, roots take up nutrients such as phosphates, nitrates and potassium from the soil where they may be in a more dilute solution than in the roots themselves. The plant uses energy to move them across cell boundaries against the concentration gradient.

How do plants respond?

Plants are sensitive to light, moisture and gravity:

- their shoots grow towards light and against the force of gravity
- their roots grow towards moisture and in the direction of gravity.

These responses are caused by **hormones**. Plants produce hormones which can collect unevenly in different parts. They will therefore cause uneven growth rates, which make the shoot or the root of the plant bend in the right direction.

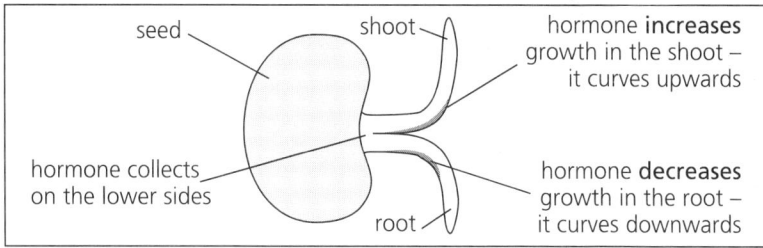

Plant hormone effects on a seedling

Plant hormones can be used to:

- help root cuttings to grow, so making large numbers of new plants quickly
- ripen fruit at the time the grower wants it to ripen
- kill weeds by making them grow so rapidly they die.

Questions

1. How are root hair cells adapted to maximise water uptake?
2. What is meant by the term 'osmosis'?
3. Use a spider diagram to show the different ways that humans use plant hormones. Put plant hormones at the centre of the diagram.

How do humans respond?

The eye

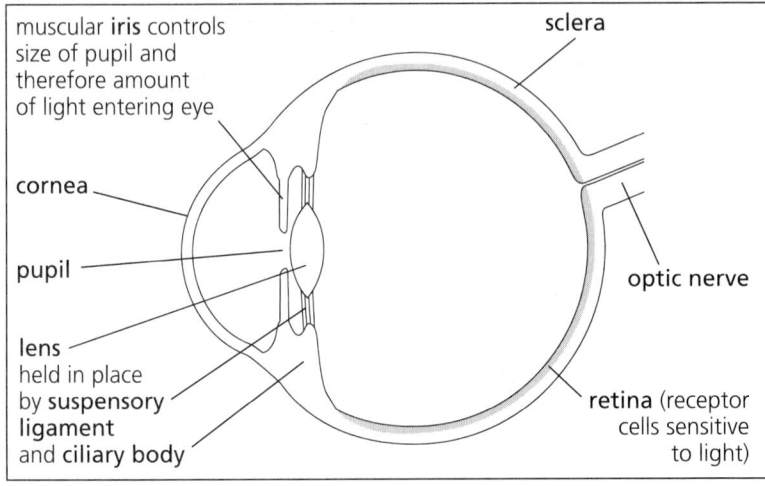

Cross-section through the human eye

When you look at an object:
- light reflected from the object enters through the cornea
- the cornea and lens focus this light on the retina
- receptor cells in the retina send impulses to the brain along the optic nerve
- the brain interprets the impulses (you 'see' the object) and co-ordinates the necessary response.

The shape of the lens can be changed to focus on near or distant objects, so:
- with near objects the light rays have to be 'bent' more – the lens is quite thick
- with distant objects the light rays need to be 'bent' less – the lens will be much thinner.

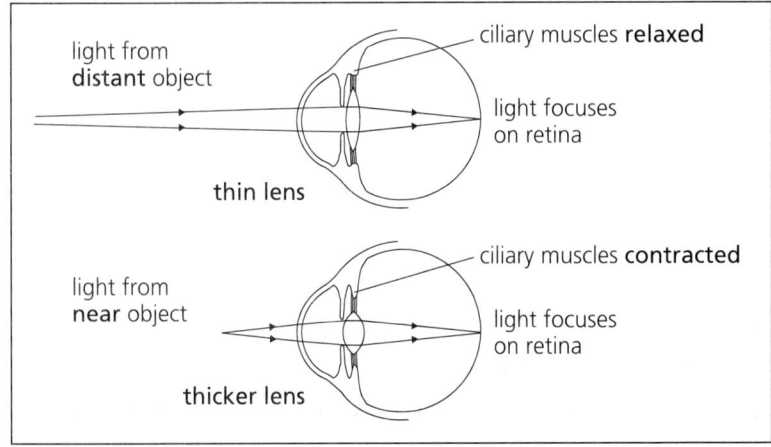

How the eye focuses

The response is automatic. You don't have to think, 'I must change the shape of my lens!' It is a reflex action.

Maintenance of Life

Reflex actions

This is a typical reflex action:
- **Receptors** (e.g. in the retina) send impulses (electrical charges) along a **sensory neurone** (e.g. in the optic nerve) to the central nervous system.
- At the junction with a **relay neurone** a chemical is released. The junction is called a **synapse**.
- This chemical triggers an impulse through the relay neurone.
- At the junction with the correct **motor neurone** a chemical is released again.
- Impulses travel along the motor neurone to the muscle or gland which will do something (the **effector**) in response to the impulse from the neurone.
- The muscle will contract or the gland will produce a hormone or enzyme.

Help
A bundle of neurones make up a nerve.

stimulus
↘ **receptor**
  ↘ **co-ordinator** (central nervous system)
    ↘ **effector**
      ↘ **response**

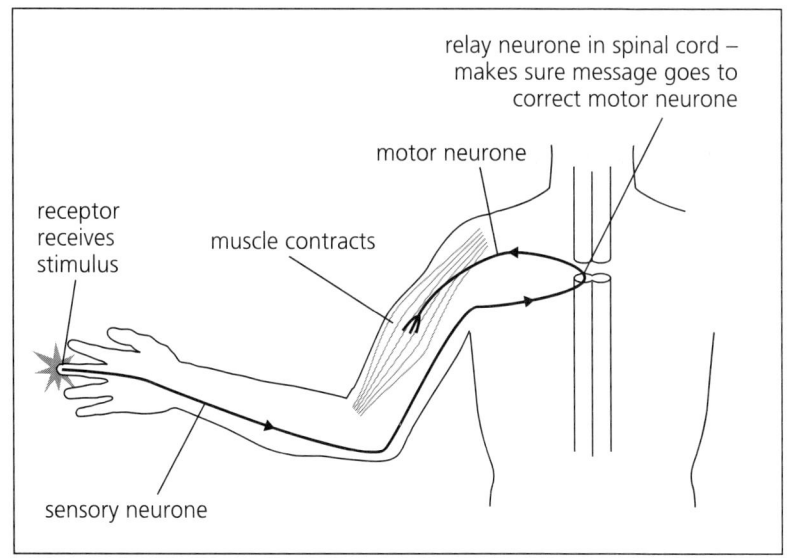

A reflex arc

Questions

1. You were watching the television but then looked out of the window at a friend walking through the gate. The television picture and then your friend were both in focus. What happened in your eye to make this happen?
2. You touch a hot kettle. You pull your hand out of the way. Describe the reflex arc which results when this happens.
3. How are impulses carried in the nervous system?

Regulating our internal environment

We produce waste and need to get rid of it. Our waste includes:

- **carbon dioxide** – produced during respiration, excreted through the lungs
- **urea** – produced in the liver by the breakdown of excess amino acids, removed by the kidneys in the urine, which is stored in the bladder.

Other internal conditions which need to be controlled include:

- **water content** of the body – water is lost from the lungs in breathing out and through the skin in sweating; excess water is lost in the urine
- the **ion content** of the body – ions are lost through sweating and in urine
- **temperature** – it is vital to maintain the temperature at which body enzymes work best
- the level of **sugar** in the bloodstream.

Hormones co-ordinate much of what happens inside us. They are carried in the bloodstream and act on specific organs.

The kidneys

Blood arriving at the kidneys contains many useful substances (e.g. glucose) as well as waste (some salts, urea and excess water). The kidneys filter the blood but:

- reabsorb all the sugar
- reabsorb some salts (ions) needed by the body
- reabsorb the water needed by the body.

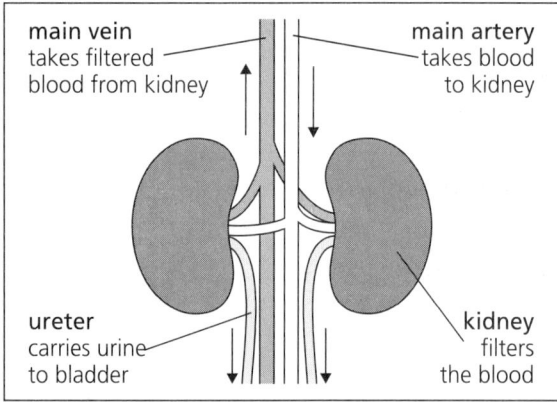

The control of water in the body

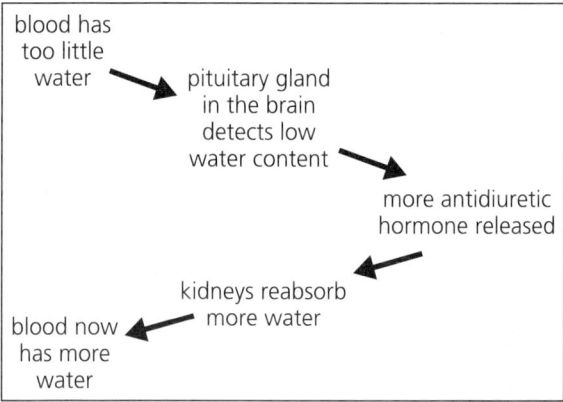

Kidney function

The filtered blood leaving the kidneys now contains only useful substances. The waste (urine) is drained from the kidneys by the ureter to the bladder.

How do the kidneys 'know' how much water to reabsorb? This is controlled by the pituitary gland in the brain.

Body temperature

This is controlled by a **thermoregulatory centre** in the brain. Sensory cells (receptors) are sensitive to the temperature of the blood flowing through the brain. Receptor cells in the skin also send messages to the centre. Most important is the core body temperature. This is the temperature in the central part of your body which contains the main organs.

Core temperature too high	Core temperature too low
blood vessels supplying capillaries in the skin dilate, so that more blood flows near the skin's surface and more heat is lost	blood vessels supplying the skin's capillaries constrict
sweat glands release sweat which uses the heat of the skin to evaporate, so cooling the body (we lose water through sweating)	muscles may 'shiver' – the respiration to provide the energy for this movement releases heat

Blood sugar level

The hormones **insulin** and **glucagon** control blood sugar levels. They are produced in the pancreas.

Sugar level too high	Sugar level too low
pancreas releases insulin into the blood – this makes the liver convert excess sugar to insoluble glycogen which is stored	pancreas releases glucagon into the blood – this makes the liver convert glycogen to glucose (sugar) which is released into the blood

Diabetes is a disease in which someone's pancreas does not produce enough insulin. Because of this the blood sugar level can rise too high and cause death. Diabetes can be controlled by a careful diet and by injecting insulin into the blood.

How do drugs affect our bodies?

Solvents, alcohol, tobacco and other drugs can harm our bodies.

- Solvents affect behaviour and may cause damage to lungs, liver and brain.
- Tobacco smoke can cause lung cancer, emphysema (lung disease) and disease of the heart and blood vessels.
- Alcohol affects the nervous system by slowing down reactions. This can lead to lack of self control, unconsciousness and possibly coma. It may also affect the liver and brain.

 *Questions*

1. After playing a game of basketball you look bright red. How would you explain this?
2. On a hot day you do not produce much urine. How would you explain this?
3. Draw a spider diagram to show the different ways tobacco smoke can harm your body. Tobacco smoke should be at the centre of the diagram.

Module test questions

1. This table is about cells and the jobs the different parts have.
   Match words from the list with each of the numbers 1–4 in the table.

   nucleus   cytoplasm
   cell wall   choloroplast

	Job
1	traps the Sun's energy for photosynthesis
2	controls the activities of a cell
3	maintains the cell's rigid shape
4	where the cell reactions take place

2. This table is about the growth of plants.
   Match words from the list with each of the numbers 1–4 in the table.

   potassium   sugars
   nitrates   carbon dioxide

	Use in plants
1	combines with water during photosynthesis
2	used to help make proteins in growth
3	used to build cellulose for cell walls
4	helps to make enzymes used to control photosynthesis

3. The diagram shows an example of an automatic response.

   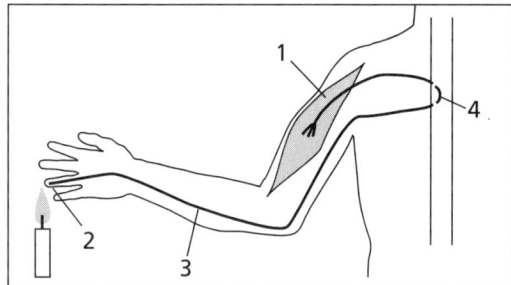

   Choose words from the list for each of the labels 1–4 on the diagram.

   relay neurone   sensory neurone
   effector   receptor

4. Which *two* of the following parts help focus light in the eye?

   A optic nerve
   B retina
   C pupil
   D cornea
   E lens

5. The *two* hormones controlling sugar in the blood are:

   A phosphate
   B glucagon
   C ADH
   D glycogen
   E insulin

6. This is a diagram of the eye.

   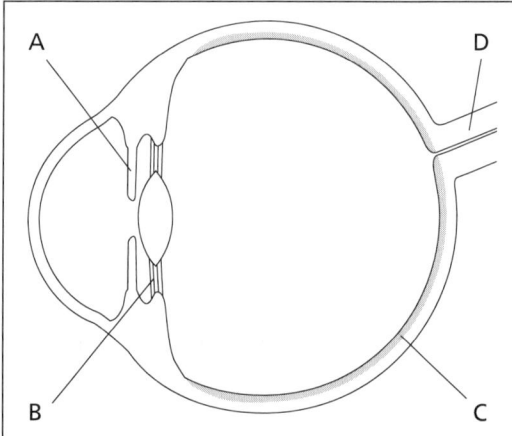

   1. Which of the parts is muscular and controls the amount of light entering the eye?
      A B C D
   2. Which part contains light sensitive cells?
      A B C D
   3. Which part of the eye is called the iris?
      A B C D
   4. Which part holds the lens in place?
      A B C D

7   This plant is photosynthesising.

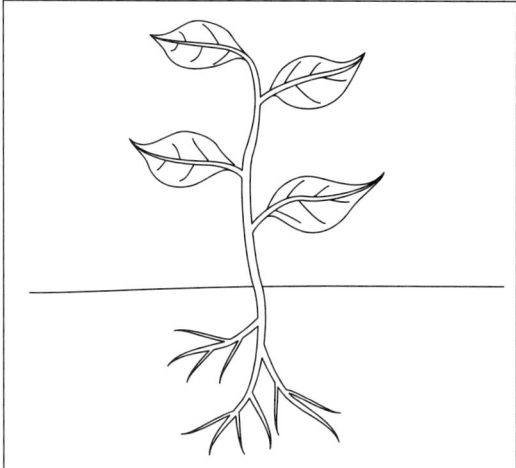

1. If the plant is stunted with yellow older leaves, what would you add to the soil?

A nitrate
B potassium
C sulphate
D phosphate

2. If the plant developed poor roots with purple leaves, what would you add to the soil?

A potassium
B sulphate
C phosphate
D nitrate

3. Which of the following substances is necessary for protein synthesis in the plant?

A potassium
B nitrogen
C phosphate
D nitrate

4. What is the use of potassium in a plant?

A it helps the enzymes controlling photosynthesis and respiration
B it helps to convert starch to sugar
C it helps to make proteins
D it allows osmosis to take place more efficiently

8   This question is about water uptake and transport in plants.

1. Carbon dioxide moves into the leaf by:

A osmosis
B transpiration
C diffusion
D evaporation

2. The evaporation of water from a leaf is known as:

A transpiration
B osmosis
C condensation
D diffusion

3. More water will evaporate from a leaf on a:

A hot, dry, windy day
B cool, dry, calm day
C hot, dry, calm day
D hot, humid, windy day

4. Osmosis is *best* described as:

A movement of water into a sugar solution
B movement of small particles from a high to a low concentration
C movement of sugar molecules to balance the concentration of two solutions
D the nett movement of water from a high to a lower concentration of water

Competition and survival

Organisms have features to help them survive in the places where they usually live. For example polar bears live in very cold areas and have very thick fur and a very thick layer of fat under their skin to help insulation. Holly leaves have a very waxy layer on the upper surface of their leaves to prevent too much water loss, especially in winter when the plant may not be able to take up very much water (as the water may be frozen).

Plants often compete with each other for:

- space
- water
- nutrients.

For example, a new seedling trying to grow underneath an oak tree is likely to die.

Animals often compete with each other for:

- space
- water
- food.

For example, birds all have their territories which they protect. This is so that they have space to breed and enough food to eat.

Animals which kill and eat other animals are called **predators**.

The animals they eat are called **prey**.

In a community of organisms:

- the animal **population** is usually limited by the amount of food (e.g. the number of foxes could be limited by the number of rabbits and other food that there is to eat)
- if the number of prey increases it is likely that the number of predators will also increase (e.g. if the number of voles increases then you might expect the number of local owls to increase)
- if the population of predators increases the number of prey is likely to decrease (e.g. if the number of owls increases then the number of voles is now likely to decrease).

The size of a population may be affected by:

- the total amount of food or nutrients available
- competition for food or nutrients
- competition for light
- predation or grazing
- disease.

Help

Weasel – a predator
Mouse – prey

Help

Population – the total number of that type of organism in an area (e.g. the number of badgers in a wood).
Community – all of the organisms living in a particular area (e.g. all of the organisms, including plants, living in a pond).

Food chains and webs

Radiation (light and heat) from the Sun provides the energy for plants – and therefore the animals which eat them. Green plants only capture a small part of the Sun's energy. The energy is then stored in the substances that make up the plant cells.

In nature it is very rare to have a simple food chain. A rabbit, for example, may eat grass but so do many other animals. A fox may eat a rabbit but so might weasels or buzzards.

If we connect up all the food chains then we create a food web, which gives us much more detailed information.

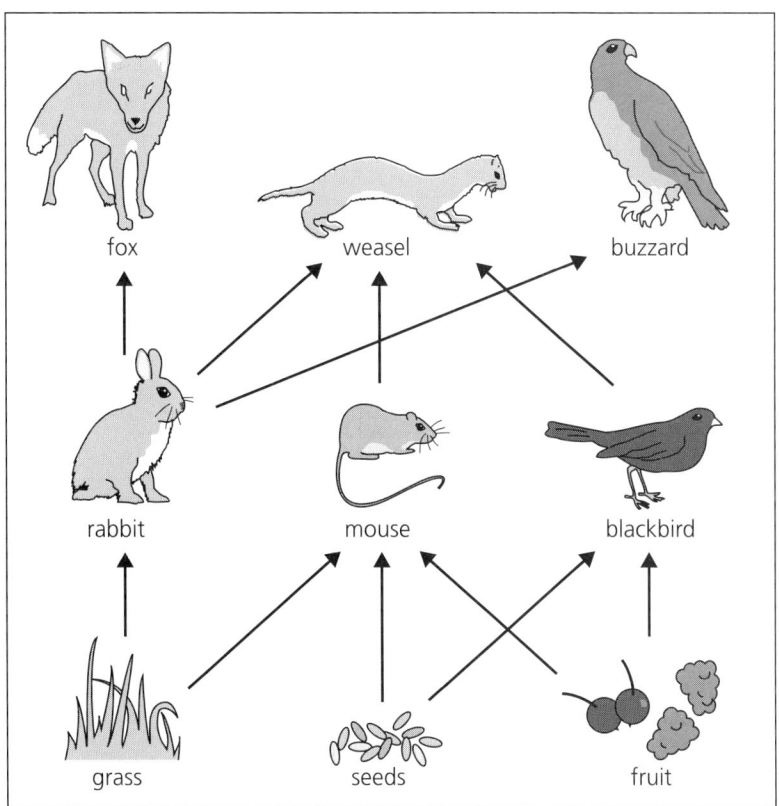

A simple food web

Questions

1. Kestrels hunt for mice along the side of a road. What is the predator and what is the prey?
2. One year there are a lot of mice. What is likely to happen to the kestrel population? What is then likely to happen to the number of mice?
3. Draw a spider diagram to show the different factors which will affect the size of a population of animals. Animal population should be at the centre of the diagram.
4. On holiday you see a kestrel hunting for small birds and mice in the hedgerow. The mice are eating seeds from some flowers and the birds are eating berries from the hedge and some of the seeds. Draw a simple food web to show this.

Pyramids of number and biomass

Food webs and chains show us how energy and material is transferred from one organism to another. The numbers of organisms involved at each stage can be shown in a **pyramid of numbers**.

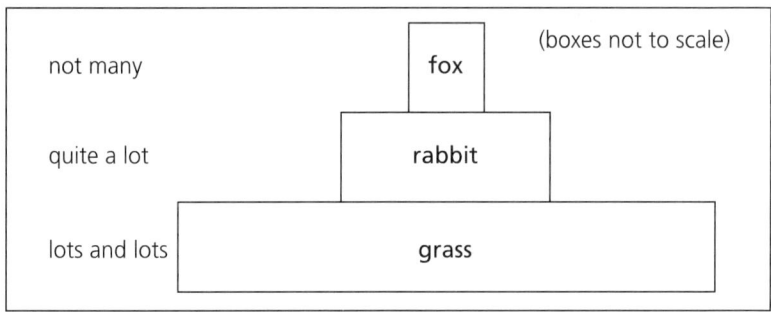

A pyramid of numbers

This pyramid shows the numbers of organisms supported in one community. Sometimes, however, a pyramid of numbers does not give a true picture of a food chain.

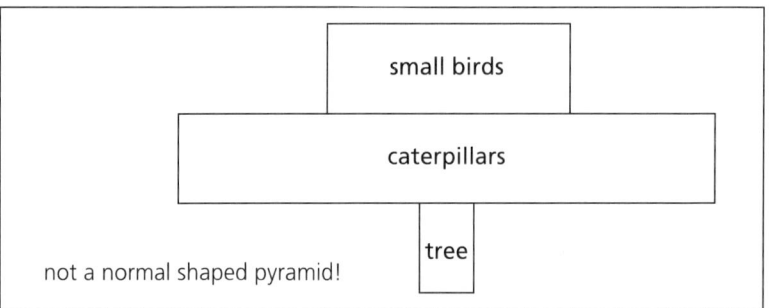

Another pyramid of numbers

A pyramid of numbers can be a strange shape if one of the organisms is large. A **pyramid of biomass** nearly always gives a good idea of the energy and material being transferred up a food chain. Biomass is the mass of living material in a community.

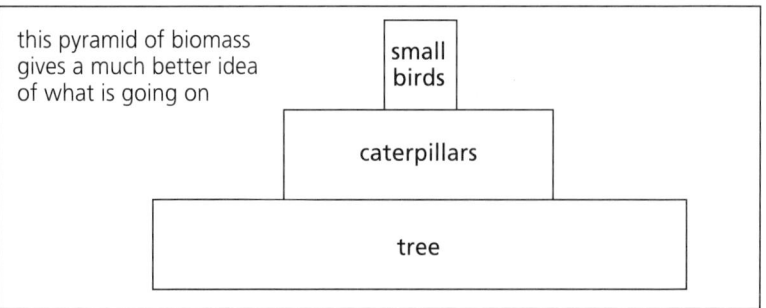

A pyramid of biomass

In the pyramids shown here, the tree is a single organism upon which many caterpillars can feed. If you consider its biomass you get a better idea of how much energy it supplies.

Losing mass through a food chain

It can be seen that as you go along the food chain less material (biomass) is contained in the organisms. There are a number of reasons for this.

All organisms use materials in respiration to release energy. The energy is used for growth and movement, and much is lost as heat to the surroundings or is excreted. Heat loss is particularly great in mammals and birds, whose bodies need to be kept at a constant temperature which is often higher than their surroundings.

The efficiency of food production (in other words, reducing losses) can be improved by:

- reducing the number of stages in the food chain (e.g. humans eating cereal grain is more efficient than feeding grain to cattle then eating the cattle)
- reducing the losses from animals by restricting their movement and controlling the temperature they are kept in (e.g. by keeping calves in crates to produce veal, the calves do not use up much energy in movement or by trying to keep warm).

This last point is, of course, a very contentious issue.

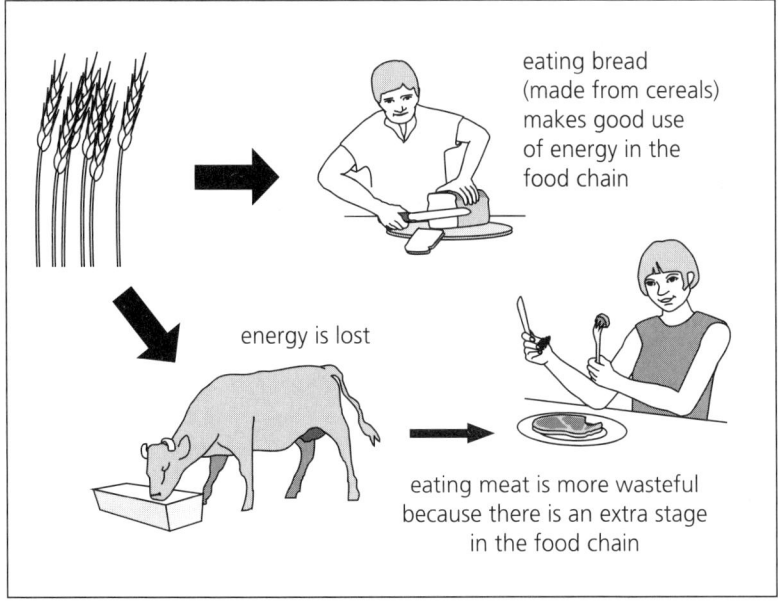

Efficiency of food production

 **Questions**

1. Why does a pyramid of biomass usually give us more accurate information than a pyramid of numbers about what is happening to the energy in a community?
2. How is energy lost between the stages of a food chain?
3. Using a food chain, suggest *one* other example of a pyramid of numbers which does not result in a 'normal' pyramid shape.

Environment

What happens to the waste?

Microbes break down dead organisms, both plants and animals. This process of **decay** releases materials which can be used again by other living organisms. The materials are continuously recycled.

There are two important cycles that you must learn. These are the **carbon cycle** and the **nitrogen cycle**.

The carbon cycle

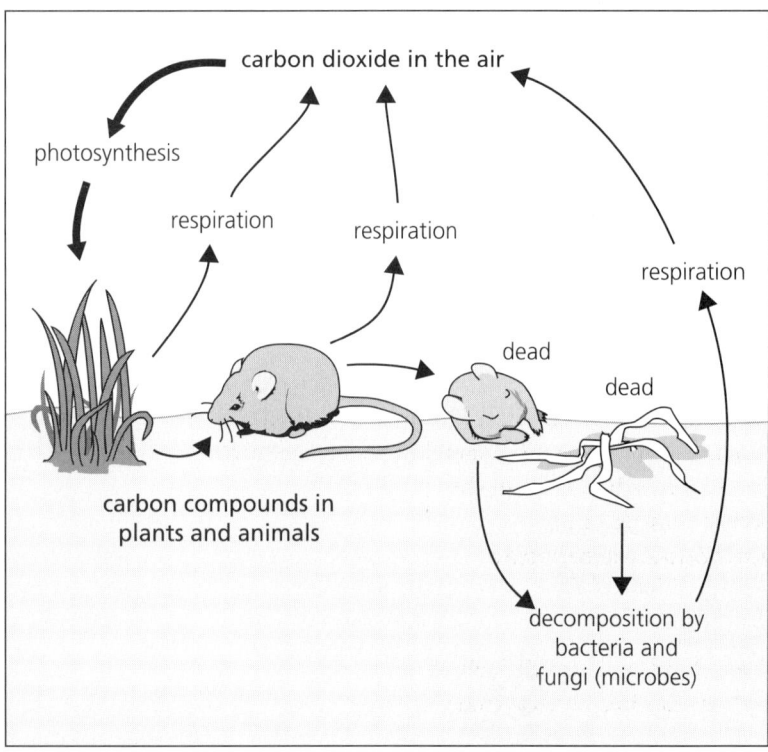

The carbon cycle

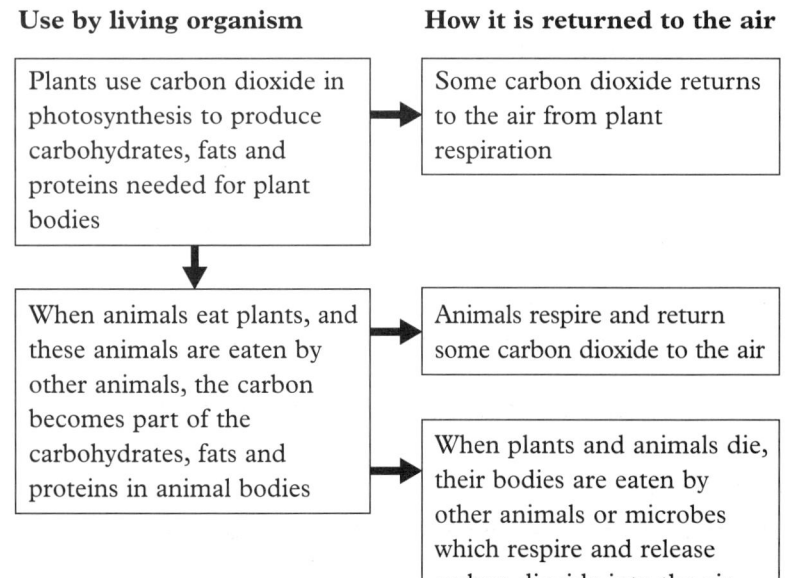

Environment

The nitrogen cycle

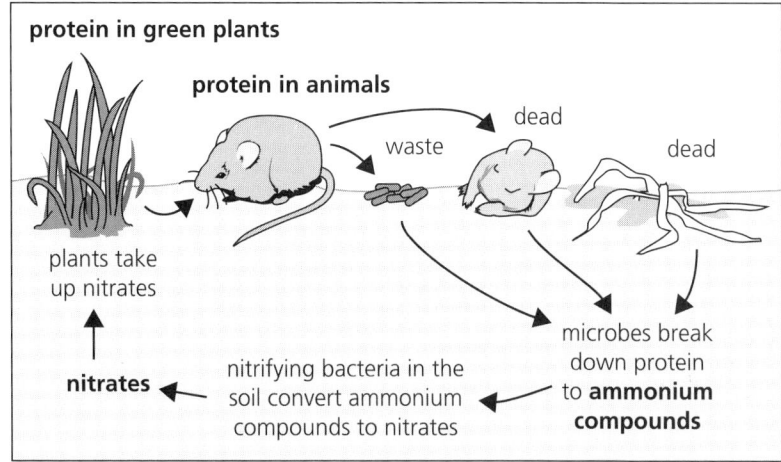

The nitrogen cycle

Use by living organism

- Green plants take in nitrogen as **nitrates** from the soil
- The nitrates are used to make **proteins**
- As animals eat the plants some of the nitrogen becomes part of the animal's bodies

How it is returned to the soil

- **Nitrifying bacteria** convert these ammonium compounds back into nitrates
- When the animals and plants die microbes break down the protein in them into **ammonium compounds**

Help

The full nitrogen cycle is very complicated. This is all that you need to know.

By the time all the protein has been broken down and recycled, all of the energy originally captured by green plants has been transferred.

If a community of organisms is **stable**, the processes of decay return as many materials (e.g. carbon and nitrogen) to living organisms as they need. The processes which use carbon and nitrogen are balanced by the processes which return them.

Questions

1. Copy and complete these sentences about the carbon cycle using words from the list. You will have to use one of the words more than once:
   respiring   decomposing   photosynthesising
   Carbon enters the carbon cycle through organisms which are _____. Organisms release carbon back into the cycle as they are _____. Dead, _____ organisms also release carbon back into the atmosphere as they are broken down by bacteria which are _____.

2. In what food types can carbon be found?

3. How is the nitrogen in animals and plants returned to the soil after the organisms have died?

How do humans affect the environment?

Acid rain

When we burn fossil fuels (e.g. coal, oil and gas) we release carbon dioxide and some sulphur and nitrogen oxides into the atmosphere. These gases can dissolve in rain and make it acidic. This rain may damage trees or fall into lakes and rivers. This may make the water too acid and as a consequence the animals and plants die.

Help

Acid conditions can kill plants and animals because enzymes work only in very specific pH conditions.

Increase in population

In the past there were not enough humans (or industry) to cause a significant problem. Now there are many humans and a great deal of industry across the world. This means that:

- the Earth's raw materials, including fossil fuels (which are non-renewable) are being used up quickly
- we produce much more waste which, unless we deal with it properly, pollutes our surroundings.

Fertilisers

These are added to the land by farmers to replace the nutrients that plants take up for growth. However, some is washed into lakes, ponds and rivers by rain.

The fertilisers result in **eutrophication.** This means that:

- the water plants grow quickly
- some plants die as a result of increased competition (those below the surface may receive little light because of the large numbers growing on the surface)
- microbes (bacteria and fungi) break the dead plants down and use up the oxygen in respiration
- animals will die (suffocate) because of a lack of oxygen.

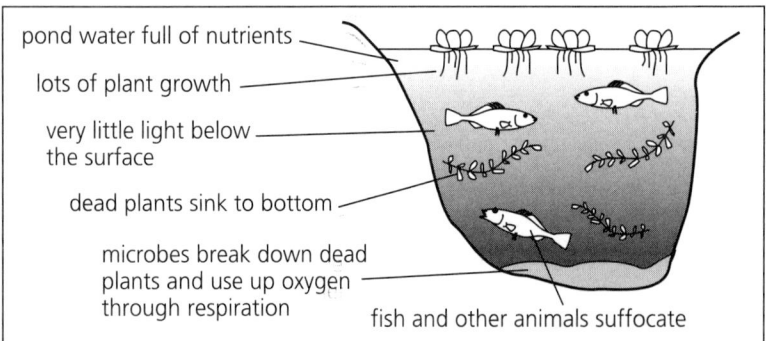

Eutrophication in a pond

You might think that with so many plants photosynthesising there would be a lot of oxygen (as the waste product) for fish to use. However, it is all used up by the respiring microbes.

Untreated sewage in rivers and streams causes the same problem because the microbes break it down and use up the oxygen.

The Greenhouse Effect

Forests are being cut down. This is called **deforestation**. The wood may be used for timber and the land for agriculture. This has several results.

- If the wood is burned then carbon dioxide is released as a product of combustion.
- If the wood is left to decay then the respiring microbes release carbon dioxide.
- Fewer trees use less carbon dioxide to photosynthesise.

Carbon dioxide in the atmosphere is also released by the burning of fossils fuels (e.g. coal for power stations, petrol from oil).

Methane gas is released into the atmosphere by cattle farming and by rice fields.

The levels of these two gases are rising. They act like a blanket, trapping some of the Sun's energy which would normally be reflected back out of our atmosphere. So the temperature of the Earth increases. This is known as the 'Greenhouse Effect'.

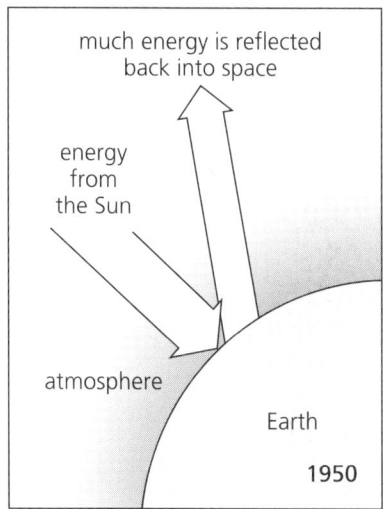 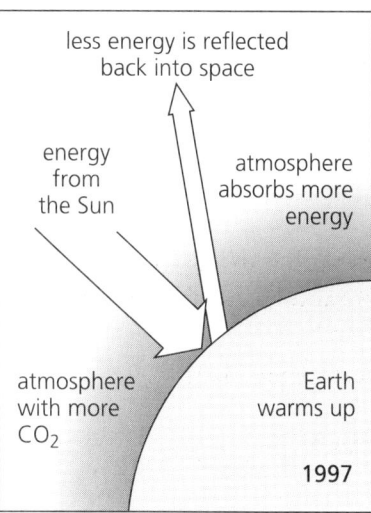

The Greenhouse Effect

A rise in temperature of a few degrees Celsius may cause:

- significant changes in the Earth's climate
- a rise in the level of the sea.

Questions

1. How can burning fossil fuels destroy life in a lake?
2. If too much fertiliser gets into a pond, why might all of the animals die?
3. Why is there more carbon dioxide in the air now than there was 100 years ago?
4. Why might the increasing amounts of carbon dioxide in the air cause the temperature of the Earth to increase?

Terminal exam questions

1 The diagram below shows a food web for a wood.

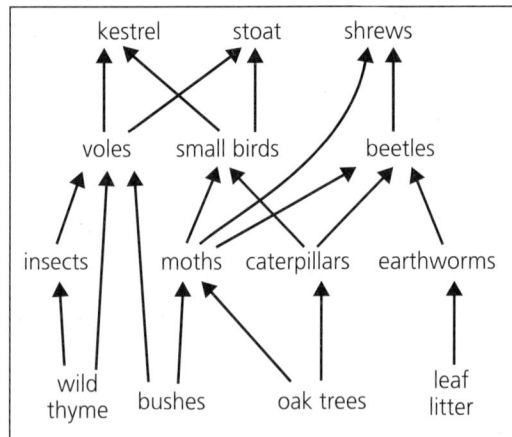

a These diagrams show a pyramid of numbers and a pyramid of biomass for the same wood.

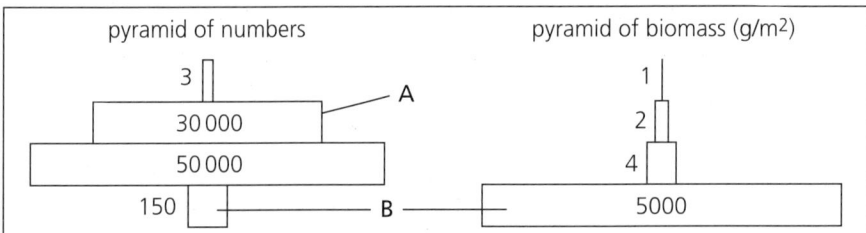

  i Name *one* organism from the level labelled A. [1]

  ii Explain, as fully as you can, why the level labelled B is such a different width in the two pyramids. [3]

b The plants in the wood capture the Sun's energy. Explain, as fully as you can, what happens to this energy. [8]

c Leaf litter is decomposing leaves. Explain, as fully as you can, how nitrogen (found as protein in the leaves) will eventually be found in other plants. [5]

d How is energy lost between the stages in a food chain? [4]

21 marks

2 Over a number of years a farmer uses fertiliser on his fields. Eventually he notices that one of the ponds is becoming full of plants. What is likely to happen in the pond over the next few years? [6]

6 marks

3 The Greenhouse Effect is thought to be an increasing problem on the planet.

  a i Name *two* 'Greenhouse' gases. [2]

  ii Why are these gases increasing in the atmosphere? [3]

  iii How is the Greenhouse Effect brought about? [3]

  b i Name *two* gases which cause acid rain. [2]

  ii Explain the problems which acid rain causes. [4]

14 marks

Environment

4   The diagram below shows a food web

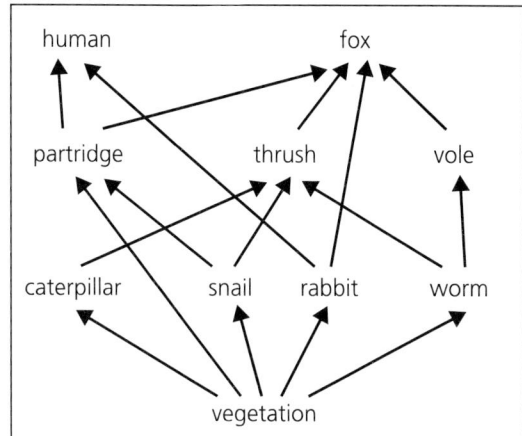

a   Draw a food chain, of four organisms, from this food web [1]
b i Name the producer in this food web. [1]
 ii What is likely to happen to the vole population if the number of worms increases? Explain your answer. [3]
 iii What is likely to happen to the number of caterpillars if the number of snails falls? [4]
c   Give *four* factors which will affect the size of an animal population [4]

13 marks

5   Here is a diagram of the carbon cycle.

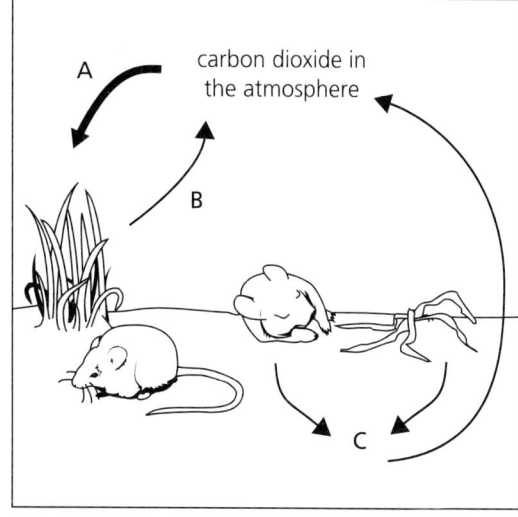

a i What process is taking place at **A**? [1]
 ii Name *three* types of substance which the plants may produce as a result of this process. [3]
b i What process is taking place at **B**? [1]
 ii Name *one* substance (other than carbon dioxide) which is produced as a result of this process. [1]
c   Explain fully how carbon dioxide is released from the dead mouse as indicated by **C** in the diagram. [4]
d   Give *two* problems that the Greenhouse Effect is likely to cause. [2]

12 marks

Total for test: 66 marks

Why are we all different?

Differences in members of the same species are due to two quite different factors:

- the different **genes** that they have inherited (**genetic**)
- the conditions they have been brought up in (**environmental**).

Usually differences are due to a combination of these factors.

Help

'Species' means a type of organism. Members of the same species can breed with each other.

Genes

Genes are found within the nucleus of a cell. The nucleus contains **chromosomes** which are made up of many genes. Each gene controls some particular characteristic of the body (e.g. eye colour). The chromosomes are found in pairs. The number of chromosome pairs in body cells is different for each species. Human body cells have 23 pairs, making 46 chromosomes in all.

Both chromosomes in each pair are made up of genes which usually control the same characteristics. This means that the genes themselves are usually paired. Some genes have different forms – these are called **alleles**.

These alleles control the same characteristics but may carry different information about them. For example, in the pair of alleles controlling eye colour, there is one allele for blue and one allele for brown.

In sexual reproduction these chromosomes are regularly shuffled so that each individual has a unique combination of alleles.

Sexual reproduction

In sexual reproduction a male sex cell and a female sex cell join together. In humans these are the sperm and the egg. Sex cells are also called **gametes**.

Sex cells are formed by cells in the reproductive organs (ovaries and testes in humans) which divide to form cells which have one from each pair of chromosomes. This process is called **meiosis**.

Meiosis

Cells in the reproductive organs, as in the rest of the body, have one pair of each type of chromosome. At the start of meiosis a copy of each chromosome is made, so that there are two pairs of each.

The cell now divides twice to make four sex cells (see the diagram on the facing page). Each of these sex cells (gametes) has one copy of each chromosome.

When the male and female gametes join at fertilisation their single chromosomes combine, making a cell with its full number of chromosomes. New pairs of chromosomes and genes have been formed in the new cell, so that the new individual will be different.

Help

In humans:
- sperm = 23 chromosomes
- egg = 23 chromosomes
- baby = 46 chromosomes.

Inheritance and Selection

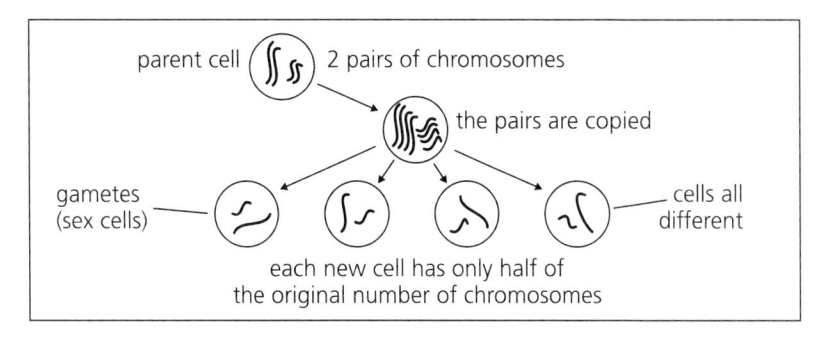

Cell division – meiosis

There is an almost infinite number of combinations of genes, and so an infinite number of possibilities for new individuals.

The new cell, formed when the gametes fuse, then divides again and again by **mitosis** to form a new individual.

Mitosis

Once the body is fully grown mitosis still takes place to replace cells which die. For example, skin cells are wearing off and being replaced all of the time.

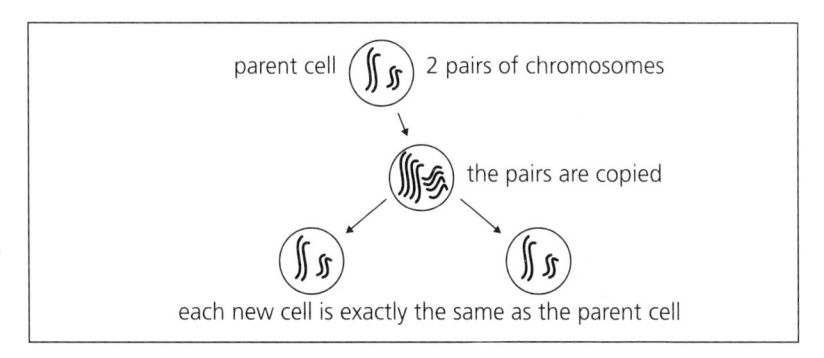

Cell division – mitosis

Mitosis is also the type of cell division used in asexual reproduction.

Asexual reproduction

No sex cells are involved in asexual reproduction, so the genetic information in the offspring is exactly the same as that of the parent. This type of reproduction is most common in plants (e.g. new plants growing from runners, tubers or bulbs). The offspring are called **clones**.

Help

In asexual reproduction new individuals are produced through mitosis.

Questions

1. What are the *two* factors causing variation between members of the same species?
2. How does a cell with 23 pairs of chromosomes divide to produce four new sex cells, with only half the number of chromosomes?
3. Why are organisms produced by asexual reproduction identical to the parent?
4. Turkeys have 82 chromosomes (in 41 pairs) in their cells. How many chromosomes do their gametes have?

Inheritance and Selection

Natural selection

How do new species evolve?

Genes may change because of **mutation**. Mutations occur naturally but the chances of one can be increased by:

- exposure to ultraviolet light
- exposure to X-rays
- exposure to other forms of radiation
- exposure to some chemicals.

Most mutations are harmful:

- reproductive cells may become abnormal or die
- body cells may multiply out of control, and the effect may spread – this is **cancer**.

Some mutations have no effect and some may even *increase* the chance of survival.

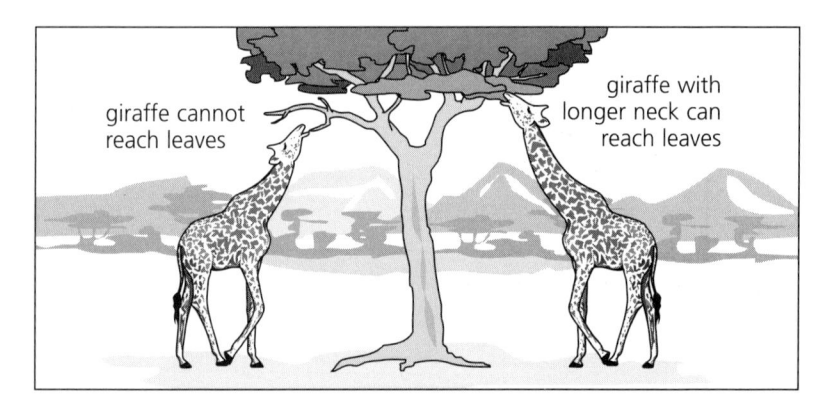

A giraffe with a longer neck than the others may be able to find food more easily because giraffes feed from the leaves on higher branches of trees. The best adapted members of a species (e.g. giraffes with longer necks) are more likely to breed as they are more likely to survive. Over many generations this will result in small changes in the species. This is called **evolution**.

Evolution of a species occurs through **Natural Selection**.

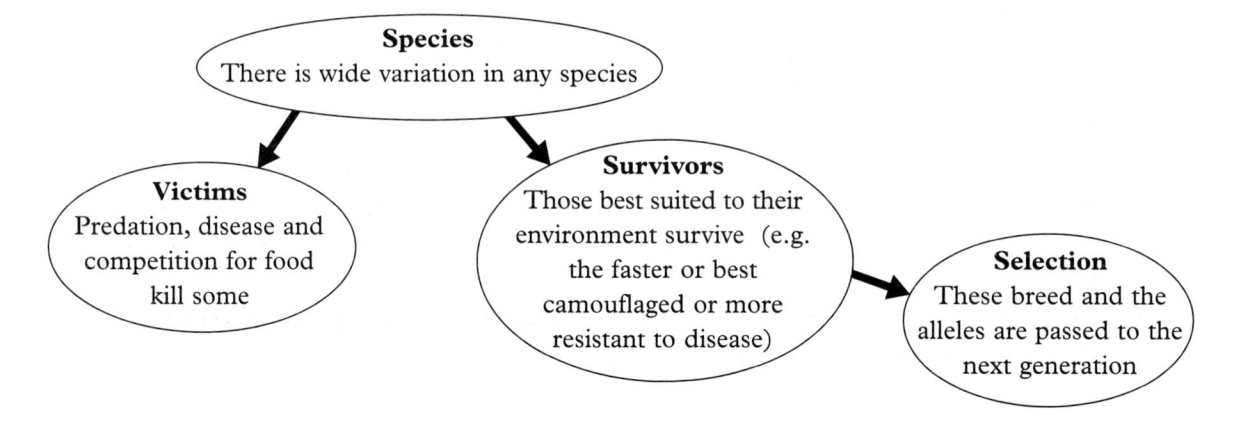

Species
There is wide variation in any species

Victims
Predation, disease and competition for food kill some

Survivors
Those best suited to their environment survive (e.g. the faster or best camouflaged or more resistant to disease)

Selection
These breed and the alleles are passed to the next generation

Inheritance and Selection

Faster antelopes get away

Help

Natural selection favours individuals in a species that are best adapted to survive and therefore breed

How do species die out?

Fossils are found in rocks. They are the remains of plants and animals that lived a very long time ago. They were formed:

- from the hard parts of animals which did not decay easily
- from other parts which did not decay because of lack of oxygen
- when parts of the organism were replaced by other materials as they decayed (e.g. chemicals may dissolve out of seashells and be replaced by minerals such as iron or silicon which then preserve the shape).

Fossils show us how species have changed over millions of years. We now know that all of the species today developed from simple life forms over three billion years ago.

Species become extinct:

- if their environment changes (e.g. change in temperature)
- if predators eat them all
- if disease kills them all
- if a new species successfully competes with them (e.g. takes all of their food source).

Help

Can't adapt to change – become extinct!

Questions

1. Fully preserved specimens of insects which are thousands of years old have been found preserved in amber (solidified sap). Explain why they are so well preserved.
2. Give *three* different causes of mutation.
3. There are two varieties of peppered moth in Britain, pale and dark. Pale moths are found in rural areas where tree trunks are mottled grey. Dark moths are found in industrial areas where tree trunks are blackened. Suggest how this distribution might have come about.
4. Draw a spider diagram to show the different ways a species might become extinct. Extinction should be at the centre of the diagram.

Controlling reproduction

Artificial selection

We can choose those individuals with the best characteristics to breed from (e.g. the fastest male and female horses). This **selective breeding** is now a very big industry. A great range of plants and animals are being 'improved' in this way.

However, selective breeding reduces the variety of alleles in a population. This is because individuals without the alleles that are desired are not used to breed, so the alleles may eventually be lost.

It might be thought that this does not matter, but it does. The environment may change, new diseases may evolve and suitable alleles may not be there to help the species survive. For example, there may be alleles in a species which prevent a certain type of disease. If individuals are bred only for their meat or ability to produce milk, then some of these alleles may be lost along the way. It would then be difficult for the species to adapt to combat the disease should it break out.

As an alternative, modern **cloning** (a type of artificial selection) can involve:

- tissue culture – using small groups of cells from part of a plant to grow into a new plant
- embryo transplants – splitting cells from a developing embryo and transplanting into a 'host' parent (this must be done before the cells become specialised).

Genetic engineering

Genes from one species can be 'cut out' of a chromosome and transferred to another species (e.g. a bacterium). The transferred gene continues to make the same protein in its new 'home'.

On a large scale, the production of **insulin** is now carried out in this way by bacteria. They produce it for humans.

It is also possible to transfer genes to 'host' organisms at an early stage of development to give 'better' characteristics (e.g. genetically modified tomatoes).

How can women control their fertility?

An egg is released every month. The thickness of the lining of the womb (uterus) increases during the month. These changes are controlled by hormones secreted by the pituitary gland (at the base of the brain) and by the ovaries.

Fertility in women can be controlled by:

- hormones that stimulate (encourage) eggs to be produced (fertility drugs)
- hormones that stop eggs being released from the ovaries (the pill).

Help

The pill is the most reliable method of contraception, but for a few women can produce unpleasant side-effects such as giddiness, nausea or occasionally thrombosis (blood clots).

Inheritance and Selection

Several hormones are involved in the menstrual cycle. The hormones controlling egg release include:

- **follicle stimulating hormone** (FSH) secreted by the pituitary gland – this causes the eggs to mature and ovaries to produce oestrogens
- **oestrogens** now inhibit (stop) more production of FSH, which stops more eggs maturing
- oestrogens also cause the pituitary gland to produce luteinising hormone (LH)
- **luteinising hormone** causes the release of an egg mid-way through the cycle.

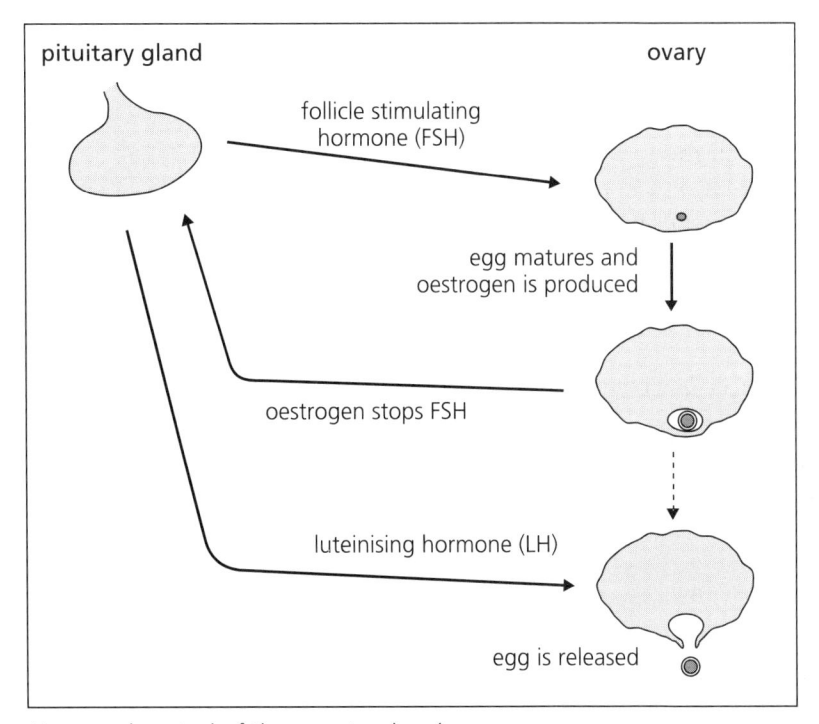

Hormonal control of the menstrual cycle

FSH can be used as a fertility drug if a woman's own production of FSH is too low. Oestrogen can be taken (as a pill) to stop FSH production so no eggs are released (birth control).

Questions

1. Describe *one* example of genetic engineering.
2. A small animal in South America is near extinction. Scientists start a breeding programme using only the most attractive animals. The number of animals in the population rises. A disease strikes the population and the scientists prove helpless to save the animals, which then die out.
   Another scientist says that it was our fault the animal became extinct. How could she explain her statement?
3. What is meant by cloning? What type of cell division does it involve?

Inheritance in humans

Determining sex

We have 23 pairs of chromosomes. One of these pairs determines the sex we are. In females the sex cells are the same (called XX because of their shape). In males they are different (called XY because of their shape). So eggs always have an X chromosome while sperm may carry an X chromosome or a Y chromosome.

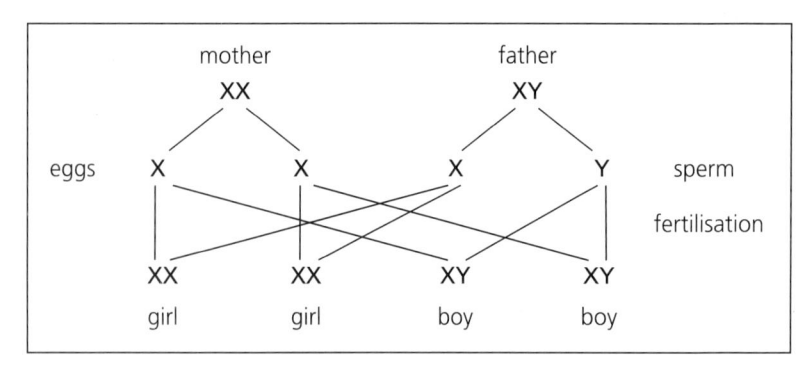

```
           mother              father
             XX                  XY
            /  \                /  \
eggs    X        X          X        Y    sperm
        |\      /|\        /|\      /|
        | \    / | \      / | \    / |    fertilisation
        |  \  /  |  \    /  |  \  /  |
        XX      XX          XY       XY
        girl    girl        boy      boy
```

There is a 50% chance of having a boy and a 50% chance of having a girl

Inherited disorders

Some forms of disease are inherited:

- Huntington's chorea – a disorder of the nervous system
- cystic fibrosis – a disorder of the cell membranes
- sickle cell anaemia – a disorder of the red blood cells.

How are they inherited?

Like many of the other features of an individual, genetic disorders are controlled by pairs of genes. The genes in these pairs often have two alleles (alternative forms).

One of these alleles is the **dominant** form. That is, when it appears in the pair it determines the characteristic which that pair of genes controls.

For example, Huntington's chorea is controlled by a dominant allele (H) – if you have the allele you will develop the disorder. So it can be inherited from one parent who has the disorder.

The other allele is **recessive** (h). If it appears in a pair with the dominant allele, it does not control the characteristic linked to that gene. It is only when both alleles are recessive that their effects show.

For example, cystic fibrosis is carried only by recessive alleles (c), so both alleles must be recessive for the individual to develop the disorder. This means that both parents must carry the recessive allele.

If individuals have two identical alleles for a characteristic, whether these are dominant or recessive, they are said to be **homozygous** (e.g. cc). If they have a dominant and recessive allele, they are **heterozygous** (e.g. Hh).

Help

You can use genetic diagrams to show the inheritance of dominant and recessive alleles clearly. The two alleles are shown by the same letter, but dominant alleles have a capital.

Inheritance and Selection

Worked examples

Q One heterozygous parent and one homozygous recessive parent for Huntington's chorea have a child. What is the chance of the child developing the disorder?

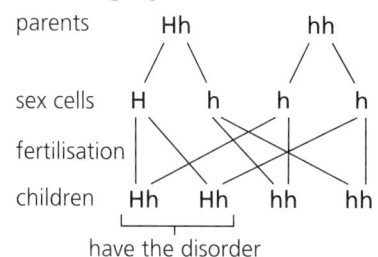

parents Hh hh
sex cells H h h h
fertilisation
children Hh Hh hh hh
have the disorder

A The chance is one in two.

Q Two heterozygous parents for cystic fibrosis have a child. What is the chance of the child having cystic fibrosis?

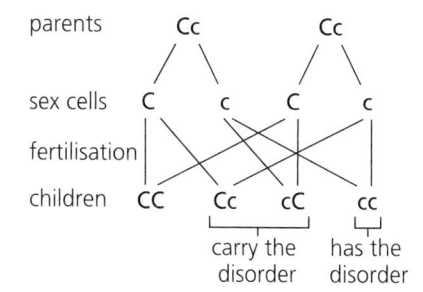

parents Cc Cc
sex cells C c C c
fertilisation
children CC Cc cC cc
carry the disorder / has the disorder

A The chance is one in four.

In sickle cell anaemia the disorder is carried by a recessive allele (s). Being heterozygous (Ss) helps to protect against malaria. This means that carrying the disorder can be an advantage in countries where malaria is common.

Worked example

Q Two parents who are heterozygous for sickle cell anaemia (so do not show symptoms) have a child. What is the chance that the child will develop the disorder?

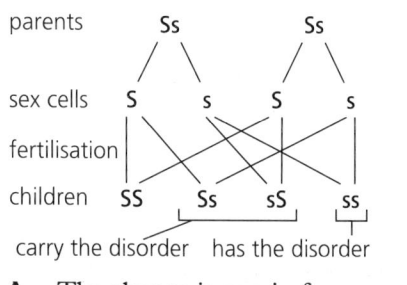

parents Ss Ss
sex cells S s S s
fertilisation
children SS Ss sS ss
carry the disorder / has the disorder

A The chance is one in four.

What are chromosomes?

They are long molecules of **DNA** (deoxyribonucleic acid). Genes are short lengths of DNA.

DNA contains the coded messages needed to produce certain proteins. It controls the order that amino acids are brought together to make these proteins.

The different proteins are responsible for the characteristics that we have.

Questions

1. One parent is heterozygous for sickle cell anaemia, the other homozygous (dominant). What is the chance of their children being carriers of the disorder? You should use a genetic diagram.

2. Two parents do not have Huntington's chorea. What is the chance, if any, of their children having the disorder?

Terminal exam questions

1. **a** State *two* differences between meiosis and mitosis. [2]

   b Plants are often reproduced asexually by taking cuttings.
   Why are new plants exactly the same as their parents? [2]

   c i What is meant by selective breeding? [3]

   ii Selective breeding is thought to be a good idea in the short term. What problems may arise in the long term if this process continues? [4]

   11 marks

2. **a i** What is meant by the term 'genetic engineering?' [1]

   ii How is the process carried out? [3]

   iii Give *one* example of genetic engineering. [3]

   b What is meant by the term 'heterozygous'? [3]

   c i What body system does Huntington's chorea affect? [1]

   ii Two parents are both heterozygous for Huntington's chorea.
   If they decide to have a child, what is the chance of it having the disorder? [4]

   15 marks

3. **a i** Name *two* methods of cloning. [2]

   ii For each of the methods you have given, explain what actually takes place. [4]

   b Two parents decide to have a child. The father is heterozygous for the disorder of cystic fibrosis and the mother does not carry a gene for the disorder.
   What is the chance of the child having the disorder? [4]

   10 marks

4. Explain the process of Natural Selection. [5]

   5 marks

5. **a i** What is meant by the term dominant? [1]

   ii What are alleles? [2]

   b i Study this diagram of meiosis.

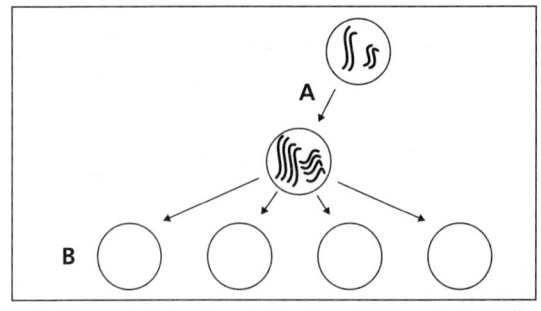

   - What is happening at **A**? [1]
   - Copy the diagram and complete the cells at **B**, showing the results of meiosis. [2]

   ii What function does meiosis serve? [1]

   c i A man heterozygous for sickle cell anaemia marries a homozygous 'normal' woman. They have a child. What is the chance of the child:
   - showing symptoms of the disease?
   - carrying the disease? [5]

   ii What is the possible advantage in being heterozygous for sickle cell anaemia? [1]

   d How do chromosomes control the characteristics we actually have? [4]

   17 marks

6. **a** Study this diagram of human egg production.

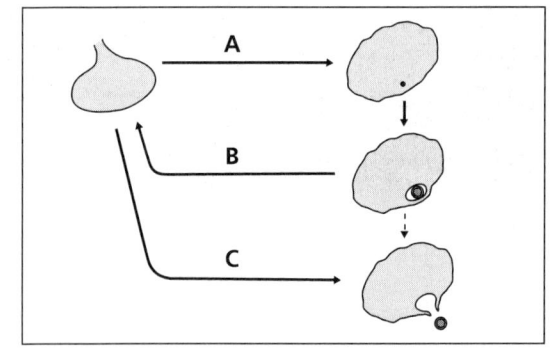

   i Explain what is happening at **A**, **B** and **C**. Name the hormones involved. [6]

   ii Which gland (in the brain) is responsible for the production of certain sex hormones? [1]

   b i Which hormone is used to increase fertility? [1]

   ii Which hormone is used in the birth control pill? [1]

   9 marks

   Total for test: 67 marks

AT3
Materials and their Properties

Metals

Earth Materials

Patterns of Chemical Change

Structures and Bonding

Metals and their uses

Properties of metals

Metals have properties which non-metals do not have. More than 75% of the elements are metals (e.g. iron, magnesium, sodium).

Metals:
- are solid at room temperature (except mercury)
- have high melting points
- are shiny (when freshly cut)
- form alloys (mixtures of metals)
- are mostly strong and tough and can be hammered or bent into shape
- are good conductors of heat and electricity (whether solid or liquid).

Some common uses

Name	Alloys	Properties	Uses
iron		strong and tough can be bent into shape	cars bridges
copper		good conductor of electricity good conductor of heat can be bent into shape easily shaped	electrical wiring saucepans water pipes
	bronze		ornaments
aluminium	duralumin, with small amount of copper	strong easily shaped low density	aircraft manufacture

Which metals are the most reactive?

We can tell by looking at how quickly they react:
- with air to produce metal oxides, e.g.

    magnesium + oxygen → magnesium oxide
    $$2Mg + O_2 \rightarrow 2MgO$$

- with water (cold, hot or as steam) to produce metal hydroxides or oxides and hydrogen, e.g.

    calcium + water → calcium hydroxide + hydrogen
    $$Ca + 2H_2O \rightarrow Ca(OH)_2 + H_2$$

- with dilute acids to produce metal salts and hydrogen, e.g.

    zinc + hydrochloric acid → zinc chloride + hydrogen
    $$Zn + 2HCl \rightarrow ZnCl_2 + H_2$$

Help

The test for hydrogen is that it burns with a 'squeaky' pop.

Metals

The most reactive metals are at the top of the reactivity list. A more reactive metal will displace a less reactive metal from its compounds.

For example, aluminium is more reactive than iron so ...

aluminium + iron(III) oxide → iron + aluminium oxide
$$2Al + Fe_2O_3 \rightarrow 2Fe + Al_2O_3$$

The reactions help us to complete a **reactivity series**.

You do not need to know this diagram.

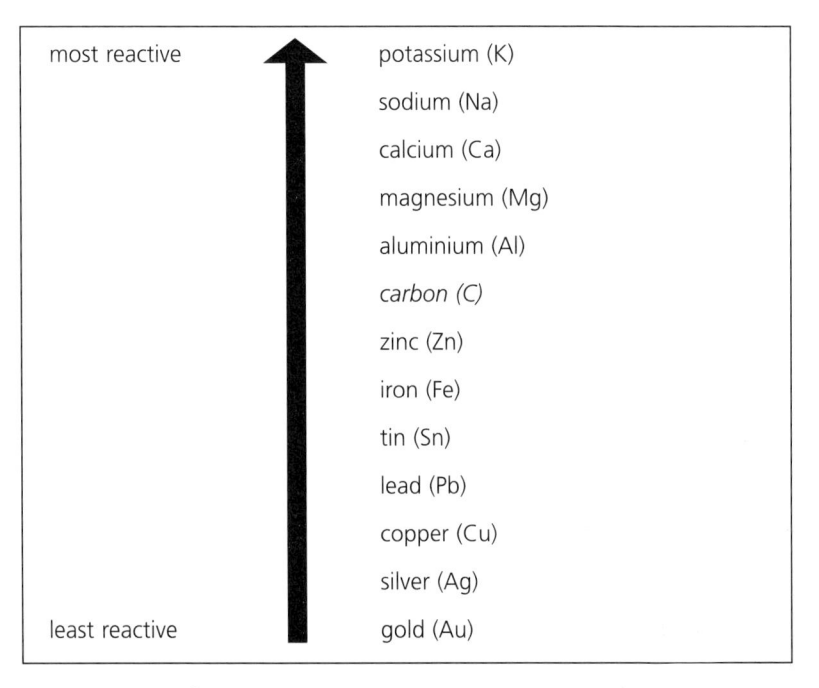

most reactive ↑	potassium (K)
	sodium (Na)
	calcium (Ca)
	magnesium (Mg)
	aluminium (Al)
	carbon (C)
	zinc (Zn)
	iron (Fe)
	tin (Sn)
	lead (Pb)
	copper (Cu)
	silver (Ag)
least reactive	gold (Au)

Some metals in order of reactivity

Non-metals

Less than 25% of the elements are non-metals.

Non-metals:

- mostly have low melting and boiling points – most are gases at room temperature
- are mostly dull in appearance
- are mostly brittle and crumbly when solid
- are mostly poor conductors of heat and electricity – whether solid or liquid.

Questions

1. Zinc is added to copper chloride solution. Predict and explain what would happen.
2. Metals have a number of properties. Draw a spider diagram to show *four* of these properties. Properties of metals should be at the centre of the diagram.
3. Mercury is a good conductor of electricity. Why is it never used for electrical wires?
4. What is the test for hydrogen gas?

Extracting metals from their ores

The more reactive the metal, the more difficult it is to extract it from its ore. This is because it readily forms strong compounds with other elements. Gold is so unreactive that it is found as a pure metal – there is no need to extract it. Most metals are more reactive.

The Earth's crust contains metals and metal compounds. They are usually mixed with other substances. There must be enough metal in the ore to make it worthwhile extracting it.

The ore is often a metal oxide, or something that is easily changed into a metal oxide. The oxygen, therefore, must be removed to leave the metal. This is known as a **reduction**. The more reactive the metal, the more difficult it is to remove the oxygen.

Extracting iron

Iron is less reactive than carbon so the following reaction is possible:

iron oxide + carbon → iron + carbon dioxide

The reaction takes place in a blast furnace.

The reaction in the blast furnace takes place in stages:

- coke (carbon) + hot air (oxygen) → carbon dioxide
- coke + carbon dioxide → carbon monoxide
- iron oxide + carbon monoxide → iron + carbon dioxide
  (a reduction reaction)

Acidic impurities go to the bottom of the furnace as waste. Limestone is added and reacts with the impurities to produce molten **slag**.

The blast furnace

Extracting more reactive metals

Many metals are more reactive than iron. It takes more energy to extract them from their ores. Aluminium is more reactive and must be extracted by **electrolysis**.

Most reactive metals form ionic compounds, where the metals are positively charged ions. When ionic compounds are either dissolved in water or melted, they can be broken down by passing an electric current through them.

When dissolved or melted the ions are free to move about. In electrolysis the positive ions are attracted to the negative electrode (cathode) and the negative ions are attracted to the positive electrode (anode). During this process gases can be given off or metals deposited on the electrodes.

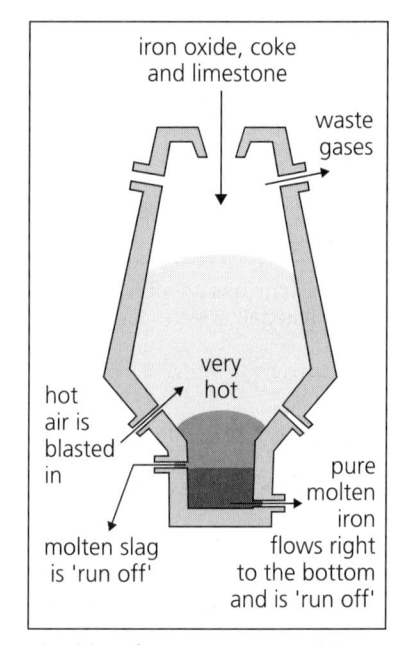

Help

Electrolysis can only take place if the substance is ionic and the ions are free to move.

Extracting aluminium

The raw materials for producing aluminium are purified aluminium oxide and cryolite. Aluminium oxide has a very high melting point, so it is dissolved in molten cryolite at a much lower temperature.

The electrodes are made of carbon. During electrolysis:

- aluminium forms at the negative electrode
- oxygen forms at the positive electrodes where it reacts with the carbon to produce carbon dioxide – this makes the electrodes burn away quickly, so they have to be replaced frequently.

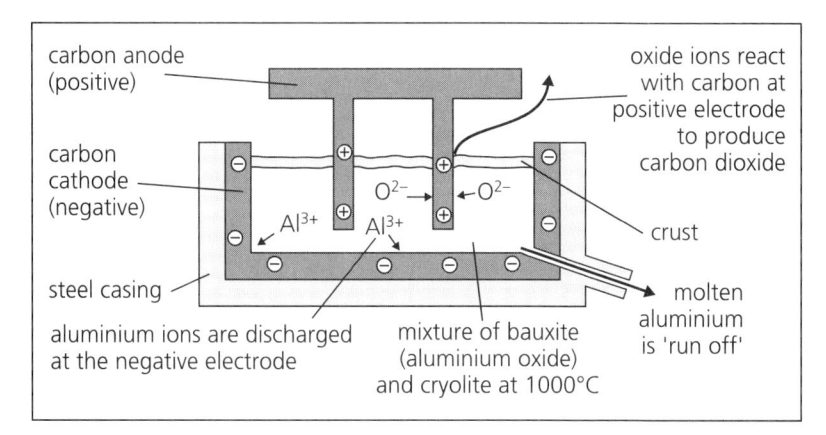

Extracting aluminium by electrolysis

Purifying copper

Electrolysis can also be used to purify copper.

Copper ions move from the impure copper positive electrode (anode) through a solution containing copper ions to the pure copper negative electrode (cathode). Here they are deposited as pure metal. So the positive electrode gets smaller and the negative electrode grows.

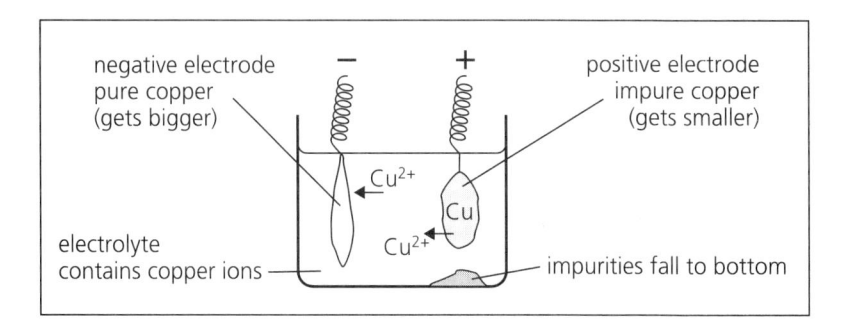

Purifying copper by electrolysis

Questions

1. Why is limestone added in the extraction of iron?
2. Why is carbon *not* used in the extraction of aluminium?
3. Why does the aluminium ore have to be melted before aluminium can be extracted? Why is cryolite used?

Forming compounds

Redox reactions

Positively charged ions gain electrons at the negatively charged electrode (**reduction**). At the positive electrode, negatively charged ions lose electrons (**oxidation**).

In a chemical reaction, if oxidation occurs then reduction must also occur – because if one ion is losing an electron then another ion must be gaining one. These are called **redox reactions**.

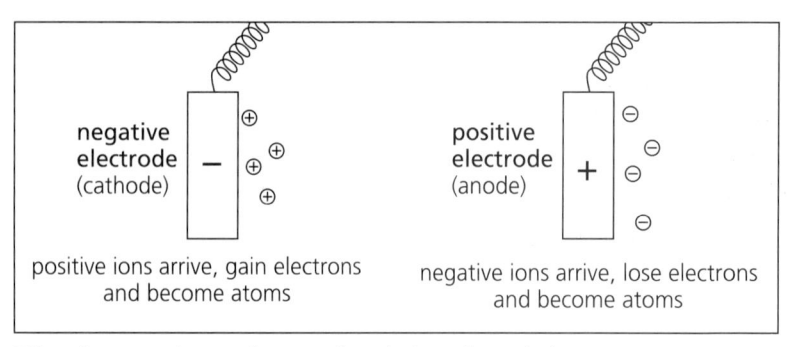

What happens in a redox reaction during electrolysis

Neutralisation

An acid and an alkali react together to produce a salt plus water – this is a **neutralisation** reaction:

acid + alkali → salt + water

The salt produced depends on:
- the metal in the alkali
- the acid used.

Neutralising hydrochloric acid produces chlorides:

hydrochloric acid + sodium hydroxide → sodium chloride + water

$HCl + NaOH \rightarrow NaCl + H_2O$

Neutralising nitric acid produces nitrates:

nitric acid + sodium hydroxide → sodium nitrate + water

$HNO_3 + NaOH \rightarrow NaNO_3 + H_2O$

Neutralising sulphuric acid produces sulphates:

sulphuric acid + sodium hydroxide → sodium sulphate + water

$H_2SO_4 + 2NaOH \rightarrow Na_2SO_4 + 2H_2O$

Help

Sodium chloride is a salt. It is also called salt. There are many other 'salts' (e.g. potassium nitrate, calcium sulphate). So salt is not the only salt!

Measuring pH

A solution may be neutral, acidic or alkaline. Water is neutral. Indicators show the pH of a liquid.

The pH scale is:

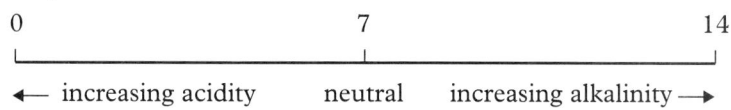

```
0                    7                    14
|_____|_____|
← increasing acidity   neutral   increasing alkalinity →
```

Properties of compounds

Some metal and non-metal compounds dissolve in water.

Soluble oxides of non-metals (e.g. carbon dioxide, sulphur dioxide and nitrogen dioxide) produce acidic solutions. For example:

carbon dioxide + water → carbonic acid
$CO_2 + H_2O \rightarrow H_2CO_3$

Some metal oxides and hydroxides (e.g. the oxides and hydroxides of sodium, potassium and, to some extent calcium) dissolve in water to produce alkaline solutions. For example:

potassium + water → hydrogen + potassium hydroxide
$2K + 2H_2O \rightarrow H_2 + 2KOH$

The potassium hydroxide dissolves in the water to produce an alkaline solution.

Questions

1. What is a redox reaction?
2. What is meant by a neutralisation reaction?
3. Predict the salts that will result from these neutralisation reactions. Copy and complete the table.

+	hydrochloric acid	sulphuric acid
potassium hydroxide		
calcium hydroxide		

4. Write down the chemical reaction between KOH and HCl.
5. Predict the reaction between sulphur dioxide and water and write down the chemical equation.

Module test questions

1. This question is about the reactivities of different elements.
   Match words from the list with spaces **1–4**.

   gold   aluminium
   carbon iron

   most reactive ↑ 1 _____
                    2 _____
                    3 _____
   least reactive   4 _____

2. This question is about the substances formed during certain chemical reactions. Match the chemical formulae from the list with each of numbers **1–4** in the table.

   NaCl   NaNO$_3$
   Na$_2$SO$_4$ Na$_2$O

	Reactants
1	hydrochloric acid and sodium hydroxide
2	sodium and oxygen
3	nitric acid and sodium hydroxide
4	sulphuric acid and sodium hydroxide

3. This question is about the different types of chemical reactions.
   Match words from the list with each of numbers **1–4** in the table.

   displacement   reduction
   neutralisation oxidation

	Description
1	the reaction between an acid and an alkali
2	when a metal oxide loses its oxygen
3	when a metal becomes a metal oxide
4	when a more reactive metal removes a less reactive metal from a compound

4. When sulphuric acid is neutralised by sodium hydroxide the *two* products of the reaction are:

   A Na$_2$SO$_4$
   B H$_2$
   C H$_2$O
   D CO$_2$
   E NaCl

5. In the electrolysis of aluminium oxide (bauxite), which *two* of the following statements are correct?

   A cryolite is used to reduce the melting point of the ore
   B the positive electrode is made of aluminium
   C oxygen forms at the negative electrode
   D negative ions gain an electron to form an atom
   E aluminium forms at the negative electrode

6. This is a diagram of a blast furnace.

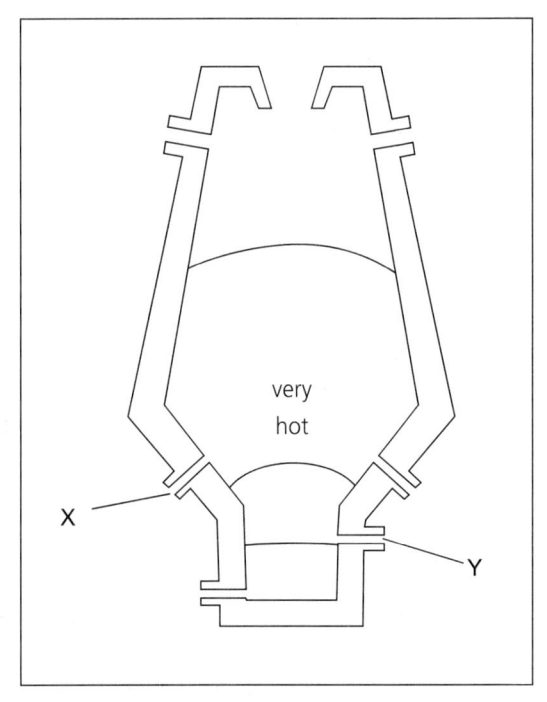

   1. What is happening at point X?

   A waste gases are escaping
   B molten iron is flowing
   C hot air is blasted in
   D molten slag is run off

2. What is happening at point Y?

A hot air is blasted in
B molten iron is flowing
C molten slag is run off
D limestone is added

3. Which substance reduces iron oxide?

A carbon monoxide
B carbon
C limestone
D carbon dioxide

4. With which of the following substances does limestone react to form slag?

A carbon monoxide
B carbon dioxide
C acid impurities
D carbon

7 Aluminium is extracted from its ore by electrolysis.

1. What happens at the negative electrode?

A negative aluminium ions gain electrons and become atoms
B negative aluminium ions lose electrons and become atoms
C positive aluminium ions gain electrons and become atoms
D positive aluminium ions lose electrons and become atoms

2. What happens at the positive electrode?

A negative oxygen ions gain electrons and become atoms
B negative oxygen ions lose electrons and become atoms
C positive oxygen ions gain electrons and become atoms
D positive oxygen ions lose electrons and become atoms

3. What happens eventually to the oxygen ions?

A they evolve as oxygen atoms
B they evolve as carbon dioxide molecules
C they form hydroxide (OH) ions
D they evolve as oxygen molecules

4. What is cryolite used for?

A to prevent the electrodes breaking down
B to conduct electricity
C to provide aluminium ions
D to lower the melting point of the ore

8 Copper is purified by electrolysis.

1. What happens at the positive electrode?

A copper atoms lose electrons to become copper ions
B copper atoms gain electrons to become copper ions
C copper ions lose electrons to become copper atoms
D copper ions gain electrons to become copper atoms

2. What happens at the negative electrode?

A copper atoms lose electrons to become copper ions
B copper atoms gain electrons to become copper ions
C copper ions lose electrons to become copper atoms
D copper ions gain electrons to become copper atoms

3. What is the liquid around the electrodes (the electrolyte)?

A water
B an acid
C a solution containing copper ions
D an alkali

4. Copper can be found 'native' (as fairly pure metal). Iron oxide can be reduced by carbon to leave iron. Aluminium oxide cannot be reduced by carbon.

What place does carbon have in the reactivity series of aluminium, carbon, copper and iron?

A it is the most reactive
B it is more reactive than copper and iron
C it is the least reactive
D it is less reactive than aluminium and copper but more reactive than iron

Structure of the Earth

The Earth is nearly a sphere. It has a layered structure, which includes:

- a thin **crust**
- an extremely viscous (thick liquid) **mantle** which goes almost half way to the Earth's centre
- a central **core** – made of nickel and iron, the outer part is liquid and the inner part solid.

The overall density of the Earth is greater than the densities of the rocks in the crust. This means that the inside is made of a material different from the rocks of the crust. It also means that the inside of the Earth must be denser than the rocks of the crust.

Continental crustal (granitic) rocks have slightly lower densities than oceanic crustal (basaltic) rocks, which is why they project above sea level.

It used to be thought that as the Earth cooled its circumference became smaller, and that this 'shrinking' forced rocks upwards to become mountains. We now know that this is not what happened.

The edges of continents are sometimes separated by thousands of kilometres of ocean. It seems that their shapes could fit together quite well (e.g. South America and Africa). They also seem to have similar patterns of rocks and fossils. This suggests that they were once joined together and have moved apart over millions of years.

Structure of the Earth

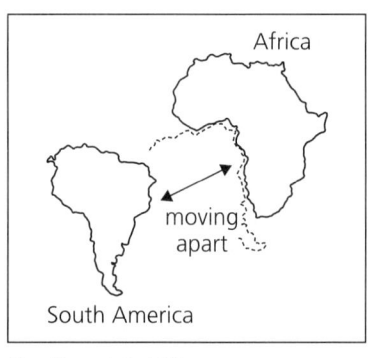

Continental drift

Plates and polarity

The Earth's crust is split into a number of very large pieces – rather like a jigsaw. These pieces are called **tectonic plates**. They are moving by a few centimetres every year, because they 'float' on the underlying mantle. This is slowly moving due to convection currents created by radioactive processes deep within the Earth.

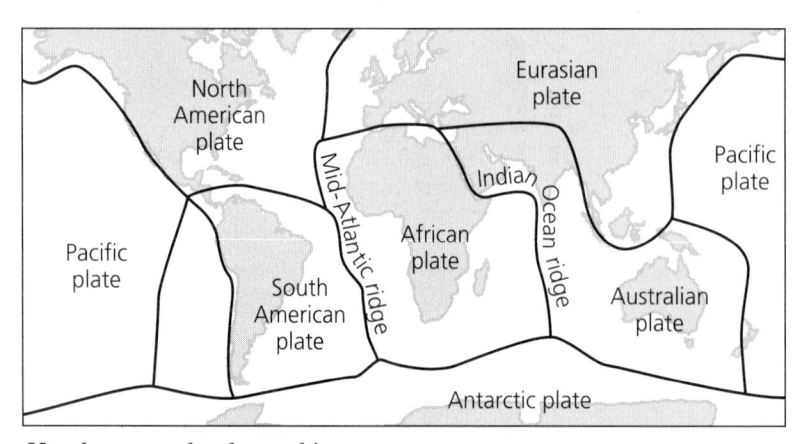

You do not need to know this map.

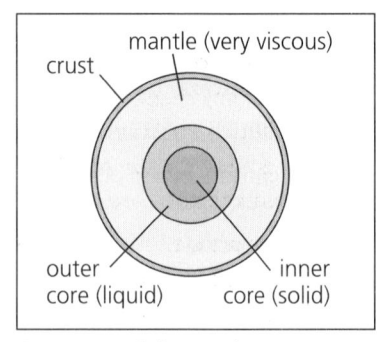

Tectonic plates

Earth Materials

Tectonic plates may:

- slide past each other and cause earthquakes (e.g. San Francisco in California)
- move towards each other – the denser oceanic plate is driven down (subducted) beneath the thicker continental plate where it melts, helping to form a layer of molten rock called **magma**. Continental crust is forced upwards. Earthquakes result and magma may rise to form volcanoes (e.g. the Andes in South America)
- move apart and magma rises to fill the gap – new oceanic crust results. This is known as sea-floor spreading. The mid-Atlantic ridge is a good example.

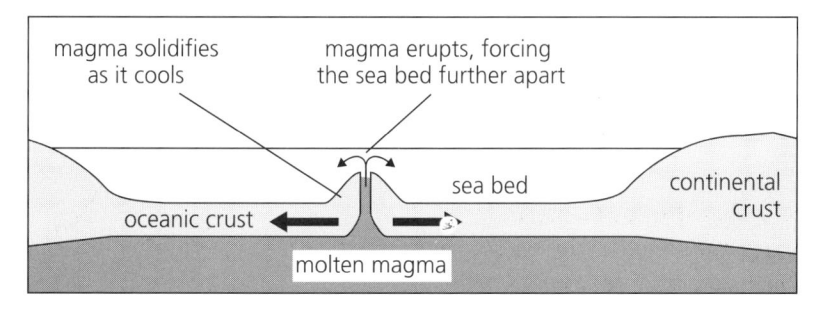

Sea-floor spreading

As the magma spreads on the sea floor the iron-rich minerals line up in the direction of the Earth's magnetic field. The polarity or direction of the Earth's field reverses every half million years or so. The iron-rich minerals align themselves with whatever direction the field takes at the time. The magma cools to form stripes alongside the ridge. By studying the patterns of these stripes we can see how the sea floor has spread and how the Earth's magnetic field has changed over time.

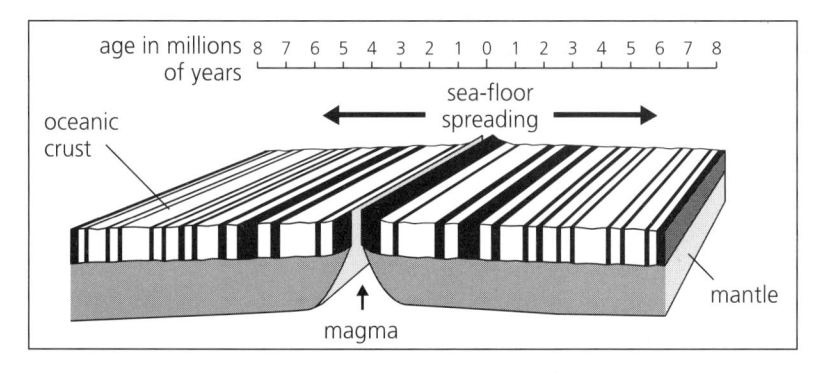

Magnetic stripes on the sea floor

Questions

1. What evidence is there that continents are moving apart?
2. In 1906 there was a disastrous earthquake in San Francisco. Recently there was a significant earthquake in Los Angeles. There are no mountains particularly near these two cities. What do you think caused the earthquakes?
3. How do the magnetic stripes on the ocean bed provide some proof that the sea floor is spreading?

Rock types and their formation

Igneous rocks

These are formed from molten rock (magma) in different ways.

- If molten rock is forced from inside the Earth up into the crust (but not onto the surface) it then cools and forms **intrusive** igneous rock (e.g. granite).
- If the molten rock erupts onto the surface (e.g. from a volcano) it forms **extrusive** igneous rocks (e.g. basalt).

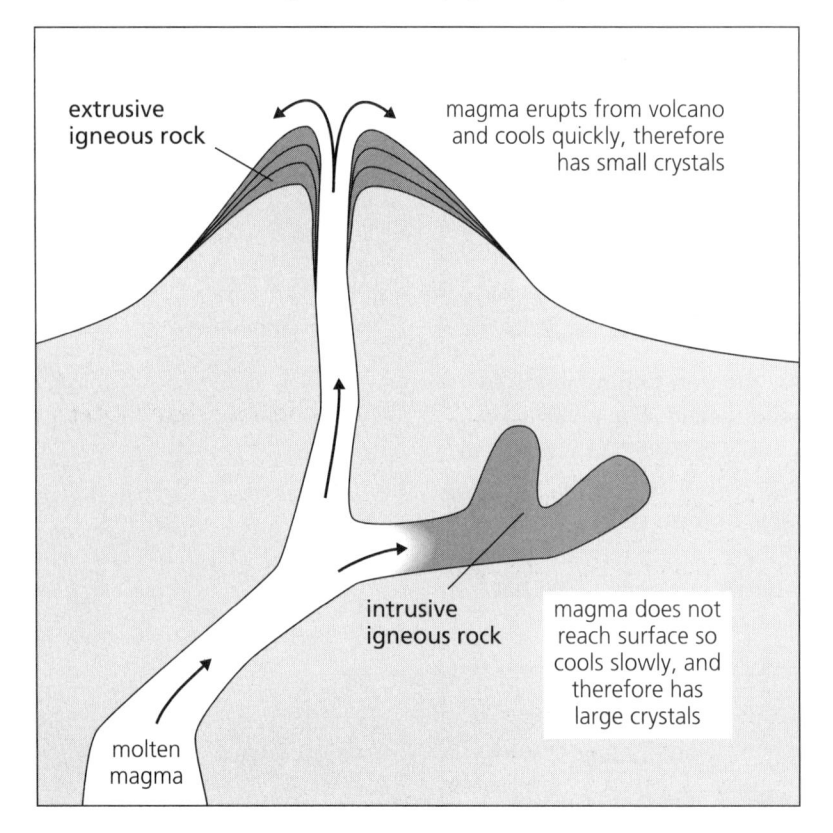

Igneous rock formation

Rocks composed of randomly arranged interlocking crystals (of a number of different minerals) are likely to be igneous. If the molten rock cools quickly (e.g. from a volcano) the crystals will probably be small. If molten rock cools slowly (e.g. below the Earth's surface) larger crystals are likely to be formed.

Sedimentary rocks

These were formed from layers of sediment deposited on top of one another on the sea floor. The weight of sediment squeezes out the water and it becomes cemented together, with other fragments, by salts crystallising out of the water. The process often takes millions of years.

These rocks include sandstone (made of grains of sand) and limestone made from calcium carbonate (often from shell remains of living organisms).

Sedimentary rocks usually lie on top of older rocks. These rock layers can be:

- tilted
- folded
- fractured (faults)
- and sometimes turned upside down!

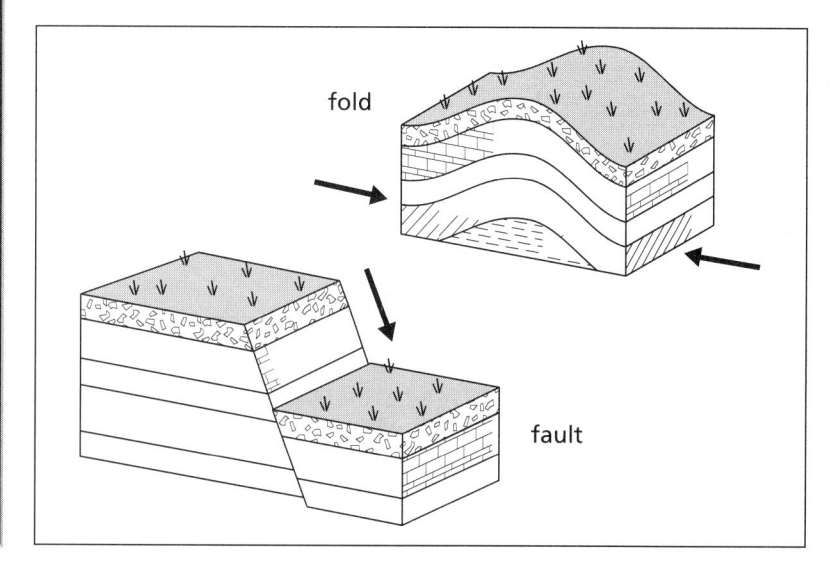

Movement of sedimentary rock

These Earth movements are caused by very large forces. Over a long time, the movements cause new mountain ranges to form (e.g. the Alps are great fold mountains formed when Africa collided with Europe). New mountains replace older mountains which have been worn down (eroded) by the weather.

Metamorphic rocks

These are often found in present-day and old mountain ranges. They are formed when there is a high temperature and pressure, often caused by the mountain building process. Metamorphic rocks are igneous or sedimentary rocks which have been buried underground by Earth movements. They become compressed and heated. Their texture may change without the rock melting.

Marble can be formed in this way from limestone. Shale can be formed from mudstone.

Rocks composed of bands of interlocking crystals are likely to be metamorphic. Schist is a good example.

Questions

1. How could sedimentary rock become magma?
2. You find a piece of granite. What type of igneous rock is granite and what size are the crystals likely to be?
3. Why do you think that metamorphic rocks are normally associated with mountain ranges?

Earth Materials

Rocks and their uses

The rock cycle

The crust of the Earth is moving all the time. This results in changes which include some mountains being formed and others being worn away. The formation and transformation of different types of rocks can be summarised in the rock cycle:

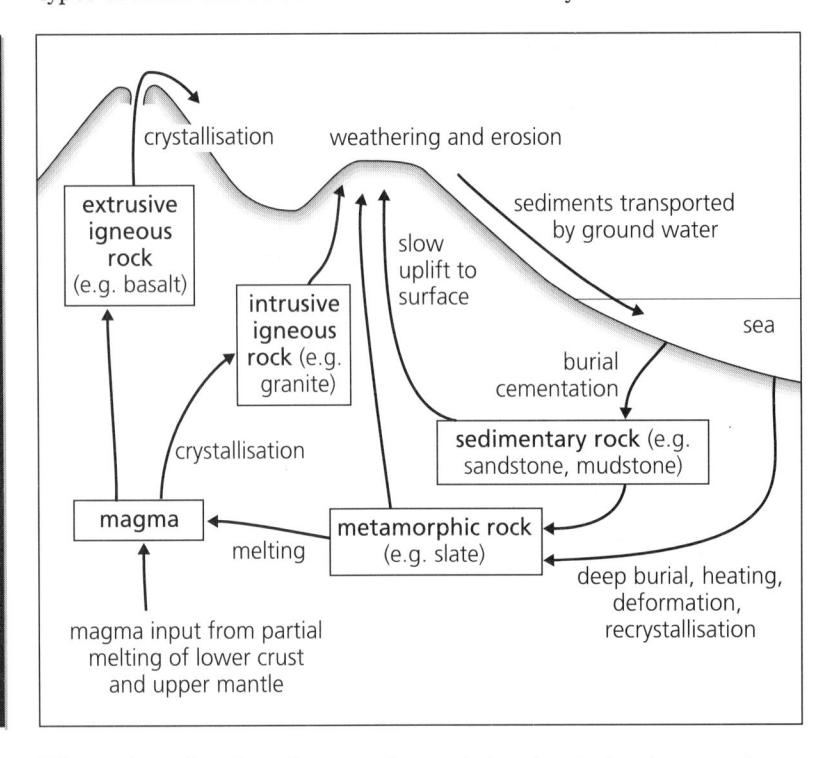

The rock cycle

The rock cycle takes place continuously but is, obviously, very slow.

As part of the rock cycle:

- sedimentary rocks may become metamorphic if they are put under sufficient heat and pressure
- metamorphic rocks may become igneous if they are buried and melt
- metamorphic rocks may become sedimentary if they are worn away and redeposited
- igneous rocks may become sedimentary if they are worn away and redeposited.

Help

Remember: the faster an igneous rock cools, the smaller the crystals.

Using limestone

Limestone, a sedimentary rock, is mainly calcium carbonate. It can be quarried and used as a building material. Powdered limestone can be used to neutralise acidity in lakes and soils.

If you heat limestone in a kiln then **quicklime** is produced (calcium oxide). This reacts with water to produce **slaked lime** (calcium hydroxide) which reduces soil acidity.

Earth Materials

Cement is made by roasting powdered limestone with powdered clay. If it is mixed with water, sand and crushed rock then a slow chemical reaction produces a hard, stone-like building material called **concrete**.

Glass is made by heating a mixture of limestone, sand and soda (sodium carbonate).

Using fossils

Sedimentary rocks often contain fossils. These are formed when the sediment is laid down and parts of plants and animals are trapped and preserved in the rock. Each layer of rock therefore contains fossils of the same age.

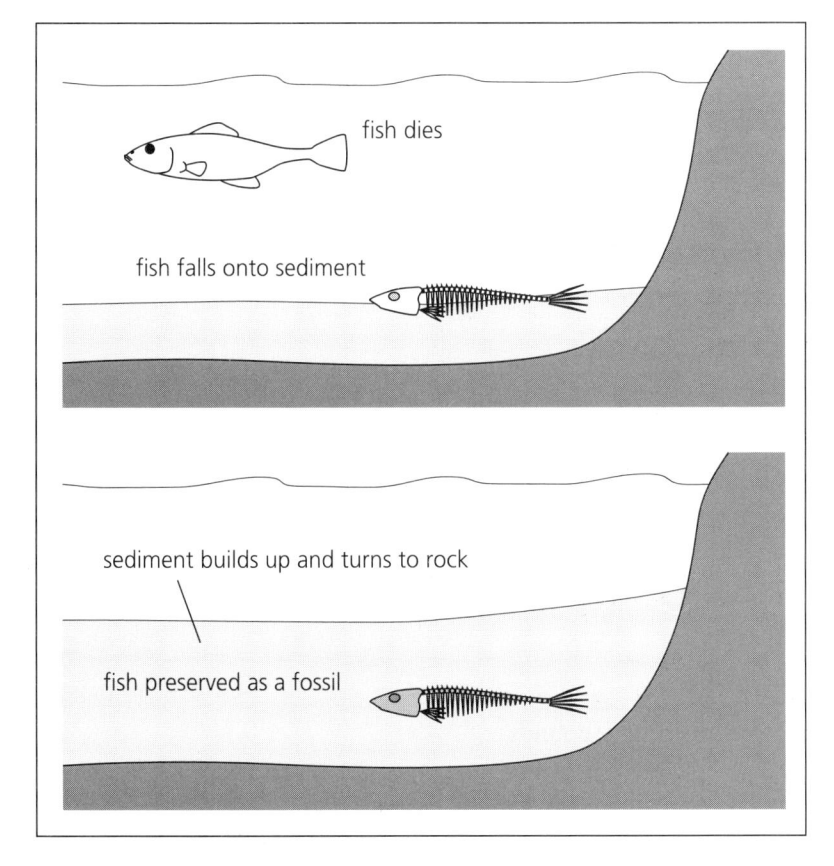

Fossil formation

Fossils can therefore be used to identify rocks of the same age in different areas. They cannot be used to date rocks accurately, but they can be used to establish if rocks are younger or older than each other.

Questions

1. How might an igneous rock eventually become a metamorphic rock?
2. Fossils are being discovered every day yet they have been there for a very long time. Suggest *two* reasons to explain why they are continually being found.
3. Why do you not find fossils in either igneous or metamorphic rocks?

Crude oil and its products

Crude oil is obtained from the Earth's crust. It is formed from the remains of organisms which lived millions of years ago. Crude oil is a fossil fuel.

Oil, like coal and natural gas, is the result of heat and pressure (over millions of years and in the absence of air) on the remains of animals and plants trapped in sedimentary rock.

Oil and gas are less dense than water. They rise to the top of porous rock. They are then trapped below non-porous rock. We obtain the oil and gas by drilling down through the non-porous layer of rock.

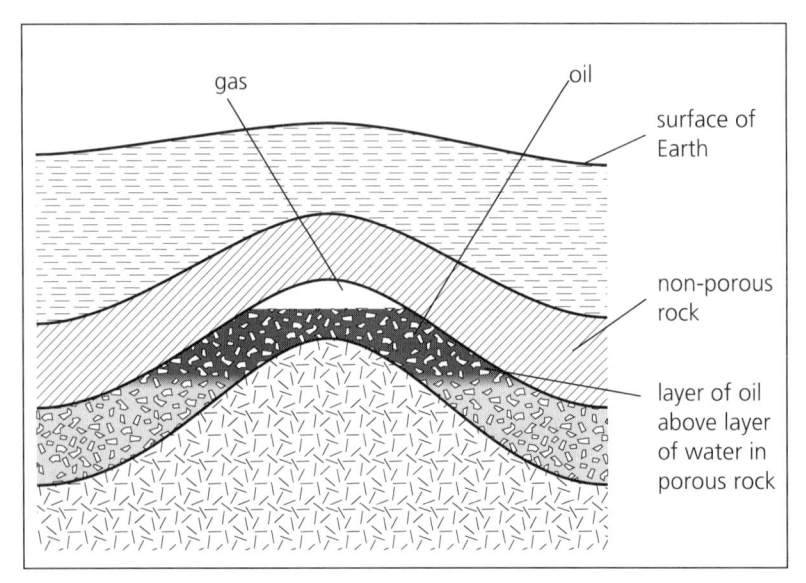

Where to find oil

Help
Porous rock allows liquids to pass through it, like a sponge.

Crude oil is a mixture of very many compounds.

A mixture is made up of two or more elements or compounds which are not chemically combined together. This means that mixtures can be separated by physical processes. Oil is separated by **distillation** (it is heated and then the liquids that come off are condensed).

Fractional distillation

Most of the compounds in oil are made from hydrogen and carbon only, and so are called **hydrocarbons**. These different hydrocarbons can be separated by evaporating the oil and allowing it to condense at different temperatures. A different 'fraction' comes off at each temperature. Each fraction consists of one type of hydrocarbon which has molecules with about the same number of carbon atoms. This is known as **fractional distillation**.

Earth Materials

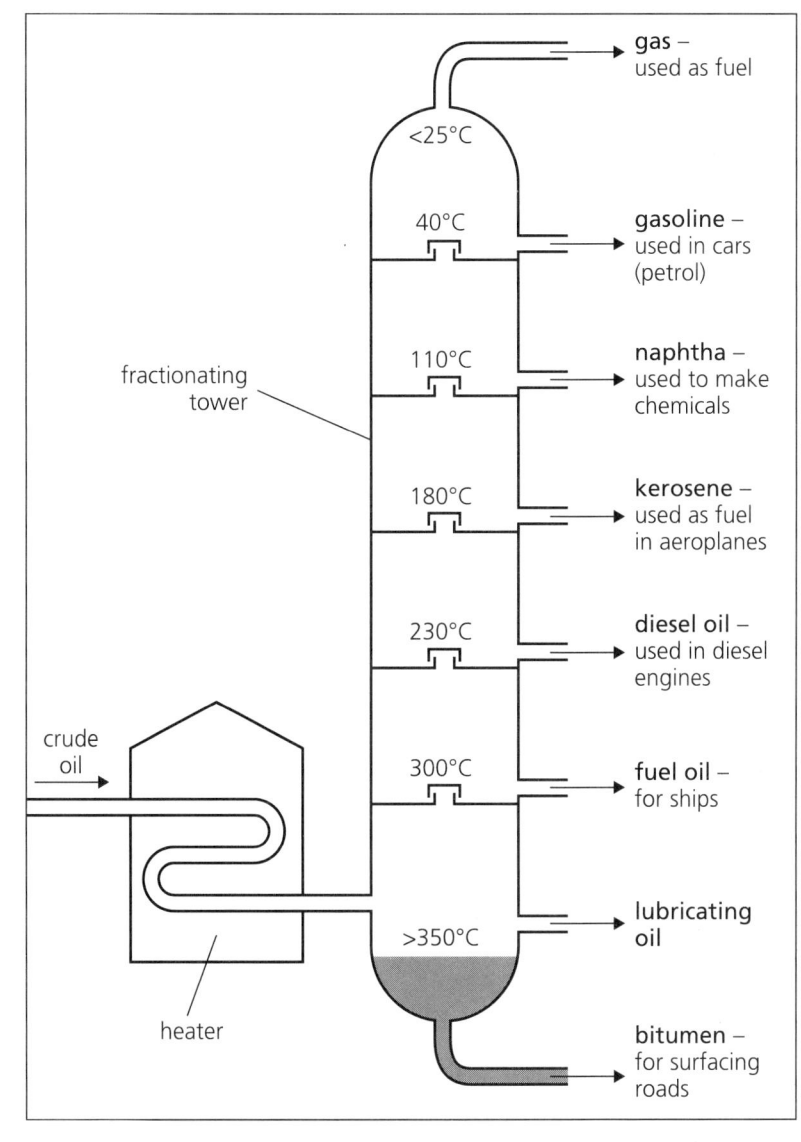

Fractional distillation

Hydrocarbon molecules in crude oil vary a great deal in size. The larger the molecules (which means that they have more carbon atoms) the:

- higher the boiling point of the hydrocarbon
- less volatile it is (this means it is more difficult to evaporate)
- less easily it flows (this means it is more viscous)
- less easy it is to ignite (this means it is less flammable).

Questions

1. Why do you find oil above porous rock and below non-porous rock?
2. Why can oil be split up into different compounds using physical processes?
3. Long-chain hydrocarbons are used to put the finishing surface on roads. Short-chain hydrocarbons are used as fuels. These hydrocarbons are never used the other way round. Explain why.

Alkanes, alkenes and polymers

Larger hydrocarbon molecules can be broken down ('**cracked**') to produce smaller, useful ones. Some are used as fuels and others to make plastics (polymers). Plastics include poly(ethene) and PVC:

- poly(ethene) (known as polythene) is used to make plastic bags
- polychloroethene (known as polyvinyl chloride or PVC) is used to make bottles, wellington boots and raincoats.

Carbon atoms form the backbone of hydrocarbon molecules.

When joined by single carbon–carbon bonds they are said to be **saturated**. These hydrocarbons are known as **alkanes**.

$$\begin{array}{c} H\ \ H \\ |\ \ \ | \\ H-C-C-H \\ |\ \ \ | \\ H\ \ H \end{array} \qquad C_2H_6$$

Ethane – an alkane

Others have double carbon–carbon bonds. These are **unsaturated** and known as **alkenes**. Some of the smaller molecules produced by 'cracking' are alkenes.

$$\begin{array}{c} H\ \ H \\ |\ \ \ | \\ H-C=C-H \end{array} \qquad C_2H_4$$

Ethene – an alkene

The bonds are all covalent. This means that:

- the electrons are shared
- molecules are formed and not ions.

Unsaturated hydrocarbons are very reactive and can be used to make many useful substances including **polymers**. These are very large molecules formed from small molecules called **monomers**. When unsaturated monomers join together to make a polymer (with no other substances produced in the reaction) the process is known as **addition polymerisation**.

The way an addition polymer is formed can be shown like this.

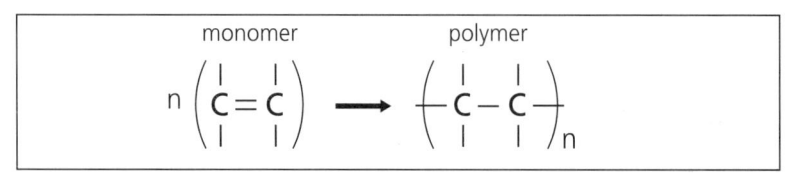

monomer → polymer

$$n \left(\begin{array}{c} | \ \ | \\ C=C \\ | \ \ | \end{array} \right) \longrightarrow \left(\begin{array}{c} | \ \ | \\ C-C \\ | \ \ | \end{array} \right)_n$$

Addition polymerisation

Help

Saturated means that the carbon atoms have no 'spare arms' to join with other atoms. In **unsaturated** hydrocarbons, one of the double carbon bonds readily breaks to join with other elements.

Earth Materials

Plastics are polymers. For example poly(ethene) is made from ethene.

```
     monomer                    polymer
     H   H             H   H   H   H   H   H
     |   |             |   |   |   |   |   |
     C = C     →     — C — C — C — C — C — C —
     |   |             |   |   |   |   |   |
     H   H             H   H   H   H   H   H
     ethene          poly(ethene) – commonly called polythene
```

Formation of polythene

PVC is not made simply from hydrogen and carbon. As the name polyvinyl chloride suggests, chlorine is involved.

```
     monomer                    polymer
     Cl  H             Cl  H  Cl  H  Cl  H
     |   |             |   |   |   |   |   |
     C = C     →     — C — C — C — C — C — C —
     |   |             |   |   |   |   |   |
     H   H             H   H   H   H   H   H
   chloroethene       polychloroethene or PVC
                         (polyvinylchloride)
```

Formation of PVC (polychloroethene)

Polystyrene is a hard, brittle plastic used for making food containers such as yoghurt cartons. If you blow air into the plastic you make polystyrene foam which is used for packaging (e.g. for electrical equipment).

```
     H   H             H   H   H   H   H   H
     |   |             |   |   |   |   |   |
     C = C     →     — C — C — C — C — C — C —
     |   |             |   |   |   |   |   |
     H   ⌬             H   ⌬   H   ⌬   H   ⌬
     styrene                polystyrene
```

You do not need to know the polymerisation reactions resulting in PVC and polystyrene. They are shown as examples of addition polymerisation.

Questions

1. Why are unsaturated hydrocarbons so reactive?
2. Why are large hydrocarbons 'cracked'?
3. Used plastic bottles cause a litter problem. One suggestion is to burn them all. Why might this not be such a good idea?

The effects of burning fuel

Burning

Burning is also known as **combustion** and is a very common type of chemical reaction. Burning produces new substances, mostly gases. When fuels burn they react with oxygen from the air. Oxidation has occurred. When a substance is burned in oxygen its elements are changed into oxides.

Most fuels contain carbon and/or hydrogen. Some also contain sulphur. The gases produced when they burn might include:

- carbon dioxide, CO_2 (from the burning of carbon)
- water vapour, H_2O (from the burning of hydrogen)
- sulphur dioxide, SO_2 (from the burning of sulphur).

There are increasing levels of carbon dioxide as a result of burning fossil fuels. The gas traps energy from the Sun in our atmosphere. The atmosphere therefore warms up (the **Greenhouse Effect**). Carbon dioxide is therefore known as a 'Greenhouse' gas.

Burning fuels results in high temperatures. This may cause nitrogen and oxygen in the air to combine and form nitrogen oxides.

Sulphur dioxide and nitrogen oxides produced by furnaces and car engines may dissolve in rain making the rain acidic. Lakes and rivers may become so acidic that living things can't survive. **Acid rain** also damages the stonework and metalwork on buildings.

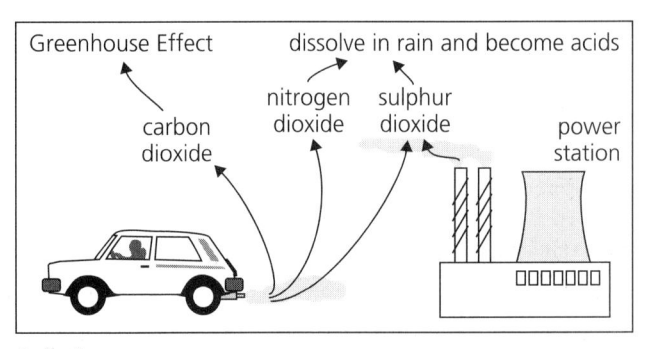

Polluting gases

The atmosphere

For the last 200 million years the atmosphere has been made up of:

- about 80% nitrogen
- about 20% oxygen
- small amounts of other gases (e.g. carbon dioxide, water and the 'noble' gases).

This is very different to the Earth's atmosphere 1 billion years ago, which was more like the atmosphere of Venus and Mars today. The atmosphere then was formed by a lot of volcanic activity and contained:

- water vapour
- carbon dioxide
- small amounts of methane
- small amounts of ammonia
- little or no oxygen.

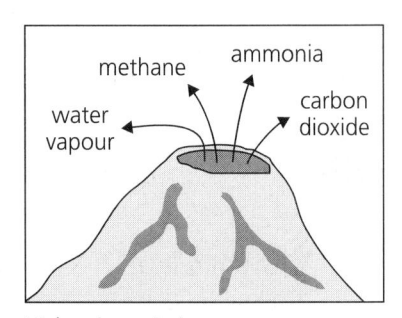

Volcanic emissions

As the Earth cooled, water vapour condensed to form the oceans.

Earth Materials

As green plants evolved, the atmosphere started to change.

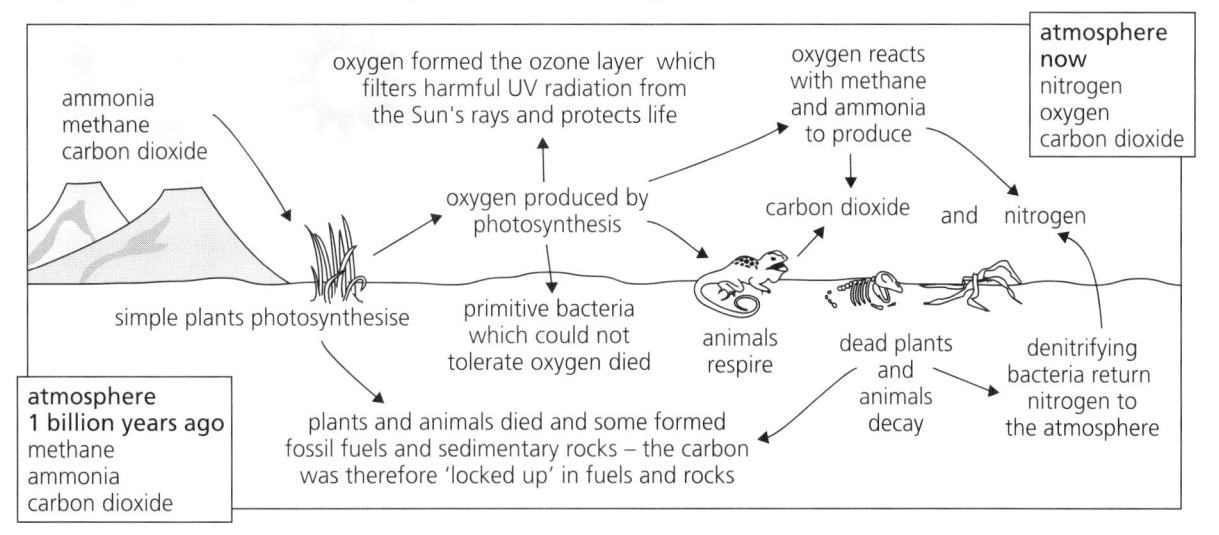

atmosphere 1 billion years ago
methane
ammonia
carbon dioxide

ammonia, methane, carbon dioxide → simple plants photosynthesise → oxygen produced by photosynthesis

oxygen formed the ozone layer which filters harmful UV radiation from the Sun's rays and protects life

primitive bacteria which could not tolerate oxygen died

plants and animals died and some formed fossil fuels and sedimentary rocks – the carbon was therefore 'locked up' in fuels and rocks

animals respire → carbon dioxide

oxygen reacts with methane and ammonia to produce carbon dioxide and nitrogen

dead plants and animals decay

denitrifying bacteria return nitrogen to the atmosphere

atmosphere now
nitrogen
oxygen
carbon dioxide

These changes in the atmosphere over 200 million years ago made it possible for new organisms to evolve and survive. There was:

- oxygen for the plants and animals to respire
- less methane which could kill them
- less ammonia which could kill them
- less carbon dioxide.

Primitive micro-organisms which had existed in the oxygen-free atmosphere could not tolerate the oxygen so died out.

Releasing carbon dioxide

Carbonates are sometimes moved deep into the Earth as a result of geological activity. If volcanic activity breaks them down, they release carbon dioxide back into the air. In addition we burn fossil fuels, releasing carbon dioxide which has been locked up for millions of years. This fast release increases the amount of carbon dioxide in the atmosphere.

The Earth can re-absorb carbon dioxide in the oceans. Carbon dioxide reacts with sea water to produce insoluble carbonates which are deposited as sediment and soluble hydrogen carbonates which remain in the sea. When there is too much carbon dioxide in the atmosphere this reaction increases, but even so the oceans cannot take all the increase in atmospheric carbon dioxide.

Questions

1. Why is the problem of acid rain increasing?
2. Explain how the amount of nitrogen gas has increased in the atmosphere over the last billion years.
3. Millions of years ago we could not have survived on Earth because of the atmosphere. Now we do survive. What changes in the atmosphere have taken place which allow us to survive?

Earth Materials

Module test questions

1. The diagram shows the rock cycle.
   Match words from the list with labels **1–4** on the diagram.

   metamorphic   **igneous**
   magma   **sedimentary**

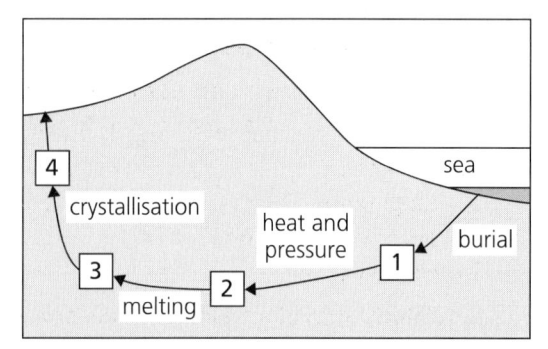

2. The diagram shows how fossil fuels may be trapped in the Earth's crust.
   Choose words from the list for each of the labels **1–4** on the diagram.

   non-porous rock   **oil**
   porous rock   **gas**

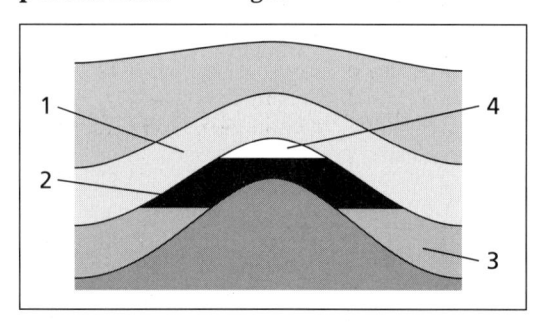

3. These sentences are about how the atmosphere changed once plants began to evolve.
   Choose words from the list for each of the spaces **1–4** in the sentences.

   nitrogen   **ammonia**
   ozone   **carbon dioxide**

   As a result of photosynthesis, oxygen began to pollute the atmosphere. ___1___ in the atmosphere became 'locked up' in fossil fuels and sedimentary rocks. Methane and ___2___ reacted with oxygen and the result of this reaction was ___3___ gas. Oxygen resulted in the production of ___4___ which filters harmful ultraviolet radiation from the Sun.

4. When the Earth was formed, which *two* of the following statements about the atmosphere were true?
   The atmosphere contained:
   A a lot of water vapour
   B very little carbon dioxide
   C a lot of oxygen
   D no methane
   E some ammonia

5. Which *two* of the following statements are true about alkanes?
   A they have only short chains of carbon atoms
   B they have carbon–carbon double bonds
   C they have carbon–carbon single bonds
   D they are more reactive than alkenes
   E they are saturated hydrocarbons

6. This is a diagram of the structure of the Earth.

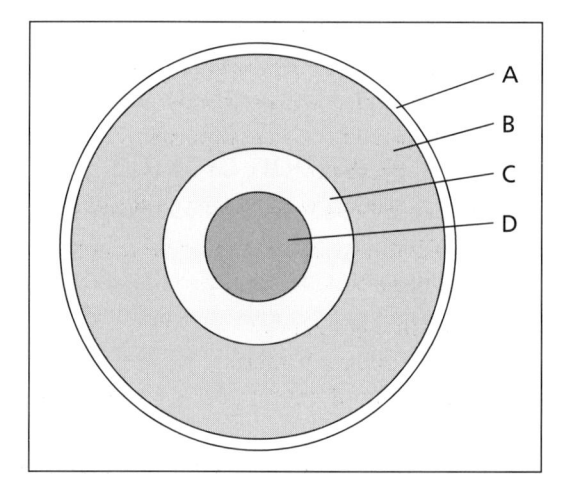

   1. Which letter represents the crust?
   A B C D

   2. Which letter represents the mantle?
   A B C D

   3. Which letter represents the part of the Earth likely to be the most dense?
   A B C D

   4. Convection currents cause the movement of the Earth's plates. Which letter represents the area where convection currents are taking place?
   A B C D

Earth Materials

7 The first atmosphere of the Earth was a result of volcanic activity.

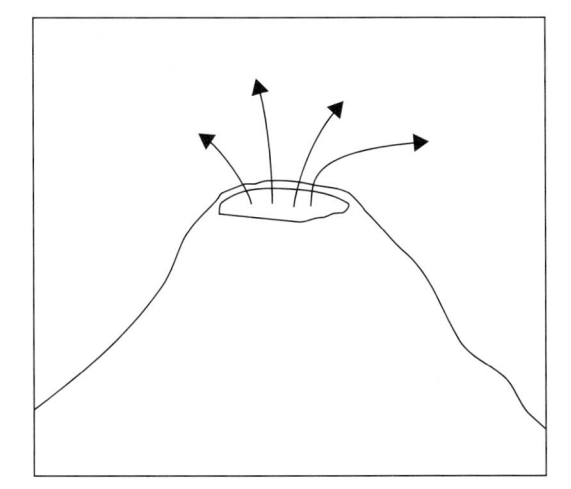

1. What did the volcanoes emit?

A oxygen, carbon dioxide and ammonia
B methane, ammonia and carbon dioxide
C nitrogen, methane and ammonia
D carbon dioxide, nitrogen and ammonia

2. What has reduced the amount of ammonia in the atmosphere?

A its reaction with carbon dioxide
B its reaction with methane
C its reaction with carbon dioxide and methane
D its reaction with oxygen and methane

3. What has caused the amount of nitrogen to increase?

A nitrifying bacteria
B denitrifying bacteria
C reaction of oxygen, carbon dioxide and ammonia
D reaction of carbon dioxide and ammonia

4. Two of the gases responsible for the increase in acid rain are:

A nitrogen oxides and ammonia
B sulphur dioxide and methane
C nitrogen oxides and sulphur dioxide
D carbon dioxide and ammonia

8 Crude oil is a mixture of compounds.

1. Which of the following statements is true of short-chain hydrocarbons compared to long-chain hydrocarbons?

Short-chain hydrocarbons:

A have a higher boiling point
B are more viscous
C are more flammable
D are harder to evaporate

2. Which is the best term for the separation of the different compounds in crude oil?

A distillation
B evaporation
C fractional distillation
D condensation

3. Which of the following statements is *not* true about alkenes?

A they contain covalent bonds
B they have double bonds
C they easily form polymers
D they are not very reactive

4. Which of the following diagrams represents polymerisation?

Important symbols about chemicals

You should be able to recognise and explain what these symbols mean:

oxidising
provide oxygen which allows other materials to burn more fiercely

harmful
similar to toxic substances but less dangerous

toxic
can cause death when swallowed or breathed in or absorbed through the skin

highly flammable
catch fire easily

corrosive
attack and destroy living tissues, including eyes and skin

irritant
not corrosive but can cause reddening or blistering of the skin

You should also be able to name one hazardous substance which is corrosive (e.g. sulphuric acid).

Rates of reaction

If you want to increase the speed of a reaction then you could:

- increase the **temperature** – to increase the speed and frequency at which the particles in the reacting chemicals bump into each other

- increase the **concentration** of the reacting chemicals – so that particles bump into each other more often

- increase the **pressure** on the reacting chemicals (if gases) – to increase the rate and frequency at which particles bump into each other

- increase the **surface area** of the chemicals (e.g. chop up a solid) – this also increases how often the particles bump into each other

- use a **catalyst** – this lowers the amount of energy needed for a reaction to take place.

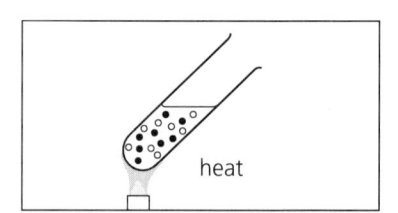

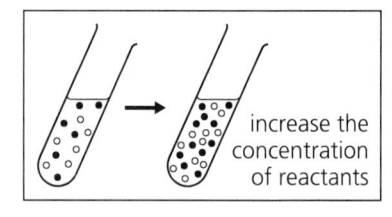

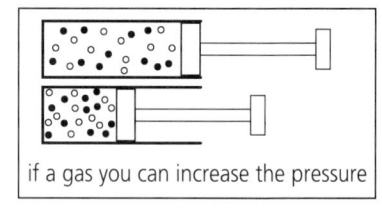

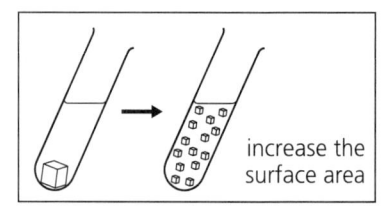

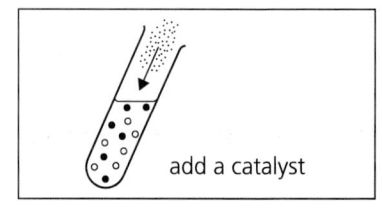

heat

increase the concentration of reactants

if a gas you can increase the pressure

increase the surface area

add a catalyst

Speeding up rate of reaction

Patterns of Chemical Change

How can you tell if a reaction has speeded up?
There are two ways:
- measure the rate products are formed (e.g. how much gas is being given off)
- measure the rate at which the chemicals disappear (e.g. a solid will get smaller).

It is possible, therefore, to compare rates of reaction. For example, when marble chips react with acid, hydrogen gas is given off and the solid chips get smaller. You can measure this.

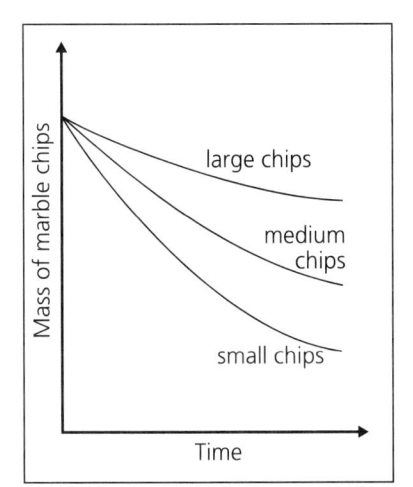

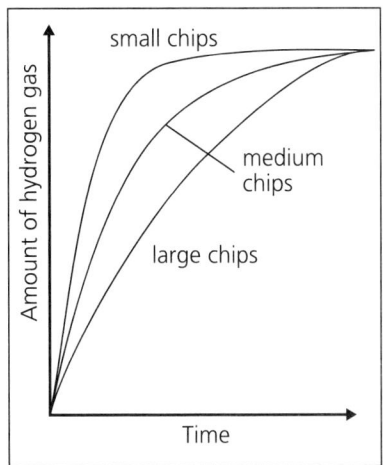

Comparing rates of reaction when marble chips are added to acid

Why speed up a reaction?
In industry, speeding up a reaction will keep costs down and therefore profits up. You will make more of your product in the same time.

Many industrial processes use catalysts. A catalyst will speed up the reaction but it is not used up itself. It can be used time and time again. Different reactions need different catalysts.

Questions
1. Suggest *three* ways of speeding up a chemical reaction. For each way explain why the reaction does speed up.
2. What are catalysts and why do industrial companies use them?
3. Suggest why industry might want to speed up reactions.

Do chemical reactions release energy?

The answer is sometimes!

An **exothermic** reaction results in energy being transferred *to* the surroundings, often in the form of heat (e.g. a fuel burning).
An **endothermic** reaction results in energy being taken *from* the surroundings.

During a chemical reaction:
- energy must be supplied to break the existing bonds between the chemicals
- energy is then released when new chemical bonds form.

In an **exothermic** reaction the energy released in forming the new bonds is *greater* than the energy used to break the original bonds – the excess energy is lost as heat. In an **endothermic** reaction the energy released in forming the new bonds is *less* than the energy used to break the original bonds – energy is therefore taken from the surroundings.

Worked example

Q Is the combustion of methane an exothermic or endothermic reaction?

A The equation for the reaction is:

methane + oxygen → carbon dioxide + water
$$CH_4 + 2O_2 \rightarrow CO_2 + 2H_2O$$

The energy needed to make or break bonds has been worked out and can be used to answer this question.

These are the bonds represented in this reaction:
- methane has 4 C–H bonds
- each oxygen has 1 O=O bond
- carbon dioxide has 2 C=O bonds
- each water has 2 H–O bonds.

The energy needed to make or break each of these bonds is shown in the table.

Bonds broken:
  4 C–H × 413 = 1652 kJ
  2 O=O × 498 = 996 kJ
    (two molecules of oxygen)
  Total = 2648 kJ energy used

Bonds made:
  2 C=O × 805 = 1610 kJ
  4 H–O × 464 = 1856 kJ
    (two molecules of water)
  Total = 3466 kJ energy released

Bond	Energy
C–H	413 kJ
O=O	498 kJ
C=O	805 kJ
H–O	464 kJ

More energy is released than used, so the reaction is exothermic.

Help

kJ = kilojoule which is 1000 joules

Help

Remember: energy is used to break bonds and energy is released when bonds are formed.

Patterns of Chemical Change

The difference between the energy used and the energy released is known as the **nett energy transfer**. If the reaction is exothermic this is negative, if it is endothermic it is positive.

The nett energy for the worked example is:

energy in	2150 kJ
energy out	3466 kJ
nett energy gain	−1316 kJ

A chemical reaction will take place only if the particles hit each other (collide) with enough energy. The minimum energy that is needed for a reaction to take place is called the **activation energy.**

The energy changes during a reaction can be shown by graphs.

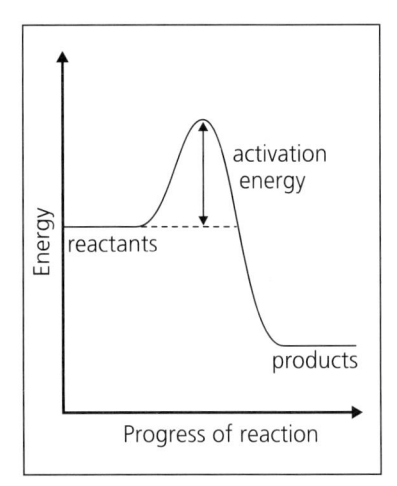

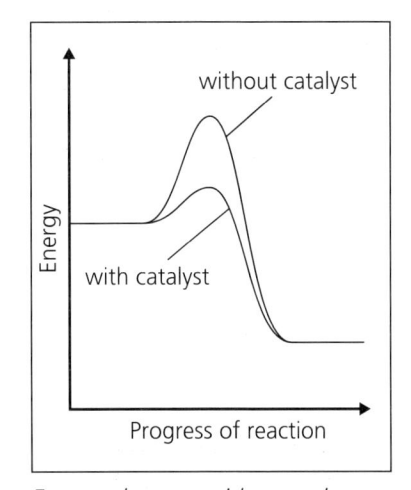

Energy changes during a reaction   *Energy changes with a catalyst*

Catalysts reduce the amount of energy required to start a reaction. They therefore reduce the activation energy.

Questions

1. What is meant by an exothermic reaction?
2. Study the graph.

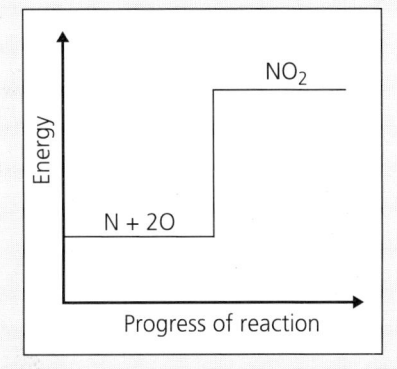

   What does the graph tell you about the reaction between nitrogen and oxygen?
3. In a reaction more energy is used in breaking the original bonds than is released in making the new bonds. Is the reaction exothermic or endothermic?

Chemistry and living organisms

Chemical reactions do not just take place in big industrial areas. They are taking place inside our bodies all the time. Our cells use chemicals to release energy from food and to make new materials. We also use some micro-organisms to make useful substances for us. For example, **yeast** cells convert:

sugar → carbon dioxide + alcohol

This is known as **fermentation** and it is used to produce:
- alcohol for wine and beer making
- carbon dioxide – the bubbles make bread rise.

Bacteria are used to make yoghurt from milk. They convert lactose sugar in the milk to lactic acid.

These reactions are faster when it is warm but *not* hot. Living organisms use catalysts called **enzymes**. These are proteins and are damaged by temperatures above about 45°C.

Help
A simple test for carbon dioxide is that it turns lime water milky.

The chemistry of fertiliser production

Nitrogen-based fertilisers help us to grow food. They replace the nitrogen taken from the soil by growing plants. This means that farmers can grow more – increase the yield of their crops. One problem with fertiliser is that it can run off the land and into ponds, rivers and lakes. This can contaminate our drinking water.

Ammonium nitrate fertiliser is made in the following way:

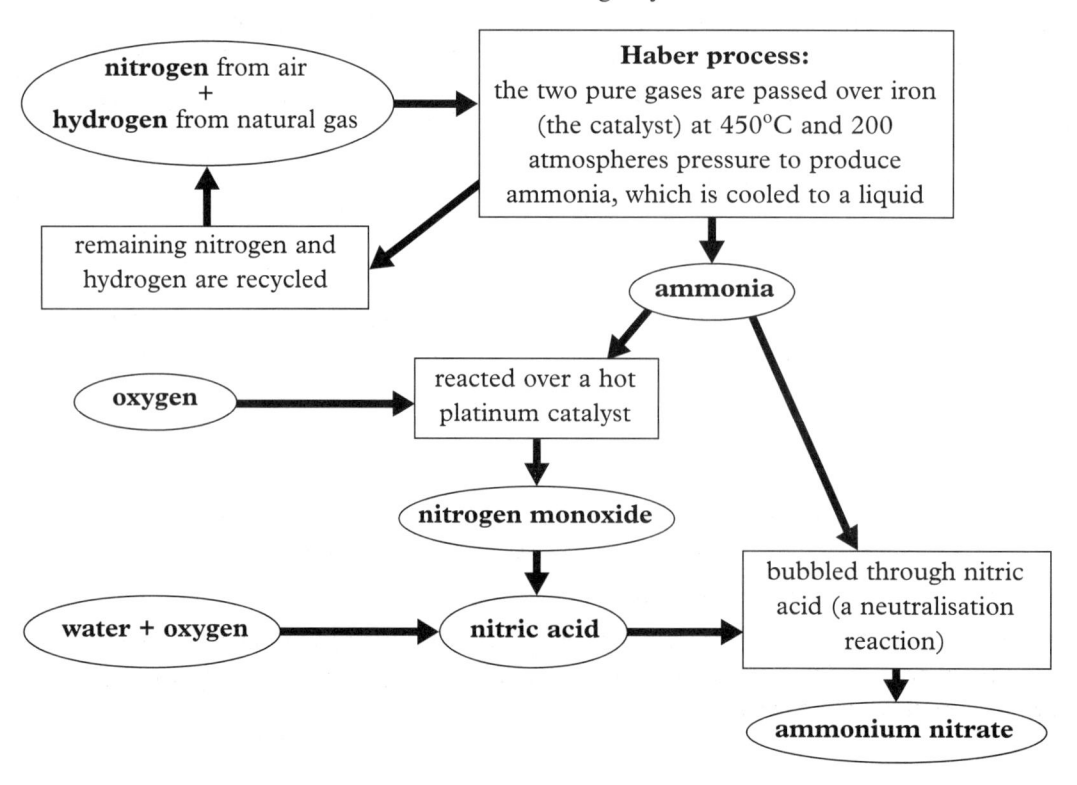

- **nitrogen** from air + **hydrogen** from natural gas → **Haber process:** the two pure gases are passed over iron (the catalyst) at 450°C and 200 atmospheres pressure to produce ammonia, which is cooled to a liquid
- remaining nitrogen and hydrogen are recycled
- ammonia + oxygen → reacted over a hot platinum catalyst → nitrogen monoxide
- nitrogen monoxide + water + oxygen → nitric acid
- ammonia + nitric acid → bubbled through nitric acid (a neutralisation reaction) → ammonium nitrate

Patterns of Chemical Change

Reversible reactions and equilibrium

The reaction between nitrogen and hydrogen to produce ammonia is **reversible**. The reaction will go either way depending on the conditions.

$$N_2 + 3H_2 \xrightleftharpoons{\text{reversible reaction}} 2NH_3$$

If the reaction is going in both directions at the same rate in a **closed system**, it is said to be in **equilibrium**. A closed system is a container where no other chemicals are involved, and where none of the products are removed from the container.

Where the point of equilibrium is between the two reactions depends on the conditions. If the forward reaction is exothermic, the back reaction must be endothermic. If you add heat energy by heating the reactants, the system will shift the reaction in favour of the back reaction which then absorbs the heat energy (you will get more reactants than products).

$$N_2 + 3H_2 \xrightleftharpoons{\text{heat}} 2NH_3$$

So whether there are more reactant molecules or more product molecules in the equilibrium 'mix' depends on temperature. This is an important principle behind the Haber process.

The Haber process

The reaction between nitrogen and hydrogen in a closed system means that you could be breaking down ammonia as quickly as you were making it! This would be useless to a manufacturer.

A German scientist called Haber found that a high temperature, high pressure and a catalyst are needed to make even modest amounts of ammonia. The yield is increased if ammonia is siphoned off as it is made, and the unused reactants continually recycled so that it becomes an open system.

This graph shows the yields of ammonia in the Haber process at various temperatures and pressures. If pressures above 200 atmospheres are used the costs for equipment would increase significantly. If the reaction was allowed to run at lower temperature it would take too long. The temperature and pressure used are the most economic way to produce ammonia.

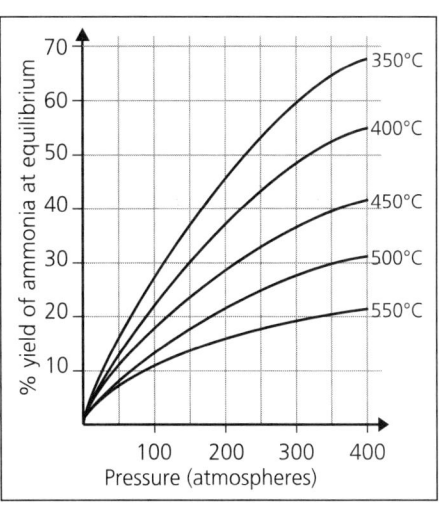

The reaction between nitrogen and hydrogen in different conditions

Questions

1. Micro-organisms can be used usefully by people. Draw a spider diagram to show these uses. Useful micro-organisms should be at the centre of the diagram.
2. What is meant by a reversible reaction?
3. To get the maximum yield of ammonia from nitrogen and hydrogen you would need to run the reaction at 350°C and 400 atmospheres pressure. Why do manufacturers using the Haber process not do this?

Chemical quantities

This topic is very much assessed in terms of calculations. You will, in the examination, have access to a data book. Here the information you need is printed in the table on the right.

A series of worked examples show the type of calculation you will be expected to do.

Relative formula mass of compounds

You must be able to calculate the **relative formula mass (M_r)** of a compound (given the formula).

> **Worked example**
>
> **Q** What is the relative formula mass of sulphuric acid (H_2SO_4)?
>
> **A** A_r hydrogen = 2 (there are two of them)
> A_r sulphur = 32
> A_r oxygen = 64 (there are four of them)
> M_r = 98

Relative atomic masses (A_r)	
hydrogen	1
carbon	12
oxygen	16
sulphur	32
calcium	40
iron	56

Percentage of elements in compounds

You must be able to work out the percentage of an element in a compound.

> **Worked example**
>
> **Q** What is the percentage of sulphur in sulphuric acid?
>
> **A** The M_r of sulphuric acid is 98
> The A_r of sulphur is 32
> Therefore sulphur represents $\frac{32}{98}$ of the compound
> This is 32.7%

Help

A_r is relative atomic mass.
M_r is relative formula mass.

Masses of reactants and products

You must be able to calculate the masses of reactants and products.

> **Worked example**
>
> On heating calcium carbonate ($CaCO_3$) it breaks down. The products of the breakdown are calcium oxide and carbon dioxide.
>
> **Q** What mass of calcium oxide can be formed from 25 g of calcium carbonate?
>
> $CaCO_3 \rightarrow CaO + CO_2$
>
> *continued ...*

Patterns of Chemical Change

> **A** From this equation:
> - 1 mole of $CaCO_3$ reacts to give 1 mole of CaO and 1 mole of CO_2
>
> M_r calcium carbonate is 100   (Ca = 40, C = 12, 3 × O = 48)
> M_r calcium oxide is 56   (Ca = 40, O = 16)
> M_r carbon dioxide is 44   (C = 12, 2 × O = 32)
>
> - Therefore 100 g of calcium carbonate will result in 56 g of calcium oxide.
> - Therefore 25 g of calcium carbonate will result in 14 g of calcium oxide.

What if the product is a gas?

You must be able to calculate the volume of a reactant if it is a gas.

From the last example, the breakdown of 1 mole of calcium carbonate will result in 1 mole of carbon dioxide. Therefore 100 g of calcium carbonate will break down to produce 44 g of carbon dioxide.

However, 1 mole of *any* gas occupies 24 litres (at room temperature and pressure). So if 1 mole of calcium carbonate breaks down, then 24 litres of carbon dioxide are produced.

If 2 moles of calcium carbonate break down, then 2 moles of carbon dioxide will be produced, or 2 × 24 = 48 litres.

Help

Carrying out calculations involving moles is simply a matter of ratios.

Help

1 mole is the relative formula mass of the compound in grams.

Working out chemical formulae

You must be able to determine the ratios of atoms in compounds from information you are given.

> ### Worked example
>
> In an investigation it is found that 5.6 g of iron react with 2.4 g of oxygen.
>
> **Q** What is the formula of iron oxide?
>
> **A**
>
> | | iron | oxygen |
> |---|---|---|
> | masses combining | 5.6 g | 2.4 g |
> | mass of 1 mole | 56 g | 16 g |
> | number of moles combining | $\frac{5.6}{56} = 0.1$ | $\frac{2.4}{16} = 0.15$ |
> | the ratios are | 1 to | 1.5 |
> | or better still | 2 to | 3 |
>
> The formula for iron oxide is therefore Fe_2O_3.

Questions

Use information on these pages to answer the questions.

1 What is the M_r of sulphuric acid (H_2SO_4)?

2 What is the percentage of oxygen in calcium carbonate ($CaCO_3$)?

Patterns of Chemical Change

Balancing equations

You must also be able to balance an equation given to you.

This is the reaction between sodium and chlorine.

$Na + Cl_2 \rightarrow NaCl$

However, there needs to be the same number of atoms of each element on each side of the equation. So this equation becomes:

$\underline{2}Na + Cl_2 \rightarrow \underline{2}NaCl$

This is the reaction of methane and oxygen:

$CH_4 + O_2 \rightarrow H_2O + CO_2$

However, there needs to be the same number of atoms of each element on each side of the equation. So this equation becomes:

$CH_4 + 2O_2 \rightarrow 2H_2O + CO_2$

Balancing half equations

If molten sodium chloride is electrolysed then chloride ions will move to the positive electrode. This is the equation for what happens at the positive electrode.

$Cl^- - e^- \rightarrow Cl_2$ (a molecule of chlorine)

However, the equation doesn't balance because one molecule of chlorine contains two atoms.

You balance the equation like this:

$2Cl^- - 2e^- \rightarrow Cl_2$

In the purification of copper, positive copper ions move to the negative electrode and are deposited as copper atoms. This is the equation for what happens at the negative electrode:

$Cu^{2+} + e^- \rightarrow Cu$

However, you must balance the equation like this:

$Cu^{2+} + 2e^- \rightarrow Cu$

Help

Balancing equations
You must have the same number of atoms on each side of the equation.

Questions

1. Balance this equation which represents the breakdown of hydrogen peroxide:
   $H_2O_2 \rightarrow H_2O + O_2$

2. 34 g of ammonia react with an excess of water. How much ammonium hydroxide will be formed?
   $NH_3 + H_2O \rightarrow NH_4OH$
   (nitrogen = 14, hydrogen = 1, oxygen = 16)

3. 48 g of magnesium react with an excess of nitric acid. What volume of hydrogen will evolve?
   $Mg + 2HNO_3 \rightarrow Mg(NO_3)_2 + H_2$
   (magnesium = 24, hydrogen = 1)

Terminal exam questions

1. Ammonium nitrate is a fertiliser used by farmers. It is manufactured on a large scale in Britain.

   a i Nitrogen and hydrogen are reacted together in the Haber Process.
   Balance the following equation.

   $$N_2 + H_2 \rightarrow NH_3 \qquad [2]$$

   ii State the conditions under which the two gases are reacted together. [3]

   iii Explain, as fully as you can, why these conditions are used. [3]

   b You will need the following information to answer this question:

Relative atomic masses (A_r)	
hydrogen	1
nitrogen	14
oxygen	16

   The ammonia is reacted with nitric acid to produce ammonium nitrate.

   $$NH_3 + HNO_3 \rightarrow NH_4NO_3$$

   i What is the relative formula mass of ammonium nitrate? [1]

   ii If 85 tonnes of ammonia are used, how many tonnes of ammonium nitrate will be produced? [4]

   13 marks

2. Ethene burns in oxygen and releases carbon dioxide as a waste product. The following equation represents the reaction.

   $$C_2H_4 + 3O_2 \rightarrow 2CO_2 + 2H_2O$$

   In terms of the bonds, the reaction can be shown as follows:

   ```
   H   H                      O    H
   |   |                      ‖     \
   C = C  + 3 O=O  →  2 C        + 2   O
   |   |                      ‖     /
   H   H                      O    H
   ```

   This table showing the energy required to break and make certain bonds will be helpful in answering the questions which follow.

Bond	Energy (kJ)
C—H	413
C=C	612
O=O	498
C=O	805
H—O	464

   a i Work out the energy changes that take place during the reaction. [5]

   ii Is the reaction exothermic or endothermic? Give a reason for your answer. [1]

   b This reaction takes place very quickly. Suggest *three* ways of speeding up a reaction that takes place slowly. [3]

   9 marks

3. You will need the following information to answer this question:

Relative atomic masses (A_r)	
sodium	23
chlorine	35
calcium	40

   a Sodium chloride (NaCl) can be broken down to produce sodium and chlorine gas. These are two useful substances.
   If 116 g of sodium chloride are broken down, what volume of chlorine gas will be released? [4]

   b In an investigation it is found that 20 g of calcium reacts with 35 g of chlorine to produce calcium chloride. What is the formula of calcium chloride? [4]

   8 marks

   Total for test: 30 marks

Solids, liquids and gases

Matter can exist in three states – **solid**, **liquid** or **gas**. If you supply sufficient energy to a substance it may change from one state to another.

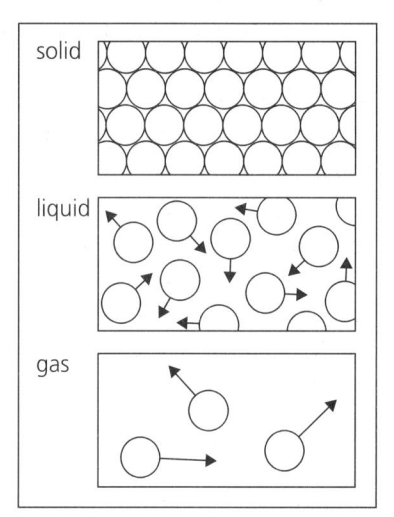

If you supply energy to a solid then the particles in the solid will vibrate more, and will therefore move more freely. Eventually the solid will melt. The temperature at which the state changes from solid to liquid is the **melting point**.

If you supply energy to a liquid then the particles will move around more quickly. If sufficient energy is supplied the liquid will boil – this is the **boiling point**. If more energy is supplied then the particles' attraction to each other will be overcome and some will escape from the liquid to form a gas. This is **evaporation.**

The particles of a gas move randomly in all directions. This is why gases spread out easily. This is known as **diffusion.**

The three states of matter

What about dissolving?

The particles in a liquid move. If a solid is added to the liquid, the particles in the liquid may separate the particles of the solid from each other. This is **dissolving** (e.g. sugar in a cup of tea).

Atomic structure

Everything we know is made from **atoms**. There are well over 90 different types of atom. A substance containing only one type of atom is known as an **element** (e.g. sodium, oxygen, hydrogen).

Atoms have a small nucleus containing protons and neutrons. Whizzing around this nucleus is a 'sea' of tiny electrons.

	Mass	Charge
proton	1	+
neutron	1	0
electron	negligible	–

In an atom there is always the same number of protons and electrons – resulting in no overall charge. All atoms of the same element have the same number of protons. The different elements have different numbers of protons. So:

- number of protons = proton number (or atomic number)
- number of protons + neutrons = mass number

In the periodic table the mass number and proton number are written at the top and bottom of the symbol for the element.

Example: mass number $^{23}_{11}Na$
proton number

Sodium has therefore got:

- 11 protons
- 12 neutrons
- 11 electrons

Help

Atoms of the same element always have the same number of protons and electrons. They have no charge.

Structures and Bonding

Isotopes

Atoms of the same element may have different numbers of neutrons. These atoms are called **isotopes** of the element (e.g. $^{35}_{17}Cl$ and $^{37}_{17}Cl$).

Electrons

Imagine that the electrons which orbit the nucleus are in different 'shells' (like layers in an onion). The shell nearest the nucleus can hold 2 electrons. The next three shells can hold 8 electrons. The shells are in fact **energy levels** (lowest energy nearest the nucleus). Electrons fill the lowest available energy levels, so they fill the shells closest to the nucleus. Atoms like to have full shells to make them stable. Noble gases have 8 electrons in their outer shells, so are very unreactive and stable.

You must be able to represent the atomic structure of the first twenty elements of the periodic table, using the periodic table in the data book. First you must work out the number of electrons and then place them in the shells. The first shell can take 2 electrons. The other shells take 8 electrons each. The last shell takes the number of electrons that are left.

Below is a diagram of an atom of sodium. It has 11 protons and 11 electrons. It therefore has no charge. The electronic structure of sodium can be written as 2, 8, 1.

Magnesium has an electronic structure of 2, 8, 2.

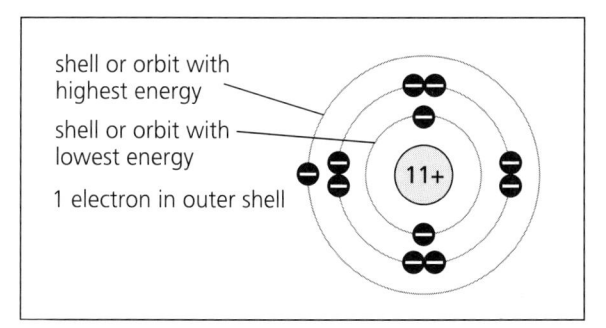

Help

An isotope is the same element but with a different number of neutrons.

The electronic structure of a sodium atom

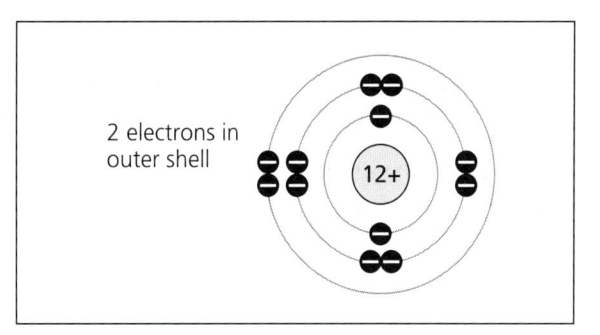

The electronic structure of a magnesium atom

Questions

1. A jug of water is left in the freezer. It turns to ice and you cannot pour it. When it melts you can pour the water. Explain what has happened.
2. Chlorine (Cl) has 17 protons. What is its electronic structure?
3. How many electrons does carbon ($^{12}_{6}C$) have in its outer shell?
4. Work out the electronic structure of magnesium ($^{24}_{12}Mg$), silicon ($^{28}_{14}Si$), argon ($^{40}_{18}Ar$) and oxygen ($^{16}_{8}O$).

Compounds

Ionic bonds

Most substances are compounds formed when two or more elements react and combine together. One way of forming a chemical bond is by losing or gaining an electron.

Look, for example, at the reaction between sodium and chlorine:

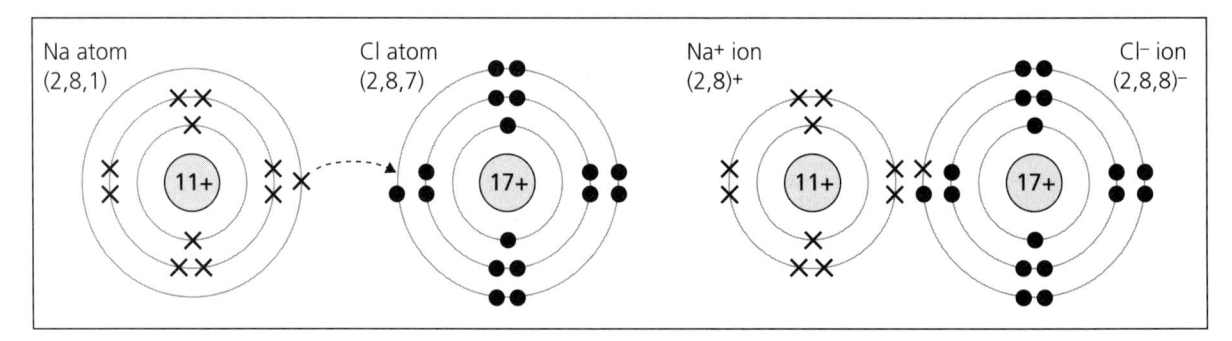

| Na atom (2,8,1) | Cl atom (2,8,7) | Na+ ion (2,8)+ | Cl- ion (2,8,8)- |

- Both elements now have a full outer shell of 8 electrons. They now have the electronic structure of noble gases.
- The sodium atom has lost one electron. It is now a positive sodium ion (it now has one more proton than it has electrons).
- The chlorine has gained one electron. It is now a negative chloride ion (it has one more electron now than it has protons).

The compound is sodium chloride (common salt). The bond between the two elements is an **ionic bond**. Ionic bonds are very strong. The compound is called an **ionic compound**.

Covalent bonds

Atoms can also form bonds by sharing electrons. These shared pairs are called **covalent bonds**. Atoms which share electrons often form molecules.

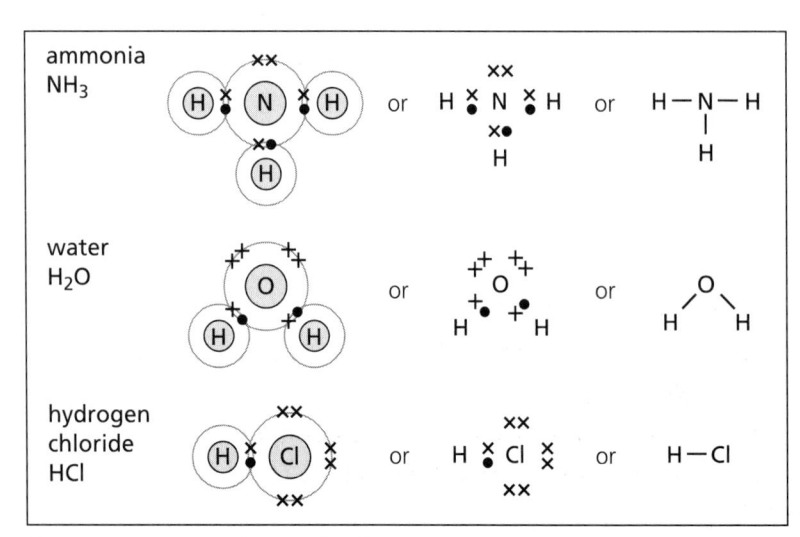

Some common covalent molecules

ammonia NH_3

water H_2O

hydrogen chloride HCl

Help

'Dot and cross' diagrams often show only the outer shell electrons

Structures and Bonding

When they are not in compounds, all of the elements which are common gases are found in diatomic molecules. This means molecules with two atoms (e.g. O_2, Cl_2).

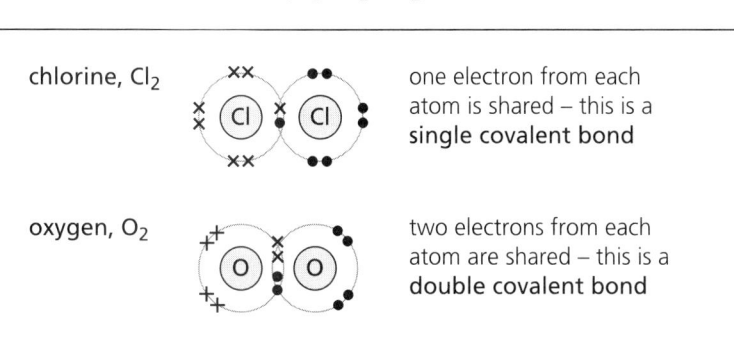

chlorine, Cl_2 — one electron from each atom is shared – this is a **single covalent bond**

oxygen, O_2 — two electrons from each atom are shared – this is a **double covalent bond**

Help

Some substances can exist in covalent *or* ionic forms. For example:
- hydrogen chloride can be HCl molecules or H^+ and Cl^- ions
- water can be H_2O molecules or H^+ and OH^- ions

The atoms in these molecules are more stable than the atoms on their own, because their highest energy levels (outer shells) are now full. Notice how oxygen (which has six electrons in its outer shell) needs to share another *two* electrons to make it stable – so forming a **double bond**.

Balancing chemical equations

The products made must have exactly the same atoms as the reactants, so:

$$Na(s) + H_2O(l) \rightarrow NaOH(aq) + H_2(g)$$

1 sodium atom   1 sodium atom
2 hydrogen atoms   3 hydrogen atoms
1 oxygen atom   1 oxygen atom

not balanced

$$2Na(s) + 2H_2O(l) \rightarrow 2NaOH(aq) + H_2(g)$$

2 sodium atoms   2 sodium atoms
4 hydrogen atoms   4 hydrogen atoms
2 oxygen atoms   2 oxygen atoms

equation now balanced

The letters (s), (l), (aq) or (g) following each reactant or product show the state of each substance.

State symbols	
s	solid
l	liquid
aq	dissolved in water (aqueous)
g	gas

Questions

1. Draw a diagram to show the electronic structure of $^{40}_{20}Ca$.
2. Predict how calcium will react with chlorine, in terms of the number of atoms reacting.
3. Show how you would represent a calcium ion.
4. Carbon dioxide has the formula CO_2. Draw a diagram of the molecule to show its covalent bonds. Write down *two* other ways of showing this bonding.
   (Atomic number of C = 6, O = 8)

Structure and properties

The structure of substances affects their properties. Ionic and covalent compounds, metals and plastics all behave in different ways which are related to their different bonding.

Ionic compounds

The ions of elements in an ionic compound have opposite electrical charges and so are held together strongly by forces of electrostatic attraction. Ionic compounds form regular structures (giant ionic lattices) in which each positive ion is surrounded by negative ions and each negative ion is surrounded by positive ions. This means that the whole lattice is held together strongly.

It is not easy to break this lattice by heating because a lot of energy is needed to pull the bonds apart. So ionic compounds have high melting and boiling points.

If, however, an ionic compound is melted or dissolved in water, the ions become free to move and will conduct electricity. So, for example, solid sodium chloride (common salt) does not conduct electricity but molten sodium chloride or a salt solution will.

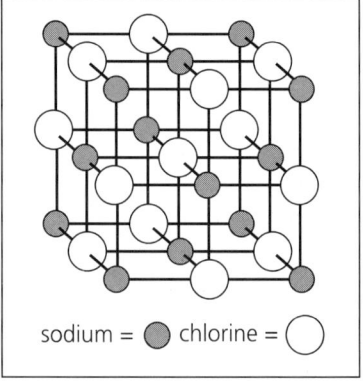

The giant lattice structure of sodium chloride

Metals

Metals consist of giant structures in which the electrons from the highest energy level (outer shell) of each atom are free to move throughout the whole giant structure. The electrons:

- hold the atoms together in a regular structure
- allow the atoms to slide over each other
- allow the metal to conduct heat and electricity.

Covalent compounds

In compounds made of molecules there are strong covalent bonds between the atoms of the molecules but *not* between the molecules themselves. This means that the molecules can be pushed apart easily, and so substances made of molecules have low melting and boiling points.

There are one or two exceptions. Sometimes, covalent compounds take the form of giant lattices rather like ionic lattices. Examples are diamond and graphite (both forms of carbon) and silica (silicon dioxide).

Within diamond each carbon atom is covalently bonded to four other carbon atoms. This makes a rigid, giant covalent structure with high melting and boiling points. Silicon dioxide forms crystals of quartz with a 3D lattice similar to diamond. In graphite each carbon atom forms three covalent bonds with other carbon atoms and they form layers which are able to slide over each other.

Structures and Bonding

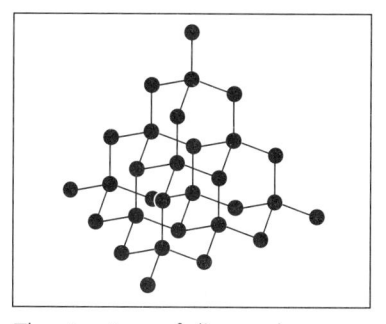

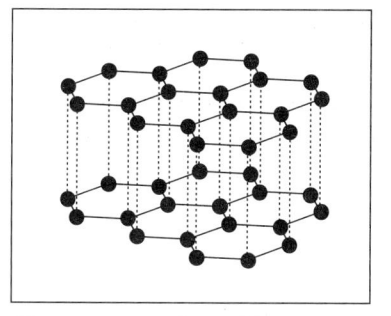

The structure of diamond

The structure of graphite

In covalent compounds the molecules have no charge because they are not made up of ions. Therefore, they cannot conduct electricity. Graphite is an exception to this because each carbon atom is only bonded to three others. This means that one electron in each atom is free to move around, and so graphite can conduct electricity.

Plastics are polymers. They are a tangled mass of very long molecules. The atoms in the molecules are joined by strong covalent bonds to form long chains.

In **thermosoftening plastic** the forces between the chains are weak. When the plastic is heated it goes soft. When it cools it goes hard again. These plastics are useful in industry when the plastic can be remoulded into various shapes during a manufacturing process. They are also useful if you need to add a colour (pigment) to the melted plastic before you let it harden. They are no use if the plastic object is going to be heated in the home (e.g. a dish for the oven).

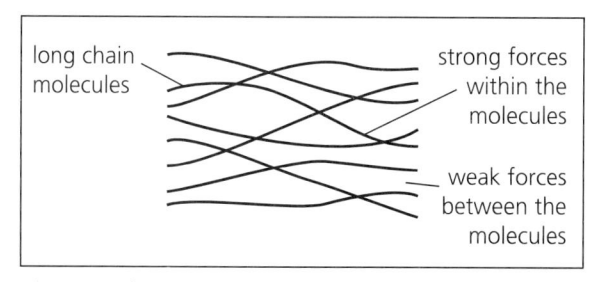

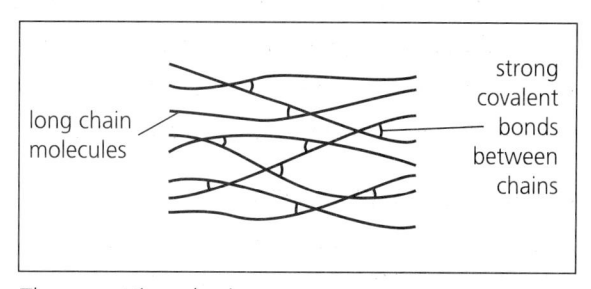

Thermosoftening plastic

Thermosetting plastic

In a **thermosetting plastic,** once it has been heated and moulded and left to cool it will never soften again. The reason is that when the plastic has been heated new covalent bonds are formed between the chains alongside each other. These strong cross linkages prevent the plastic from softening again. The plastics cannot, therefore, be remoulded.

Questions

1. Why are molecular substances often liquids or gases at room temperature?
2. Diamond is so hard that it is used to cut other materials. Explain this in terms of its structure.

The periodic table

The elements can be arranged in order of their proton (atomic) number. This means that they are also arranged in terms of their electronic structure.

This list can then be arranged so that elements with the same number of electrons in their outer shells are in the same columns or groups. So, for example, the elements in group 1 (e.g. lithium, sodium, potassium) all have only 1 electron in the outer shell. These groups are like families of similar elements.

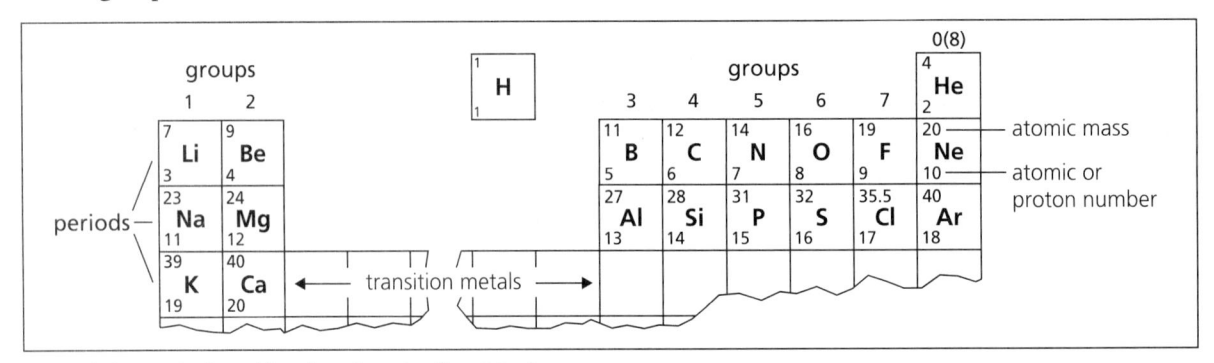

Part of the periodic table, showing the first 20 elements

The history of the periodic table

For a long time chemists searched for patterns which might explain and predict the behaviour of elements. Around 1800, John Dalton introduced the idea that chemical elements were made up of atoms, and that atoms of different elements but with similar properties could be grouped into threes or triads (e.g. lithium, sodium and potassium, which are all soft reactive metals).

In 1863 Newlands introduced the idea of arranging elements in order of their atomic masses in groups of eight (octaves). A few years later Mendeléev published the first clear table, grouping elements by their atomic mass *and* properties. Not all of the elements were known at the time, so this early table had gaps. When the elements were eventually found which fitted the gaps, it strengthened the idea of the periodic table.

Group 1 elements

These are called the alkali metals, because when they react with water an alkaline solution is produced. The alkali metals:
- are soft metals
- react with non-metals to form ionic compounds
- form ions that usually carry a 1^+ charge (as they lose their outer electron)

$$2Na + Cl_2 \rightarrow 2Na^+Cl^-$$

- react with water releasing hydrogen and forming an hydroxide which dissolves in the water to form an alkaline solution

$$2Na + 2H_2O \rightarrow 2NaOH + H_2$$

Structures and Bonding

When placed in cold water, alkali metals float and may well move around on the surface. The more reactive the metal, the more vigorous its reaction with water.

The further down a group the metal is:
- the more reactive it is
- the lower its melting and boiling point.

So, potassium is more reactive than sodium, which is more reactive than lithium.

Why do these metals have different levels of reactivity, given that they all have 1 electron in the outer shell?

The answer is that the higher the proton number (and so the number of electrons), the further the outer electron is from the nucleus. It is at a higher energy level. The further away from the nucleus, the:
- more easily the electron is lost
- less easily electrons are gained.

The electronic structure of lithium is: 2, 1
The electronic structure of sodium is: 2, 8, 1
The electronic structure of potassium is: 2, 8, 8, 1

Group 0 elements (noble gases)

These are sometimes called group 8 elements as they have 8 electrons in their highest energy levels. The noble gases:
- are very stable (unreactive)
- all exist as individual atoms, not as molecules like other gases
- are used to replace air inside light bulbs (because oxygen in air *is* reactive, and would cause the filament to burn away).

Noble gases include helium, neon and argon.

Transition metals

These elements are in the centre block of the periodic table. Examples are iron (Fe) and copper (Cu). These metals:
- have high melting points
- are often used as catalysts (e.g. iron in the Haber process)
- form coloured compounds (e.g. iron oxide, which is red).

Questions

1. You may have seen sodium and potassium react with water. Both are very reactive but potassium is noticeably more reactive than sodium. Explain this in terms of its structure.
2. Why are group 1 metals often called 'alkali' metals?
3. Why are the noble gases so unreactive?
4. Xenon exists as atoms. Chlorine is a molecule and is diatomic. What do these statements mean?

The halogens

The halogens are the elements in group 7 of the periodic table. They are called the halogen gases.

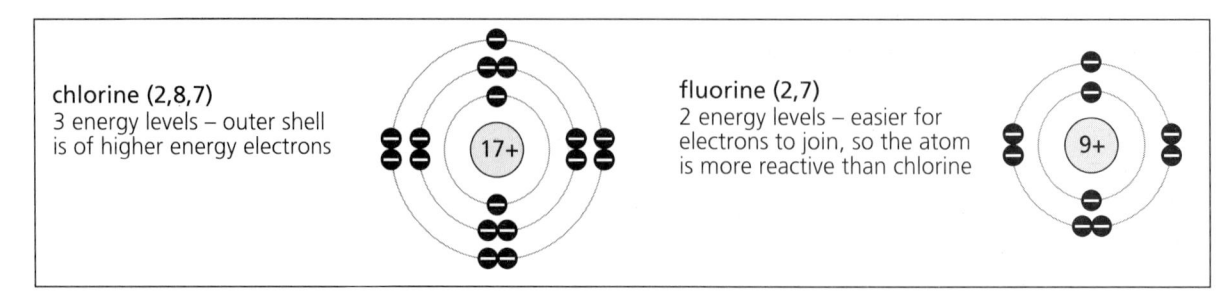

chlorine (2,8,7)
3 energy levels – outer shell is of higher energy electrons

fluorine (2,7)
2 energy levels – easier for electrons to join, so the atom is more reactive than chlorine

Halogens:

- have 7 electrons in the outer shell and so need gain only 1 electron to react
- if they react the halogen ion (halide) has a 1⁻ charge
- are non-metals
- have coloured vapours (e.g. chlorine is green)
- consist of molecules which are made up of pairs of atoms (e.g. chlorine Cl_2, bromine Br_2)
- form ionic salts with metals (e.g. potassium chloride, calcium bromide)

The further down the group you go the:

- less reactive the gas
- higher the melting and boiling points.

Halogens are less reactive as you go down the group. This is because bigger atoms have more electrons, which occupy higher energy levels. Extra electrons need to have sufficient energy to fill the highest energy level (outer shell). This means that the atoms find it increasingly difficult to accept electrons to make ions.

The order of reactivity (from highest to lowest) is: fluorine, chlorine, bromine, iodine.

A more reactive halogen gas can displace a less reactive halogen from an aqueous solution of its salt. For example:

$$2NaI + Cl_2 \rightarrow 2NaCl + I_2$$

The chlorine is more reactive than the iodine.

Metal–halogen compounds

Sodium chloride is a metal–halogen compound. It is common salt and is found in large quantities in the sea and underground (salt mines).

It can be broken down, when in solution, by electrolysis. This is an important industrial process.

Help

Sodium (a reactive metal) reacts with *chlorine* (a reactive non-metal and poisonous gas) to produce *sodium chloride* (common salt) which you put on your fish and chips!

Structures and Bonding

Chlorine gas is formed at the positive electrode (chloride ions are negative) and hydrogen gas at the negative electrode (hydrogen ions are positive). A solution of sodium hydroxide is also formed.

There are uses for these products.

- Chlorine is used to kill bacteria in drinking water and in swimming pools.
- Chlorine is used in the manufacture of disinfectants, bleaches and in the plastic polymer PVC (polyvinyl chloride).
- Hydrogen is used in the manufacture of ammonia (the Haber process) and margarine.
- Sodium hydroxide is used in the manufacture of soap, paper and ceramics.

What happens during electrolysis?

In the electrolysis of molten sodium chloride, Cl^- ions arrive at the positive electrode. Each chloride ion loses an electron. This makes it electrically neutral – a chlorine atom again:

$$Cl^- - e^- \rightarrow Cl$$

However, you need two atoms to make chlorine gas so:

$$2Cl^- - 2e^- \rightarrow Cl_2$$

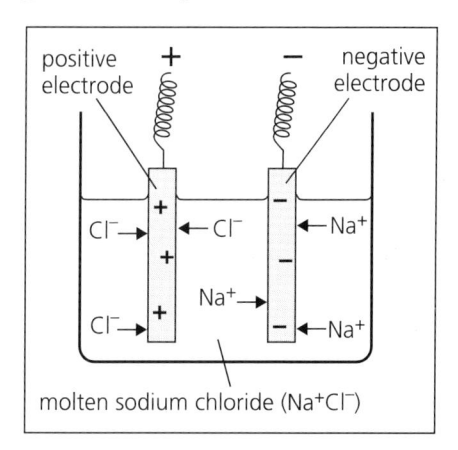

Help

A simple test for chlorine gas is that it bleaches damp litmus paper.

More uses for the halides

Silver chloride, bromide and iodide (the silver halides) are reduced to silver by the action of light, X-rays and radiation. They are used to make photographic film and photographic paper.

Hydrogen halides (e.g. hydrogen chloride) are gases which dissolve in water to produce acidic solutions.

Questions

1. The electrolysis of aqueous sodium chloride produces a number of useful substances. Draw a spider diagram which shows the substances and their uses in industry. Useful substances from the electrolysis of aqueous sodium chloride should be at the centre of the diagram.
2. What happens at the positive electrode during the electrolysis of molten sodium chloride?
3. Why are the halogens so reactive?
4. Give *one* example of a displacement reaction involving the halogens.

Terminal exam questions

1 a All of the elements are represented in the periodic table. Potassium is represented in this way: $^{39}_{19}K$

  i What is the atomic mass of potassium? [1]

  ii How many protons has potassium? [1]

  iii How many neutrons has potassium? [1]

b Sodium is represented in this way: $^{23}_{11}Na$

Draw a diagram to show the electronic structure of a sodium atom. [3]

c Lithium has the electronic structure 2, 1 and chlorine has the structure 2, 8, 7.

  i Draw an electronic diagram to show how the two atoms react with each other to produce lithium chloride. [3]

  ii What type of bond has been formed? [1]

  iii During this reaction the lithium atom becomes an ion. What is an ion? [2]
  How does lithium become an ion? [2]

14 marks

2 a What is a molecule? [3]

b Draw a diagram of an ammonia molecule (NH_3) to show the bonds present. You should show the arrangement of the electrons. [3]

c Why do molecules generally have lower melting and boiling points than ionic compounds? [2]

8 marks

3 Group 1 metals are also known as the alkali metals. They react with water to produce metal hydroxides.

a i Balance the following equation:

$$K + H_2O \rightarrow KOH + H_2$$ [1]

  ii Sodium is less reactive than potassium. Explain why. [3]

b The alkali metals react with the halogen gases to form metal halides. If sodium iodide and chlorine react together the result is sodium chloride and iodine.

$$2NaI + Cl_2 \rightarrow 2NaCl + I_2$$

Explain this reaction. [2]

6 marks

4 Sodium chloride can be broken down into sodium and chlorine gas. This is done by electrolysis.

a Why must the sodium chloride be molten before it can be electrolysed? [2]

b During the electrolysis, what would you expect to happen at the cathode? [3]

c i Give two uses of chlorine. [2]

  ii What is the test for chlorine gas? [3]

10 marks

5 This is a diagram of a molecule of hydrogen chloride.

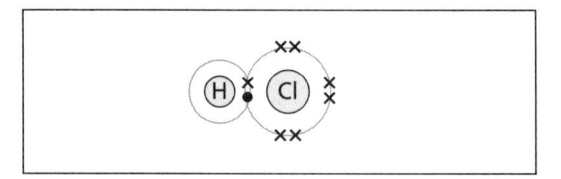

a i What does this tell you about the molecule? [3]

  ii Hydrogen is shown in the periodic table like this: ^1_1H.
  What does this tell you about the structure of the hydrogen atom? [3]

b i What is meant by a diatomic molecule? [1]

  ii Use an electron diagram of an oxygen molecule to show its structure. [3]

c The bond in the hydrogen chloride molecule is covalent. Covalent bonds are also present in both thermosoftening and thermosetting plastics.
Why are thermosetting plastics unable to be softened again on re-heating? [3]

d Molecules tend to have low melting and boiling points. Diamond is molecular but has a high melting point. Explain why. [4]

17 marks

Total for test: 55 marks

AT4
Physical Processes

Energy
Electricity
Forces
Waves and Radiation

Heat transfer

Conduction

Substances may be hotter in one part than another part (e.g. a metal bar may be heated at one end). If energy (heat) moves through the substance from the hotter to the cooler part (without the substance itself moving) this is known as **conduction**.

Metals are good **conductors** and non-metals are usually poor conductors (**insulators**). Gases (which are non-metals) are also very poor conductors.

When a metal is heated its free electrons move more quickly. These bump into adjacent electrons and make them move more quickly as well, so energy is transferred to other parts of the metal.

Convection

Liquids and gases can flow, so they are able to **transfer** energy in the form of heat from hotter to cooler areas by their own movement. This is called **convection**.

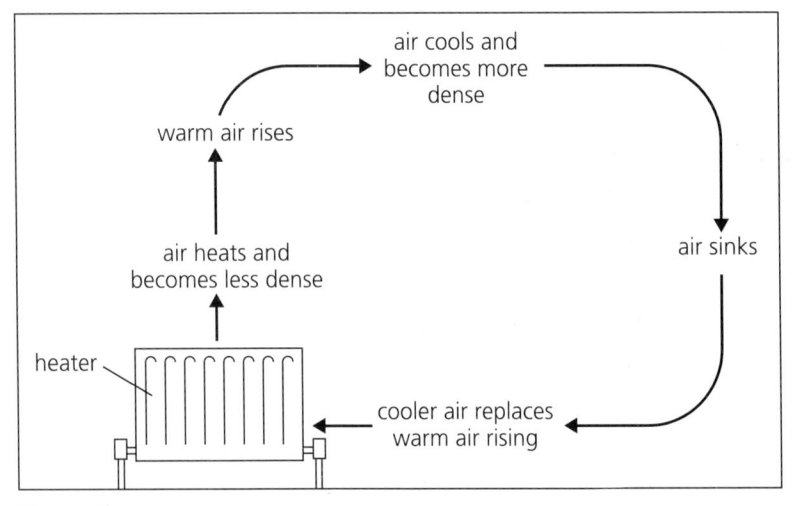

Convection

As a liquid or gas gets hotter its particles move faster. The liquid or gas expands and becomes less dense. This means that the gas will rise, or warmer liquid will rise above surrounding cooler liquid.

Radiation

The energy transfer in **radiation** is by waves. Particles are not involved. This energy transfer can take place through space. Hot bodies (e.g. the Sun) give off mainly infrared radiation. The hotter the body, the more radiation is given off.

Dark, matt surfaces emit more radiation than shiny, white surfaces (at the same temperature). Dark, matt surfaces are also good absorbers of radiation, and shiny white surfaces are good reflectors of radiation.

Help

Houses and cars in sunny Spain are usually white to reflect heat. People in hot countries (e.g. Saudi Arabia) often wear white clothing.

Energy loss from buildings

A lot of energy escapes from buildings in the form of heat, especially from windows and roofs. Some of the main ways in which this heat loss can be reduced include:

- double glazing – air between the two panes of glass is a very poor conductor and therefore a good insulator
- fibreglass lagging in a roof – air trapped between the fibres gives good insulation
- cavity walls – air between the bricks gives good insulation
- cavity wall insulation – air provides good insulation but if warmed it will rise and more heat lost as a result. Special foam in the cavity wall helps prevent the air rising (by convection), and so results in better insulation
- draught excluder – strips of foam around a door frame make a tight-fitting door, so warm air cannot escape.

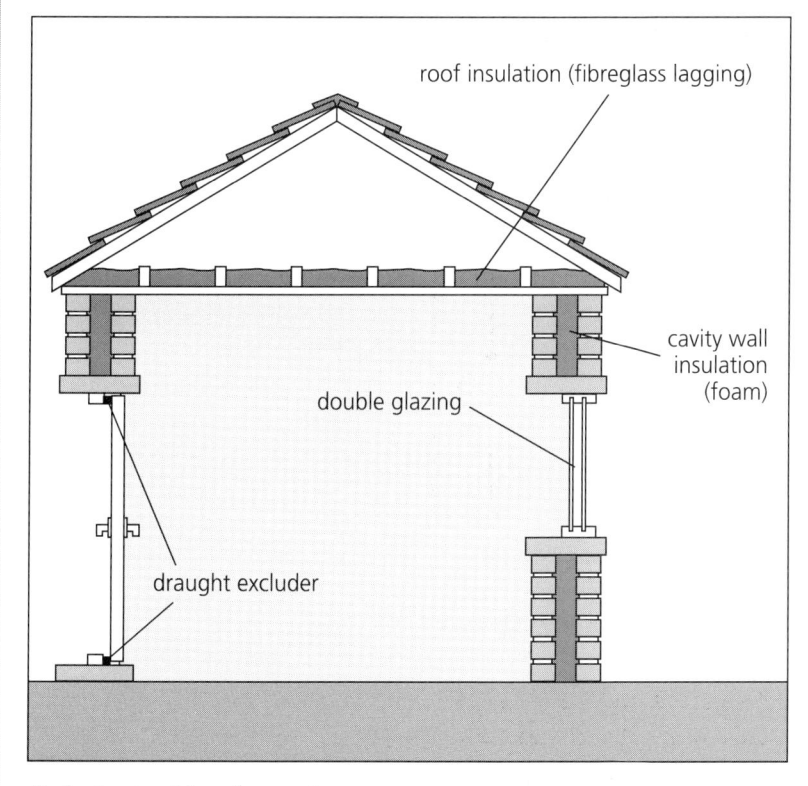

Reducing heat loss from a house

Questions

1. Which type of energy transfer results in heat reaching us from the Sun?
2. A radiator is turned on in a room. You are sitting at the other side of the room. You become warmer. Explain why.
3. Cavity wall insulation is expensive. Why do some houses have it, when the air in the cavity between the bricks is a good insulator anyway?

Using electricity

Electrical appliances

An electrical appliance transfers energy from electricity to heat, light, sound or movement. The amount of electrical energy an appliance transfers depends on two factors:

- how long the appliance is switched on
- how fast the appliance transfers energy (this represents the power of the appliance).

Measuring power

Energy is normally measured in joules. Power is a measure of how fast this energy is transferred. The greater the power rating of an appliance, the more energy is transferred in the same time.

You do not have to remember this formula but must be able to use it:

$$\textbf{power (watt, W)} = \frac{\textbf{energy transferred (joule, J)}}{\textbf{time taken (second, s)}}$$

1 watt is therefore the transfer of 1 joule of energy in one second.

Worked example

Q A light bulb transfers 1000 J of energy in 25 seconds. What is the power rating of the appliance?

A $\text{power} = \frac{\text{energy transferred}}{\text{time}}$

$\text{power} = \frac{1000}{25} = 40 \text{ watts}$

Help

In this worked example the unit for time is in seconds. Beware – in the examination it may be in minutes.

However, the joule is a small amount of energy compared to the amounts used at home for lighting and heating. Electricity suppliers use a much bigger unit called the **kilowatt hour**. This is based on **kilowatts** which are 1000 watts.

energy transferred = **power** × **time**
(kilowatt hour, kWh) (kilowatt, kW) (hour, h)

The amount of electrical energy transferred from the mains is measured in kilowatt hours or **units**.

Worked example

Q The power of a food mixer is rated at 20 kW and is switched on for 30 minutes. How much energy is transferred?

A energy transfer = 20 × 0.5 (half an hour) = 10 kWh

Help

In the examination you often have to convert units before carrying out the calculations

Energy

You can calculate the cost of energy, given the information:

cost of energy = number of units × cost per unit

Worked example

Q A house owner receives an electricity bill. The previous meter reading was 1487 units and this has risen to 1923. The cost per unit is 43.5p. How much is the cost of the electricity used?

A cost of energy = number of units × cost of each unit
= (1923 − 1487) × 43.5 = £189.66

Gravitational potential energy

Electrical and heat energy are not the only forms of energy. There are other forms. One of these is **gravitational potential energy**.

Gravitational potential energy is the energy stored in an object which has been lifted against the force of gravity. The higher the object is lifted, the more energy it has.

You do not have to remember this formula but must be able to use it:

change in gravitational = weight × change in vertical height
potential energy (J)   (N)   (m)

Worked example

Q You weigh 500 N and you climb a mountain 3000 m high. What is your change in gravitational potential energy?

A change = weight × change in vertical height
= 500 × 3000 = 1 500 000 or 1.5 million (J)

Help

The higher you climb, the more gravitational potential energy you have.

Electrical energy can be transferred as gravitational potential energy (e.g. a crane lifting a steel bar).

Worked example

Q A crane lifts a steel bar weighing 1200 N to a height of 25 m. What is the change in gravitational potential energy of the bar?

A change = weight × change in vertical height
= 1200 × 25 = 30 000 J

Questions

1. A heater transfers 1500 J of energy in one minute. What is the power rating of the appliance?
2. You weigh 500 N and climb a mountain 2300 m high. What is your change in gravitational potential energy?

Energy efficiency

When energy is transferred from electricity some of it is usefully used and some of it is not. For example, when a radio is switched on the useful energy is the sound which you hear – however, some energy is wasted as heat.

All energy which is transferred (whether it was useful or 'wasted') eventually ends up in our surroundings, which then warm up. Once the energy has spread out like this it is very difficult to use again as it is difficult to trap.

That part of the energy which is usefully transferred gives us the efficiency of the appliance.

You do not have to remember this formula but must be able to use it:

$$\text{efficiency} = \frac{\text{useful energy transferred}}{\text{total energy supplied}}$$

Worked example

Q A nightlight bulb has a power rating of 10 W and is switched on for 10 minutes. However, only 4500 J of the energy is used in a useful way. How efficient is this light bulb?

A energy supplied = power × time
= 10 × 600 (seconds)
= 6000 J

$$\text{efficiency} = \frac{\text{useful transfer}}{\text{total energy supplied}}$$

$$= \frac{4500}{6000}$$

= 0.75 (or 75%)

Help

No appliances or machines are 100% efficient.

The diagrams show appliances or machines that usefully transfer energy. Each also wastes energy.

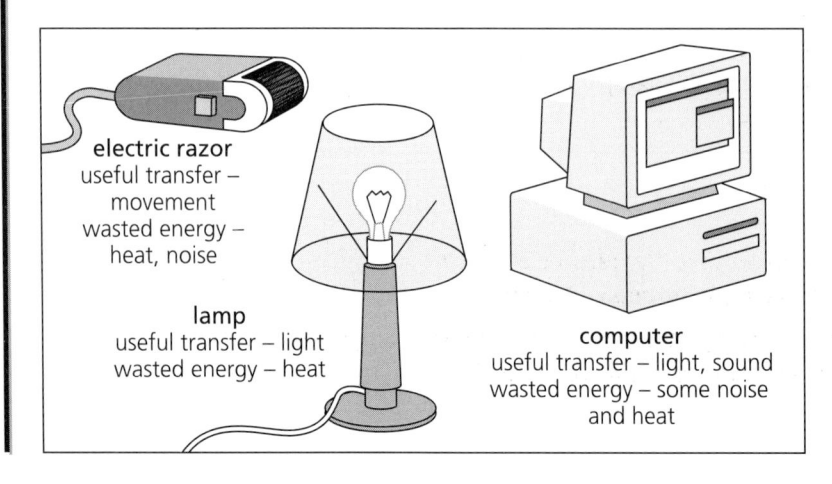

electric razor
useful transfer – movement
wasted energy – heat, noise

lamp
useful transfer – light
wasted energy – heat

computer
useful transfer – light, sound
wasted energy – some noise and heat

Energy transfers in household appliances

As you saw earlier in this module, houses also lose energy. It is a waste of money heating a house simply for all of the heat to 'disappear' through windows, ceilings or walls. Houses are therefore insulated against this heat loss. There are various methods all shown earlier in the module. Some cost more than others, and some are more effective that others.

Worked example

This table shows various ways to insulate one particular house against heat loss. Against each method the cost and how much it would save per year are given.

Insulation method	Cost of installing (£)	Saving per year (£)
double glazing	2000	80
draught excluders	30	40
cavity wall insulation	1000	30
extra roof insulation	300	100

Q Which method represents the best value for money in terms of reducing heat loss?

A You must work out the 'payback period' for each method. The most cost effective method will have the shortest payback time.

- The **double glazing** costs £2000 and saves £80 per year.
  It takes $\frac{2000}{80}$ years to pay for itself. This is **25 years**.
- The **draught excluders** cost £30 and save £40 per year.
  It takes $\frac{30}{40}$ years to pay for itself. This is **9 months**.
- The **cavity wall insulation** costs £1000 and saves £30 per year.
  It takes $\frac{1000}{30}$ years to pay for itself. This is **33.3 years**.
- The **extra roof insulation** costs £300 and saves £100 per year.
  It takes $\frac{300}{100}$ years to pay for itself. This is **3 years**.

Draught excluders are therefore the most cost effective in this house. The extra roof insulation saves you the most per year. The other two are expensive with long payback periods.

Questions

1. How do the following appliances usefully transfer energy?
   hair drier   toaster   television   vacuum cleaner

2. In the worked example above, suggest a reason why someone might still double glaze their house even though they know it is not cost effective.

Energy sources

Electricity is very convenient but it needs to be produced.

In most power stations energy from fuel is used to heat water. The steam produced drives turbines, and these drive the generators which produce the electricity.

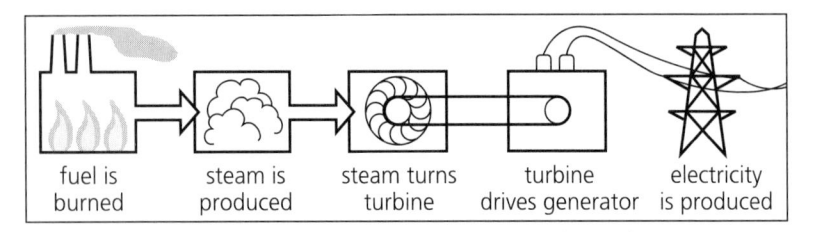

Generation of electricity

fuel is burned → steam is produced → steam turns turbine → turbine drives generator → electricity is produced

But how is the water in power stations heated?

In Britain:

- many power stations use fossil fuels (coal, oil, gas)
- some use nuclear fuel (uranium/plutonium).

Other ways of generating electricity

There are potential environmental problems associated with all the ways described above. The waste from fossil fuels can cause acid rain and global warming. The waste from nuclear reactors is difficult to dispose of safely because it is radioactive and stays so for thousands of years. Another problem is that all of the above methods rely on fuels which will run out. These are all **non-renewable energy** sources.

However, there are **renewable energy** sources which are obviously 'cleaner' for the environment. These convert other forms of energy (e.g. kinetic, electromagnetic and heat energy) into electricity. They include:

- **wind farms** – the generator is driven by the turning of the sails of many wind turbines

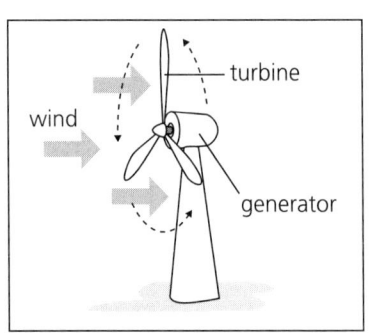

Wind power

- **tidal power** – rising and falling sea levels are used to power turbines which generate electricity

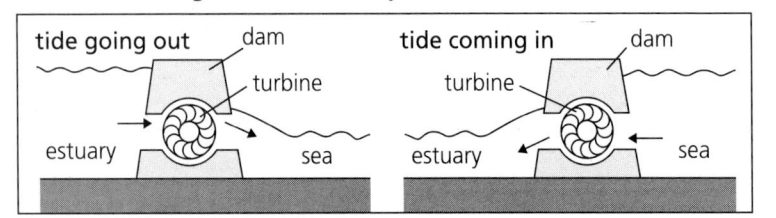

Tidal power

Help

Non-renewable sources of energy include coal, oil, gas and nuclear sources.
Renewable sources of energy include solar, wind, tidal, hydroelectric and hot rocks.

- **hydroelectric power** – the flow of water from high points to low points can also be used to power turbines

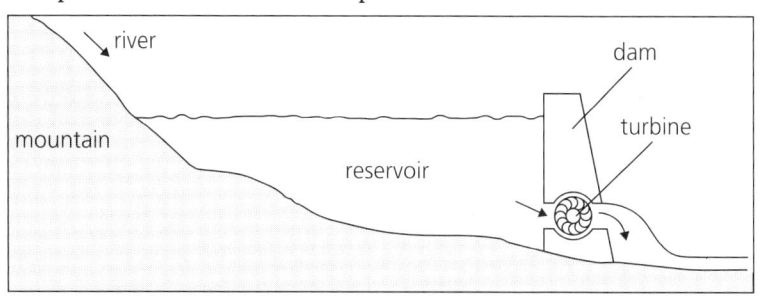

Hydroelectric power

- **solar power** – heat energy from the Sun is harnessed by solar panels to heat water; solar cells are used to convert electromagnetic energy from the Sun into electricity

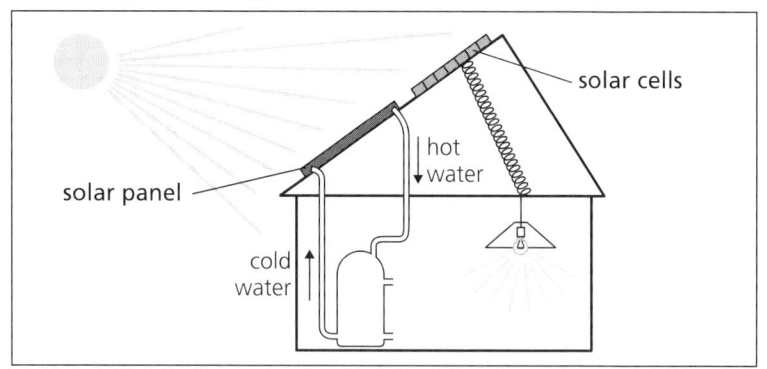

Solar energy

- **steam** can also be produced by pumping water through **hot rocks** well below the surface of the Earth. The rocks are hot because at this depth below the surface radioactive elements are decaying slowly and releasing heat – just like a slow nuclear reactor.

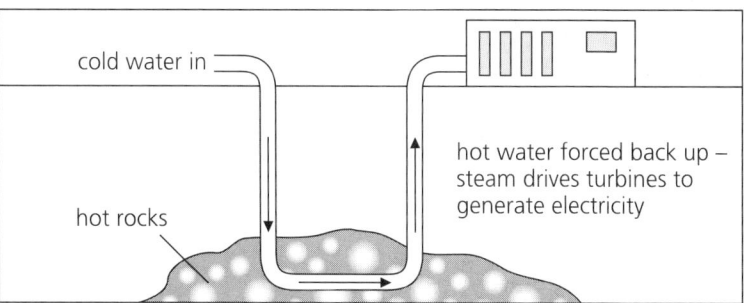

Geothermal energy

Questions

1. Draw and complete the table to show *one* advantage and *one* disadvantage of each type of energy source.
2. Which of the sources of energy in question 1 are renewable energy sources?
3. Suggest, with reasons, suitable areas to build wind farms.

Energy source	Advantage	Disadvantage
coal		
hydroelectric		
nuclear		
wind turbine		
tidal		

Module test questions

1. This question is about different sources used in the generation of electricity.
   Match words from the list with each of the numbers 1–4 in the table.

   wind   nuclear
   coal   solar

	Information about the source
1	there is no air pollution but cloud cover reduces the amount of electricity generated
2	there is little, if any, air pollution in normal circumstances but the costs of closing down are high
3	there is no air pollution but areas of natural beauty can be affected
4	there is air pollution and the resource will run out in the not too distant future

2. This question is about units.
   Match words from the list with numbers 1–4 in the table.

   watt   joule
   newton metre

	The unit is relative to
1	calculations involving energy
2	changes in vertical height
3	calculations involving weight
4	calculations involving power

3. These sentences are about energy transfer. Match words from the list to the spaces 1–4 in the sentences.

   vacuum   radiation
   waves   conduction

   In ___1___ the energy transfer is by ___2___ and the transfer can take place through a ___3___. In ___4___ the energy is transferred from a hotter part of a substance to a cooler part.

4. Which *two* statements about cavity wall insulation are correct?
   A radiation of heat is prevented by the foam in the cavity wall
   B air is a good insulator and so helps to prevent heat loss
   C air conducts heat quite well but the foam prevents it
   D the foam completely fills the space forcing the air out
   E the foam prevents convection of the air in the wall

5. Which *two* of the following statements about convection are correct?
   A as a gas or liquid heats it becomes less dense
   B as a gas or liquid heats the particles move closer together
   C the particles within the gas or liquid transfer the energy as heat
   D as a gas rises it cools down
   E the energy transfer is able to take place through space

6. These are diagrams illustrating four ways of generating electricity.

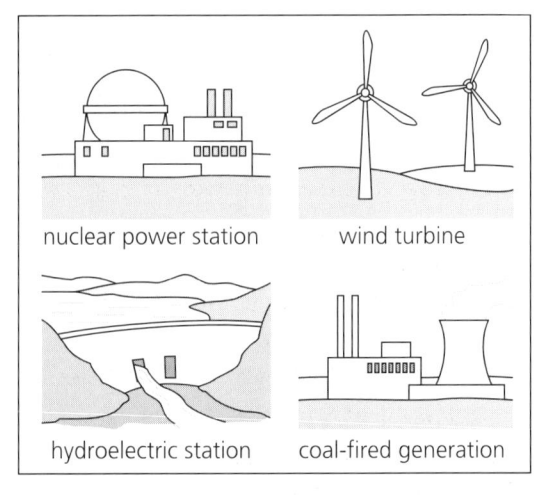

   nuclear power station   wind turbine
   hydroelectric station   coal-fired generation

   1. In electricity generation, what is the function of steam?
   A to lubricate the machinery
   B to drive the turbines
   C to dissolve impurities made in the process
   D to drive the generators

2. Which of these methods of generating electricity is the most expensive to close down safely (decommission)?

A wind generators
B hydroelectric power stations
C nuclear power stations
D coal-fired power stations

3. Which of these pairs of methods of electricity generation do not rely on the production of steam?

A nuclear and coal
B hydroelectric and wind
C hydroelectric and nuclear
D wind and nuclear

4. Which *one* of the following pairs of methods of electricity generation is generally agreed to be the 'cleanest' for the environment?

A hydroelectric and wind
B nuclear and wind
C hydroelectric and nuclear
D wind and coal

7 This question is about the transfer of energy as heat. This is a diagram of a cup of tea cooling down.

1. How is heat energy being lost at point X?

A convection into the wooden bench
B radiation into the wooden bench
C convection through the cup followed by radiation into the bench
D conduction into the wooden bench

2. How is heat energy being lost at point Y?

A convection of the air
B conduction into the air
C radiation followed by conduction
D convection followed by radiation

3. Which type of surface would result in the cup radiating more heat energy?

A dark and shiny
B bright and shiny
C dark and matt
D bright and matt

4. Which sentence best describes radiation?

A the transfer of heat energy through a solid
B the movement of air
C the transfer of heat between two substances touching each other
D the transfer of heat by waves

8 This toaster has a rating of 840 W.

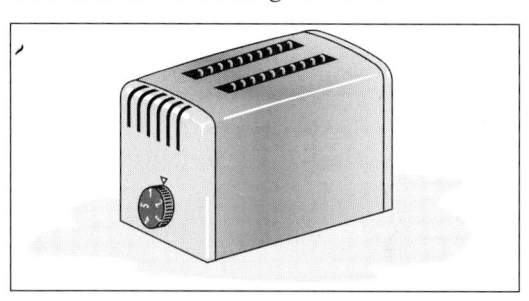

1. If it is switched on for 1 minute, how much energy does it transfer?

A 840 J
B 50 400 J
C 7 J
D 8400 J

2. If the toaster is used for 20 minutes, how much energy will have been transferred in terms of kilowatt hours?

energy transferred = power × time
(kWh)   (kW)   (h)

A 16 800 kWh
B 280 kWh
C 0.28 kWh
D 42 kWh

3. Which of the following is useful energy transferred by the toaster?

A heat
B noise
C movement
D light

4. You can heat food by placing a saucepan on top of the hot plate of a cooker. What type of energy transfer is mainly responsible for heating the food?

A convection
B radiation
C waves
D conduction

Measuring electricity

An electrical current is a flow of **charge**. It is transferring energy in the form of electricity from the mains or battery to an appliance. If this current has to pass through something which offers **resistance** (a **resistor**) the energy is converted to heat. In light bulbs this heat also provides light.

The current flowing in a circuit is measured in amperes (A) using an ammeter connected in series with the component.

Potential difference (p.d.) across a component is measured in volts (V) using a voltmeter connected across the component.

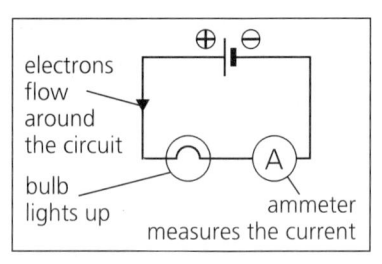

The rate of energy transfer

The speed at which energy is transferred in a circuit is measured in watts (or kilowatts).

power (watts) = **potential difference** (volts) × **current** (amps)

The amount of energy transferred

How can we calculate how many joules of energy are transferred? Our equipment measures volts and amps, not joules. This formula helps us part of the way:

energy (joules) = **potential difference** (volts) × **charge** (coulombs)

A coulomb is the unit of charge. One coulomb equals one ampere passing through in one second, so:

charge (coulombs) = **current** (amperes) × **time** (seconds)

You can now use the reading from your ammeter to find the charge in a circuit and combine this with your readings from your voltmeter to find the amount of energy transferred.

An ammeter is connected in series

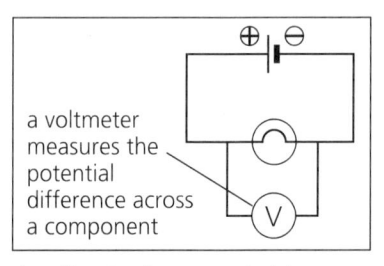

electrons flow around the circuit
bulb lights up
ammeter measures the current

a voltmeter measures the potential difference across a component

A voltmeter is connected in parallel

Worked example

Note: at the highest examination levels you have to use the results of using one formula to work out the final answer using a second formula.

Q A current of 15 A flows through an appliance for 2 minutes. The voltage supplied to the appliance is 230 V. How much energy has been transferred?

A energy transferred = potential difference × charge.

We only know the potential difference but we can work out the charge from:

charge = current × time
= 15 × 120 (time is in seconds) = 1800 coulombs
energy transferred = p.d. × charge
= 230 × 1800 = 414 000 J

Help

Potential difference is the difference in energy between two points in an electrical circuit. It is also called **voltage**.

Circuits

In circuits with the components connected in **series**:

- the total resistance is the sum of the resistances of the individual components
- the same current flows through each component (as the current has no alternative but to flow through all of the components)
- the total potential difference of the supply is shared between all of the components.

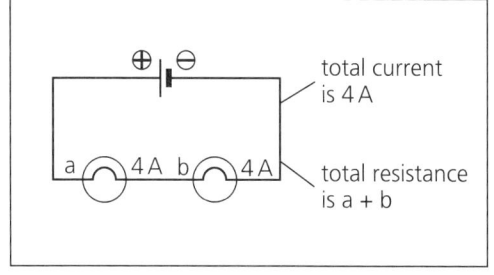

A series circuit with two lamps

In circuits with the components connected in **parallel**:

- there is the same potential difference (p.d.) across each component
- the current through each component depends on the resistance of the component – the greater the resistance, the smaller the current (this is because in a parallel circuit the current can flow around the circuit of least resistance)
- the total current through the whole circuit is the sum of the current running through the individual parts.

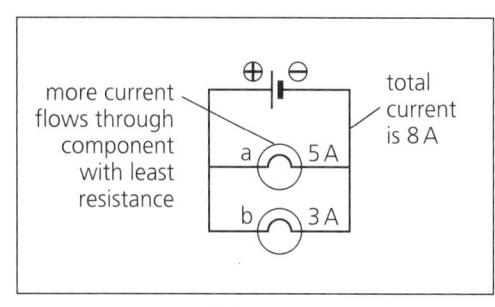

A parallel circuit with two lamps

Power supplies

The potential difference provided by each of the cells connected in series in a circuit must be added together to find the total potential difference supplied by the cells.

You must know these circuit symbols for the examination:

Help

Several *cells* connected in *series* is called a *battery*.

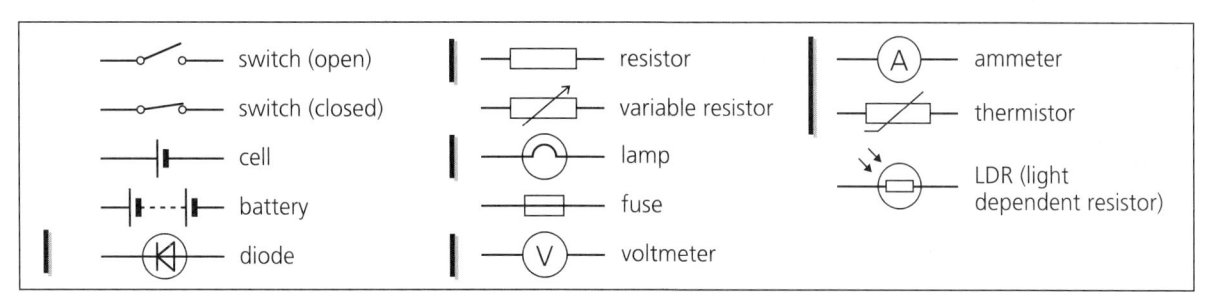

switch (open)	resistor	ammeter
switch (closed)	variable resistor	thermistor
cell	lamp	LDR (light dependent resistor)
battery	fuse	
diode	voltmeter	

Questions

1. Power can be expressed as the amount of energy transferred in one second:

   $$\text{power (watts)} = \frac{\text{energy transferred (joules)}}{\text{time (seconds)}}$$

   Use this formula for finding the amount of energy transferred, to show how power can be calculated by the formula:

   power (watts) = potential difference (volts) × current (amps)

2. You turn on the light switch in your bedroom. Why does the bulb give out light?

Resistance

This is the measure of how difficult it is for the current to flow. The bigger the resistance, the smaller the current produced by a particular voltage.

$$\text{resistance (ohm, } \Omega \text{)} = \frac{\text{potential difference (volts, V)}}{\text{current (ampere, A)}}$$

Current–voltage graphs are used to show how the current flowing through a component varies with the voltage across the component. So the gradient of the graph shows how much resistance the component presents.

These current–voltage graphs show the effect of sending the voltage in either direction through the component:

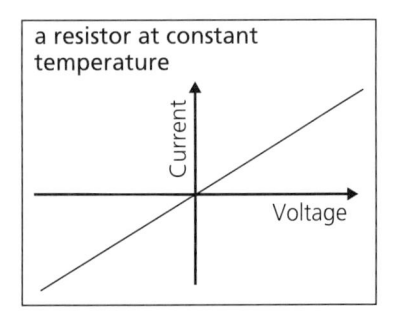

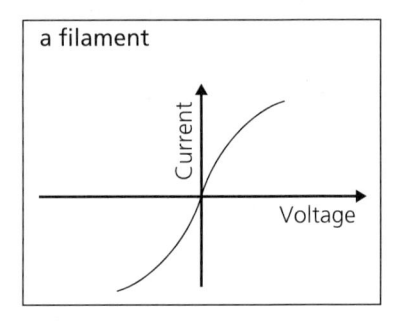

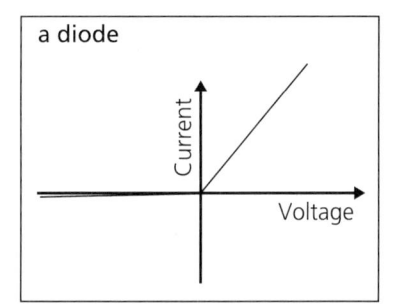

a resistor at constant temperature

a filament

a diode

- The current through a resistor is proportional to the voltage across the resistor at the same temperatures. This means that as the voltage increases, the current increases at the same rate.
- The resistance of a filament lamp increases as the temperature of the filament increases.
- The current through a diode flows in one direction only – it has a very high resistance to current trying to flow the wrong way.

Light and temperature dependent resistors

The resistance of a light-dependent resistor decreases as the light intensity increases (e.g. a burglar alarm). The resistance of a thermistor decreases as the temperature increases (e.g a thermostat).

Static electricity

In solid conductors like copper wires the electric current is a flow of electrons. Metals are good conductors because some of the electrons from their atoms can move freely through their structure.

However, many materials which are not good conductors (i.e. through which electrons will not flow freely) can build up an electrical charge. If you take two such materials and rub them together, electrons will pass from one to the other. The materials losing electrons become positively charged. The material gaining electrons becomes negatively charged. This is **static electricity** and the materials are **electrostatically charged**.

Electricity

Static electricity can be generated by rubbing strips of clear plastic and polythene on a dry woollen cloth. The polythene gains electrons and becomes negatively charged. The plastic strips lose electrons and become positively charged.

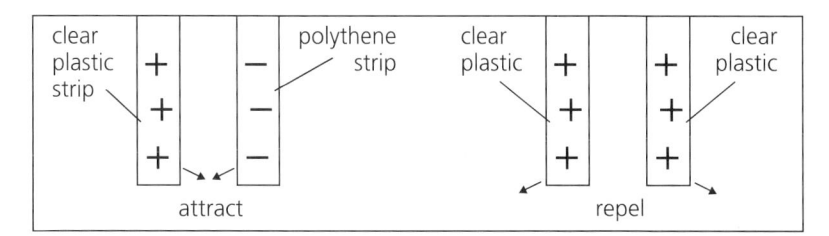

Static electricity

The greater the charge that an object picks up, the greater the potential difference (measured in volts) between the object and the Earth. If this voltage becomes large enough a spark will jump across the gap from the object to any earthed conductor. Lightning is the most dramatic example of this.

One danger: An aeroplane flying may become charged when it 'rubs' against the air as it flies. Static charges could build up in the fuelpipes, causing a spark during refuelling. However, an earth lead clamped to the metal frame of the aeroplane allows the charge to be conducted safely to Earth and prevents an explosion.

One use: A charged, fine wire mesh is present in the chimneys of coal-burning power stations. The fine particles of ash, produced by the burning of coal, have an opposite charge so 'stick' to the mesh. This prevents them going into the atmosphere.

Electrolysis

Ionic compounds are held together by electrostatic attraction. They will conduct electricity if melted or dissolved in water. Negatively charged ions (e.g. Cl^-) will move to the positive electrode. Positively charged ions (e.g. Na^+) move to the negative electrode.

The ionic compound is therefore broken down and simpler substances (products) released at the electrodes.

The amount of product released depends on:

- the size of the current
- the length of time the current is switched on.

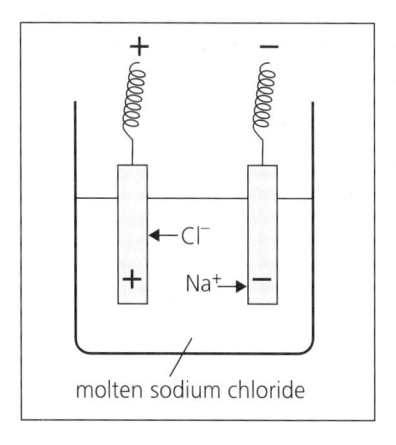

Questions

1. Study the current–voltage graphs on the facing page. Describe what each graph tells you about how the current varies with the voltage through the three different components.
2. Explain why you should not stand under an umbrella during a thunderstorm.

Using electricity

Mains electricity is alternating current (a.c.). This means that the current is constantly changing direction. The frequency of change is 50 cycles per second (50 hertz or Hz).

Cells and batteries supply current flowing in one direction only – this is direct current (d.c.).

Electrical safety

Wiring plugs correctly
A correctly wired plug should look like this.

You may be given diagrams showing incorrect or unsafe wiring. You must be able to 'spot the difference'.

The **neutral** wire is earthed back at the power station. The voltage it carries, therefore, is usually close to zero.

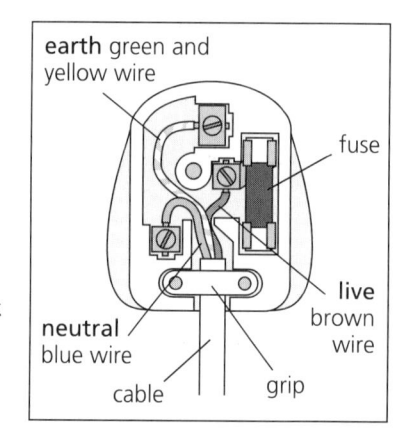

A 3-pin plug

The **live** wire is very dangerous. Mains electricity supply is alternating (a.c.), so the live wire alternates between carrying a voltage which is sometimes positive (with respect to the neutral wire) and sometimes negative.

Fuses
Fuses protect electrical appliances. If there is a fault and an increased current flows as a result, then the fuse becomes hot and eventually breaks or 'blows'. This breaks the circuit. The fuse rating should therefore be a little higher than the current that normally flows around the circuit. If it is the same or just slightly higher than the 'normal' current then the fuse will break all of the time.

Earthing appliances
Appliances with metal covers need to be earthed. The **earth** pin in the plug is connected to the metal cover through the green/yellow wire. It is possible to get an electric shock from some appliances if this is not done.

Example: If one element of an electric fire breaks or bends and touches the metal case a large current will flow. If the fuse is blown this is reasonably safe, but if the fuse is not blown and you touch the case you might receive a fatal electric shock.

any current above 5A causes the fuse wire to break

A 5 amp fuse

Circuit breakers

Many household appliances have fuses, but circuit breakers are increasingly used instead in some appliances. They contain an electromagnet. When the current becomes high enough then the strength of the electromagnet increases sufficiently to separate a pair of contacts. This breaks the circuit. Circuit breakers work more quickly than a fuse and are easy to reset by pressing a button.

Electromagnets

If an electric current is flowing through a coil of wire it causes the coil of wire to behave like a magnet. One end of the coil becomes a North pole and the other end a South pole, like a magnet. The magnet is switched on and off, depending on whether electricity is flowing or not. So the coil is behaving as an **electromagnet**.

You can increase the strength of an electromagnet by:

- placing an iron core inside the coil
- increasing the number of turns on the coil
- increasing the size of the current flowing through the coil.

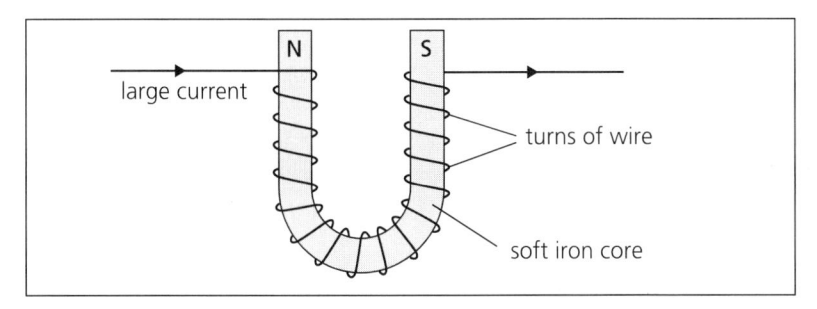

A simple electromagnet

If you reverse the current, you reverse the poles of the magnet.

If you place a wire in a magnetic field it experiences a force. The size of this force can be increased by:

- increasing the strength of the magnetic field
- increasing the size of the current flowing through the wire.

If the direction of the field or the current is reversed, the wire experiences an opposite force.

A whole range of electrical appliances and components (i.e. those with electric motors) are based on wires acting like magnets when electric currents flow through them.

Questions

1. What is meant by an alternating current?
2. Suggest *two* ways in which circuit breakers are better than fuses.
3. You make a simple electromagnet by passing a small current through a coil of wire. Give *three* ways of increasing the power of your electromagnet.

Using electromagnets in appliances

The door bell

The electromagnet in this case is used to cause a bell to ring.

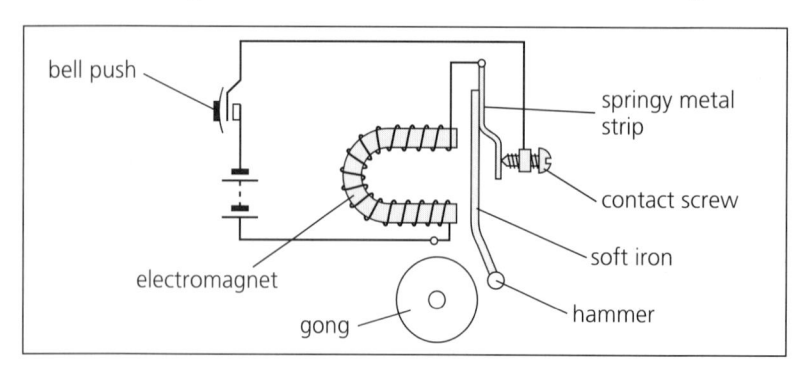

This is how it works:

- You press the bell push. The circuit is complete and a current flows.
- The electromagnet works and pulls the soft iron. The hammer hits the gong.
- The contact screw is not now contacting the springy metal strip. The circuit therefore breaks and the electromagnet stops working.
- The hammer springs back. The contact screw is now in contact again with the springy metal strip, so the circuit is complete again and the current flows.
- The bell continues to ring (the hammer keeps hitting the gong) until you take your finger off the bell push and break the circuit.

Help

When you press the bell push, the circuit is continually broken and remade. So the hammer doesn't just hit the gong once, but continues to do so until you release the bell push.

The d.c. motor

An electromagnet is used to turn a coil.

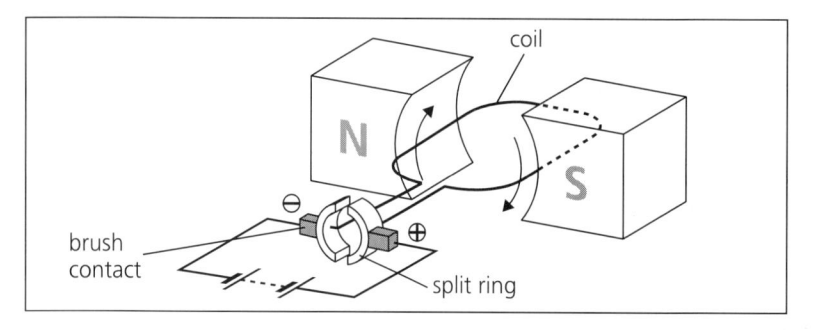

This is how it works:

- The battery is turned on. The current flows. The coil turns due to the force fields from the magnets at either side.
- When the coil is vertical the forces are equal, but the momentum of the coil carries it over.
- The split ring keeps switching the direction of the current so that it flows first one way and then the other, and the coil keeps spinning.

Electricity

The loudspeaker

An electromagnet is used to create sound waves.

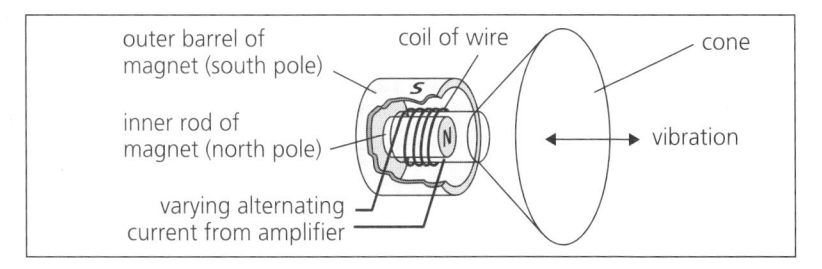

This is how it works:

- As a current flows through the coil it develops a magnetic force.
- The magnet also has a field and the two interact.
- The cone moves (vibrates) in and out and these vibrations result in sound waves.

Relay

An electromagnet is used to help a weak current trigger a strong current.

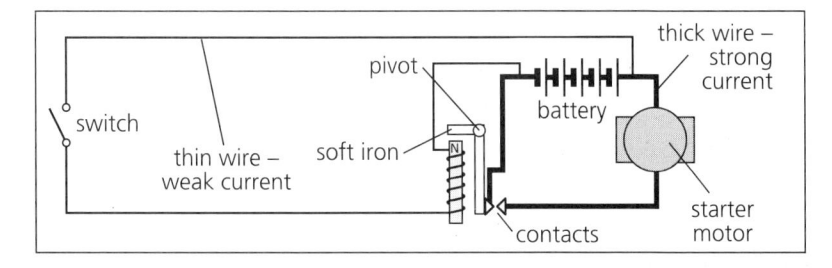

The starter motor of a car requires 100 A to work. The current is carried in short, expensive, thick wires from the car battery. An electromagnet is used to link the switch on the dashboard, the starter motor and the battery.

This is how it works:

- The long, thin, cheap wires from the switch on the dashboard carry current which causes the electromagnet to work.
- This attracts the soft iron at the top of the pivot. The movement of the pivot closes the contacts and the circuit to the battery is complete.
- One circuit therefore results in another being 'switched on' for a short period. This is called a **relay**.

Questions

1. Explain, in your own words, how the d.c. motor works.
2. In the loudspeaker, why does the cone move in and out?
3. Why is a relay used when starting a car?

Electricity

Making and supplying electricity

The a.c. generator

If you rotate a coil of wire in a magnetic field (or rotate magnets around a coil of wire) then you will induce an electric current. This is how the **generator** works.

As the coil of wire cuts through the lines of force of the magnetic field, a voltage (p.d.) is produced between the ends of the wire. If the wire is part of a complete circuit then a current will flow.

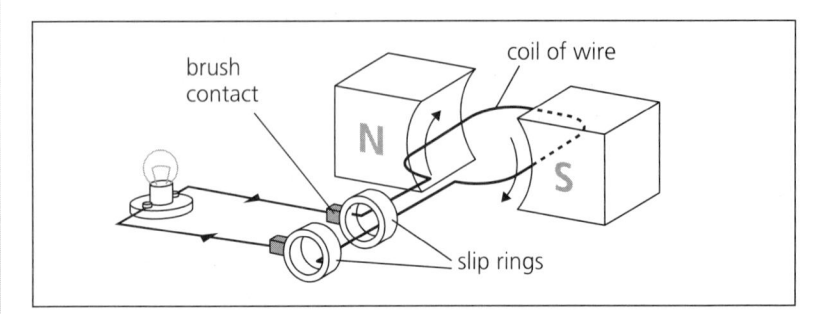

Help

The generator
spinning movement within magnetic field
= electrical current

The motor
electrical current within magnetic field
= spinning movement

You can increase the size of the voltage by doing any, or all, of the following things:

- move the coil of wire faster
- increase the strength of the magnetic field
- increase the number of turns on the coil
- increase the area of the coil.

Why is alternating current produced?
As the coil spins, the poles will keep reversing relative to the coil. Each time they reverse, the current will flow in the opposite direction through the coil.

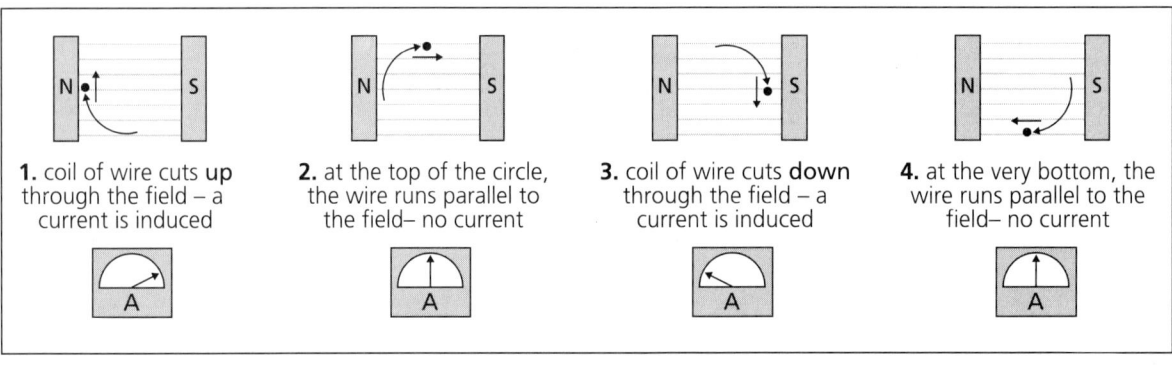

1. coil of wire cuts **up** through the field – a current is induced
2. at the top of the circle, the wire runs parallel to the field – no current
3. coil of wire cuts **down** through the field – a current is induced
4. at the very bottom, the wire runs parallel to the field – no current

Alternating current

What are the slip rings used for?
The current has to be taken away from the generator. With the coil spinning, ordinary wires would twist and break. Two continuous slip rings are used to prevent the wires twisting and to ensure that the current is a.c. (Brush contacts are used to transfer current to and from the slip rings.)

This is the principle behind electricity generating power stations. Steam is used to drive turbines which in turn drive the generators. The generators then produce electricity.

Using tidal power or hydroelectric power, it is water that drives the turbines. Steam does not need to be produced by burning fuels. These are, therefore, environmentally more 'friendly'.

Transformers

These are used at power stations to produce very high voltages for transmission through power lines. Transformers near houses then reduce this voltage so that it is useable with household appliances.

The higher the voltage transmitted in our power lines, the smaller the current needed to transmit electricity at the same rate. A high current would heat up the power lines, resulting in a waste of energy.

How does a transformer work?
A transformer consists of two separate coils wound around an iron core. When an alternating voltage is supplied to one coil (the primary coil) it induces (causes) an alternating voltage in the other coil.

The calculations are simply a matter of using ratios. The formula is:

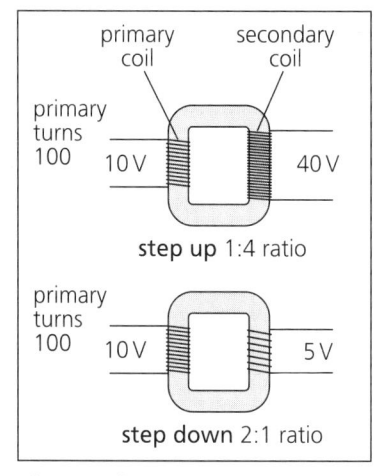

The transformer

$$\frac{\text{voltage across primary coil}}{\text{voltage across secondary coil}} = \frac{\text{number of turns on primary coil}}{\text{number of turns on secondary coil}}$$

Worked example

Q 200 V is supplied to the primary coil in a transformer. This coil has 50 turns. The secondary coil has 200 turns. What voltage is induced in the secondary coil?

A In terms of ratios, the secondary coil has 4 times as many turns as the primary coil. This means the induced voltage will be 4 times as great (4 × 200 V), which is 800 V.

Using the formula:

$$\frac{\text{voltage across primary}}{\text{voltage across secondary}} = \frac{\text{number of turns on primary}}{\text{number of turns on secondary}}$$

$$\frac{200}{x} = \frac{50}{200} \text{ or } \frac{1}{4}$$

$$x = 4 \times 200 \text{ or } 800 \text{ V}$$

Questions

1. A transformer is supplied with 200 V. The primary coil has 50 turns and the secondary coil has 2500 turns. What is the voltage induced?

2. You supply a transformer with 5000 V but you want to step the voltage down to 200 V. What must you make the ratio of primary to secondary turns on the coils?

Module test questions

1. These diagrams show some components which may be found as part of an electrical circuit.
   Choose words from the list for each of the components 1–4 in the drawings.

   resistor
   diode
   fuse
   thermistor

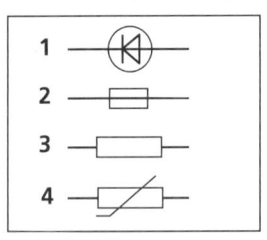

2. The table gives information about how current flows through various electrical components.
   Match words from the list with each of the numbers 1–4 in the table.

   thermistor   diode
   LDR   resistor

	How the current flows
1	current flows in one direction only
2	the resistance decreases as light intensity increases
3	the resistance decreases as the temperature increases
4	the current is proportional to the voltage at the same temperature

   (LDR = light dependent resistor)

3. These sentences are about how a d.c. motor works.
   Choose words from the list for each of the spaces 1–4 in the sentences.

   force field   battery
   current   split ring

   When the ___1___ is turned on a current flows. The coil turns because of the ___2___. When the coil is vertical momentum carries the coil over. Because of the ___3___ the ___4___ now flows the other way and the coil keeps spinning.

4. Which *two* of these statements are true of the graph showing current against voltage?

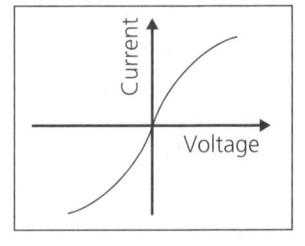

   A there is no current if the voltage is reversed
   B as the voltage increases so does the current, but eventually the current increases more slowly
   C the current is directly proportional to the voltage
   D as the voltage is reversed the current still increases as the voltage increases
   E the current is inversely proportional to the voltage

5. You can increase the strength of an electromagnet by doing which *two* of the following things?

   A increasing the current
   B making the turns on the coil larger
   C increasing the number of turns on the coil
   D increasing the resistance of the wire
   E moving an iron core out of the coil

6. This is a diagram of an a.c. generator.

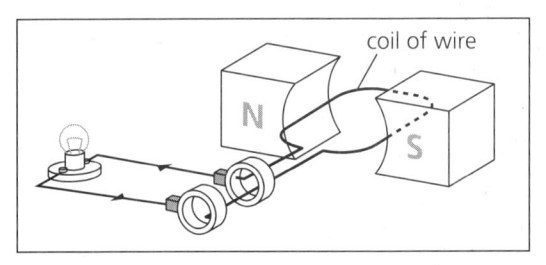

   1. What happens when the coil spins?

   A a voltage is induced
   B the resistance of the coil increases
   C a current is induced
   D the coil sets up its own magnetic field

   2. Which of the following would not increase the voltage?

   A increasing the strength of the magnetic field
   B decreasing the area of the coil
   C moving the wire faster
   D increasing the number of turns on the coil

3. In which of the following forms of power generation is water not turned into steam?

A coal-fired   B nuclear
C gas-fired   D hydroelectric

4. Why are transformers used at power stations?

A to decrease the resistance of power lines
B to alter the voltage
C to allow a greater current to flow
D to increase the temperature at which the wires transmit the electricity

7   The graphs show how current (I) varies with voltage (V) for three different components.

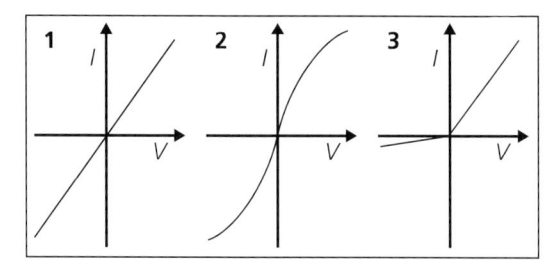

1. The best description of how current varies with voltage in graph **1** is:

A as voltage increases so does current, but it will only flow in one direction
B as the voltage increases the current decreases
C as the current increases the voltage decreases
D as the voltage increases the current increases

2. The best description of how current varies with voltage in graph **2** is:

A voltage and current are directly proportional to each other
B as the voltage increases so does the current, but at a certain point the current increases less
C current increases with the voltage but the current will only flow in one direction
D as the current increases so does the voltage, but at a certain point the voltage increases less

3. The best description of how current varies with voltage in graph **3** is:

A as the voltage increases so does the current, but the component will only allow the current to flow in one direction
B the current will flow in both directions but the voltage will not
C as the current increases so does the voltage and the current will flow in both directions
D the current and voltage are always directly proportional to each other

4. Which of these is likely to be the component in graph **3**?

A resistor
B filament
C variable resistor
D diode

8   This is a diagram of a d.c. motor

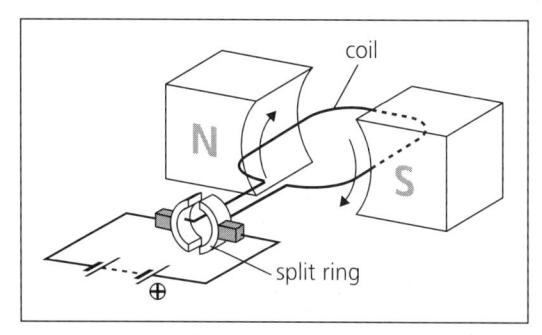

1. What causes the coil to pass the vertical position?

A it is attracted by the South pole
B it is repelled by the North pole
C the momentum of the coil
D the voltage in the wire

2. The function of the split ring is to:

A maintain current flowing in the same direction
B increase the current
C switch the direction of the current
D increase the voltage

3. An a.c. generator produces alternating current. What is the frequency of alternating current measured in?

A hertz   B ohms
C watts   D coulombs

4. A supply of 250 V reaches the primary coil of a transformer. The primary coil has 50 turns. You would like a voltage of 50 V from the secondary coil. How many turns should there be in the secondary coil?

A 300   B 12 500
C 200   D 10

Speed, velocity and acceleration

Speed

If an object moves in a straight line, the distance it has gone (from a certain point) can be shown by a distance–time graph.

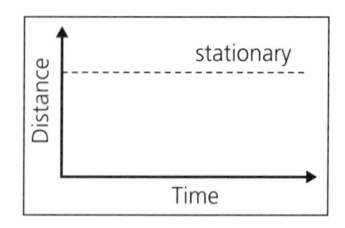

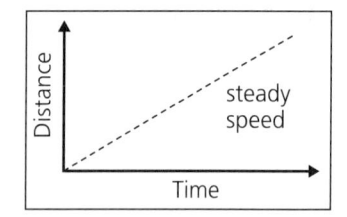

The steeper the slope of the graph, the greater the speed this represents.

The speed of an object moving in a straight line and at a steady speed can be calculated using this formula:

$$\text{speed (m/s)} = \frac{\text{distance travelled (m)}}{\text{time (s)}}$$

So, for the distance–time graph shown on the right:

$$\text{speed} = \frac{40 \text{ m}}{5 \text{ s}} = 8 \text{ m/s}$$

You must be able to calculate the gradient of a distance–time graph.

Worked example

Q A train travels 1000 m in 40 seconds. What is its speed?

A $\text{speed} = \dfrac{\text{distance}}{\text{time}}$

$= \dfrac{1000}{40} = 25 \text{ m/s}$

Help

m/s = metres per second
m = metres
s = seconds

Velocity

Velocity is the speed of an object in a straight line and in a given direction.

Velocity–time graphs represent the movement of an object travelling at a constant velocity or at a constant acceleration.

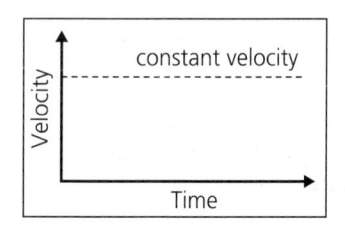

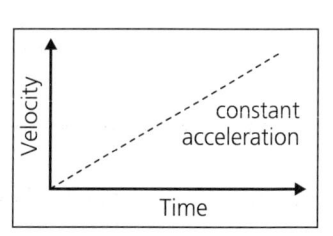

Acceleration

The acceleration of an object is the rate at which its velocity changes. For an object moving in a straight line with steady acceleration, its acceleration can be calculated by taking the change in its velocity between one point and another, and then dividing this by the time taken to get from the first point to the second.

$$\text{acceleration (m/s}^2\text{)} = \frac{\text{change in velocity (m/s)}}{\text{time taken for the change (s)}}$$

Worked example

Q A car accelerates from 0 to 30 m/s in 10 seconds. What is its acceleration?

A acceleration = $\frac{\text{change in velocity}}{\text{time}}$

= $\frac{30}{10}$ = 3 m/s² (always remember the units)

Help

Always remember to include units unless they are given. Examiners may use km or other units – don't be tricked!

Velocity–time graphs

You must be able to calculate:

- the gradient of a velocity–time graph (and interpret this as acceleration)
- the area under a velocity–time graph for an object moving with constant acceleration (and interpret this as distance travelled).

Worked example

Q An aeroplane accelerates towards take-off. The graph shows how its velocity changes in the first four seconds. What distance does it travel in this time?

A
- The area of the graph is 80 (4 × 20)
- The area under the velocity–time line is 40 (0.5 × 4 × 20)
- So the distance travelled is 40 m.

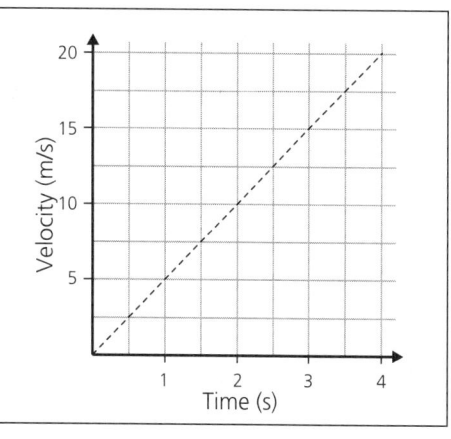

Questions

1. A car travels 60 m in the first 4 seconds of its journey. Calculate its average velocity and acceleration.
2. You get on your bike to go to the local shop. You accelerate until you reach a constant speed. As you get closer to the shop you slow down, before stopping very suddenly as you press the brakes too hard. Draw a very simple graph to illustrate this.
3. How is velocity different to speed?

Speeding up and slowing down

Balanced forces

Wherever two objects interact they exert a force on each other. If the forces are equal and opposite they cancel each other out – they are **balanced forces**. This means that if the object is still to start with, it will not move.

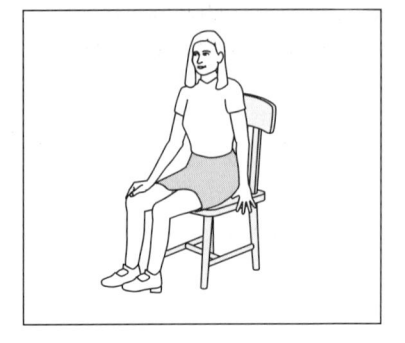

Balanced forces

If an object is moving and the forces on it are balanced, it will carry on moving at the same speed. When a car is travelling at an unchanging speed the forces are balanced – the force from the engine is the same as the force opposing it.

Unbalanced forces

If the forces are not balanced, a stationary object will move. The forces are said to be **unbalanced**. In the example on the right, if the force exerted downwards by the person is more than the force exerted upwards by the chair, then the person will crash through the chair!

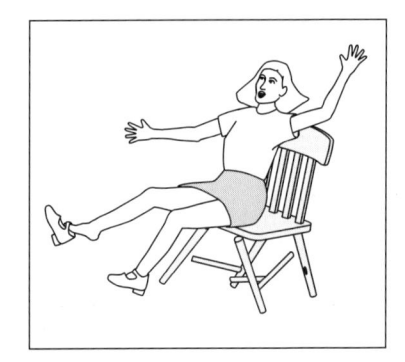

Unbalanced forces

A car starts to move because the engine exerts a greater force than the forces opposing it.

Unbalanced forces

Unbalanced forces are also needed for the car to accelerate.

A stationary object always moves in the direction of the unbalanced force, and the object moving in that direction will speed up. The greater the force, the greater the acceleration of the object. Any object moving in the opposite direction slows down. The greater the force, the more it slows down.

Downwards acceleration

Objects moving downwards are accelerated by the force of gravity. On Earth this is about 10 N/kg. Your weight is actually your mass in kilograms multiplied by the force of gravity. (This formula will be given in an examination.)

> **Worked example**
>
> Q A person on the Earth has a mass of 70 kg. What is that person's weight?
>
> A weight = mass × force of gravity
>   = 70 × 10
>   = 700 N (remember the units)

Help

Weight is often wrongly expressed in kilograms – bathroom and kitchen scales show kilograms. This is actually your *mass*. Your weight should be expressed in *Newtons*.

Kinetic energy

Kinetic energy is the energy an object has because of its movement.

An object has more kinetic energy:

- the greater its mass
- the greater its speed.

kinetic energy (J) = ½ × **mass** (kg) × **speed**^{2} (m/s)

You do not have to remember this formula but must be able to use it.

> **Worked example**
>
> Q A rock has a mass of 30 kg and falls with a speed of 20 m/s. What is its kinetic energy?
>
> A kinetic energy = ½ mass × speed^2
>   = (0.5 × 30) × 20^2
>   = 15 × 400
>   = 6000 J

Questions

1. Find out your mass in kg. Multiply this figure by 10 to work out your weight in newtons.
2. A boat is floating on the water. Describe the forces that are acting on the boat.
3. A car reverses out of a parking space. Describe the forces acting on it.
4. An aeroplane is sent to deliver relief supplies to people without food. It is unable to land because of the dangers involved. It drops a 100 kg package which falls at 30 m/s. What is the kinetic energy of the package?

Friction and work

Friction

A force of **friction** acts:

- when an object moves through air or water
- when solid surfaces slide over one another.

Friction is always opposite to the direction in which an object is travelling. It slows the object down. It also heats the object up and wears it away (e.g. an aeroplane is both slowed down and heated up due to the friction of the air). The surface of an object may 'wear away' due to friction (e.g. tyres on a car).

Brakes use friction between solid surfaces to slow cars down. The greater the speed of a car:

- the greater the braking force needed to slow the car down in the same time *or*
- the longer it takes to slow the car down, if you use the same braking force.

If you brake too hard then the car will skid as there is not enough friction between the car and the road surface.

The stopping distance of a car depends on:

- the distance the car travels during the driver's 'thinking time'
- the distance travelled while the brakes are applied.

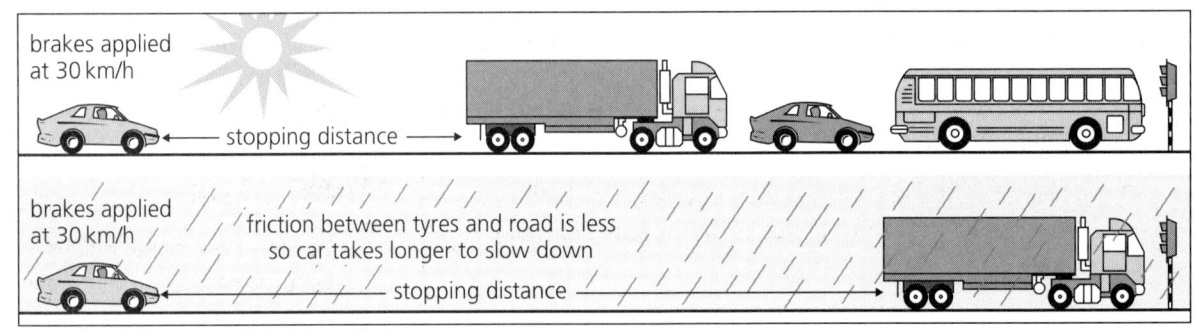

Wet surfaces reduce friction

The stopping distance of a car increases if:

- the car is travelling faster
- the driver's reactions are slow (due to drink, drugs, tiredness)
- the road conditions are poor (wet, icy, poor visibility)
- the car is poorly maintained (worn brakes or tyres).

The faster something falls through air or a liquid, the greater the force of friction. When a body falls:

- at first it accelerates due to the force of gravity
- the force of friction eventually balances the force of gravity
- the object now falls at **terminal velocity** which is a steady speed.

force of friction

force of gravity

terminal velocity is reached when the forces are balanced

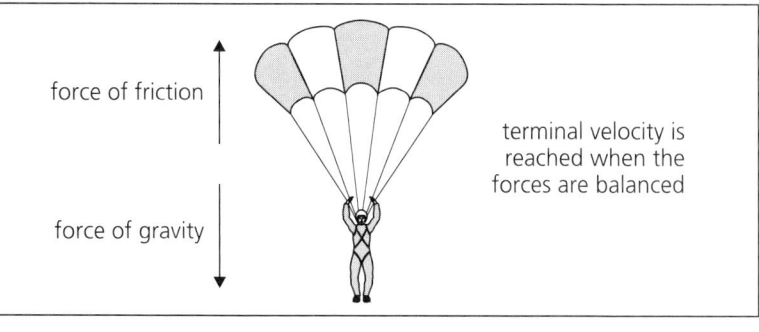

Terminal velocity

Force, mass and acceleration can all be linked in the following formula:

force (N) = **mass** (kg) × **acceleration** (m/s²)

Worked example

Q A parachutist has a mass of 70 kg and accelerates at 8 m/s². What force is being exerted?

A force = mass × acceleration
= 70 × 8
= 560 N

Help

You may have to rearrange any equation in an examination.

Doing 'work'

When a force moves an object then energy is transferred and work is done (e.g. you carry a bag across a room).

work done (J) = **force applied** (N) × **distance moved** (m)

Worked example

Q Chris carried a bag of potatoes weighing 50 N for 25 m from the shop to the car. Calculate the amount of work done.

A work done = force × distance
= 50 × 25
= 1250 J

Help

In physics, 'work done' means that energy has been transferred from one object to another.

Questions

1 A car slows down at a rate of 6 m/s². It has a weight of 10 000 N. What force is being applied to slow the car down?

2 The same car travels 50 m. What work has been done by the engine? (Assume that there is no friction).

3 A mountaineer dislodges a stone. At first the stone accelerates down the cliff-face. After a few seconds the stone falls at a steady speed. Explain what has happened.

Pressure and stretching forces

Stretching force

If you stretch a metal wire or a spring it will return back to normal, as long as the **elastic limit** is not reached. If this limit is reached then it will remain stretched – it is permanently deformed.

Elastic potential energy is stored in the spring as it is stretched. This means that the spring is able to do work.

Pressure

The greater the force over an area the greater the pressure. Pressure is measured in pascals.

$$\text{pressure (pascal or N/m}^2\text{)} = \frac{\text{force (N)}}{\text{area (m}^2\text{)}}$$

This applies when a force acts at right angles to an area (e.g. pushing a drawing pin into a wall).

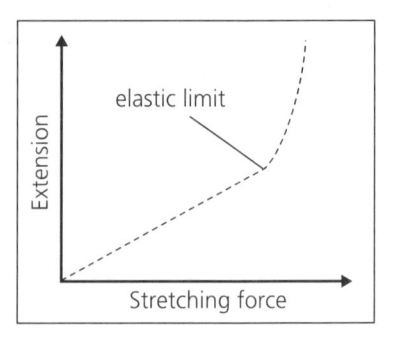

Help

Pressure is given in N/m^2 or pascals.
1 pascal is equal to 1 N/m^2

Worked example

This example includes a couple of 'tricks' that you should be aware of.

Q A fox is standing on the snow. It exerts a force of 100 N and each of its feet has an area of 18 cm². What pressure (N/m²) does it exert on the snow?

A pressure = $\frac{\text{force}}{\text{area}}$

72 cm² = 0.0072 m² (the fox has four feet!)

pressure = $\frac{100}{0.0072}$

= 13 900 N/m² = 13 900 pascals

You must be careful in an examination to work in the correct units and to think about a question before you start. Convert the cm² to m² before you start to get your answer in the right units. This is a particularly difficult example.

Hydraulic systems

These are used as **force multipliers**. For example, if you press on the brake pedal of a car the car will stop. The force you have applied to the brake pedal is multiplied sufficiently for the car brakes to stop the car.

What is happening?

The brake pedal is pressed. The brake fluid is put under pressure. The liquid puts pressure on the slave piston which exerts pressure on the brake (see worked example on facing page).

The pressure in a liquid (or gas) acts equally in all directions, so force can be multiplied in whichever direction you require. In a liquid, pressure increases with depth.

Forces

Worked example

Q What force will be exerted on piston B?

A You must first work out the pressure that piston A exerts.

$$\text{pressure} = \frac{\text{force}}{\text{area}}$$

$$= \frac{1}{0.01}$$

$$= 100 \text{ N/m}^2$$

Now using this information, the force exerted by piston B can be worked out.

$$\text{pressure} = \frac{\text{force}}{\text{area}}$$

therefore:

force = pressure × area

= 100 × 0.5

= 50 N

force 1 N — load

liquid

master cylinder piston A (0.01 m²)

slave cylinder piston B (0.5 m²)

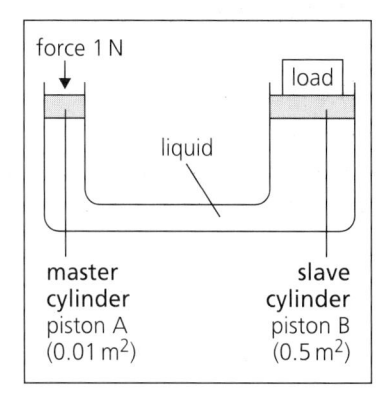

If you simply used ratios, then the master cylinder has an area 50 times smaller than the slave cylinder. The slave cylinder will therefore exert 50 times the force.

50 × 1 newton = 50 N.

Gases

When the pressure on a gas increases and the temperature of the gas stays the same then the volume of the gas decreases.

initial pressure × initial volume = final pressure × final volume

You may be asked to use pascals or atmospheres as units of pressure.

Worked example

Q The pressure on 500 cm³ of a gas is increased from 100 N to 200 N. What volume will it now occupy?

A initial pressure × initial volume = final pressure × final volume

On the left-hand side of the equation
100 × 500 = 50 000

On the right-hand side of the equation
50 000 divided by the pressure will give the new volume (50 000 ÷ 200).

The new volume is therefore 250 cm³.

Questions

1. A master cylinder has a surface area of 0.1m². A force of 20 N is exerted on it. The slave cylinder has an area of 0.4m². What force will the slave cylinder exert?

2. Why is it so difficult to explore the deepest parts of the oceans?

Moving in space

Gravity

The Earth, Sun and Moon (in fact all bodies) attract each other with a force called **gravity**. The greater the distance between bodies the smaller the force of attraction. Larger bodies have greater gravitational attraction than smaller ones.

A smaller body will stay in orbit around a larger one (e.g. the Moon around the Earth) because of the combination of its high speed and the force of attraction between the bodies. To stay in orbit at a particular distance, smaller bodies (including planets, moons and satellites) must move at a particular speed around larger bodies. The further away an orbiting body is away from the larger body, the longer it takes to make one orbit. The planets therefore move at different speeds around the Sun.

The orbits of the planets are slightly squashed circles (ellipses) with the Sun quite close to the centre.

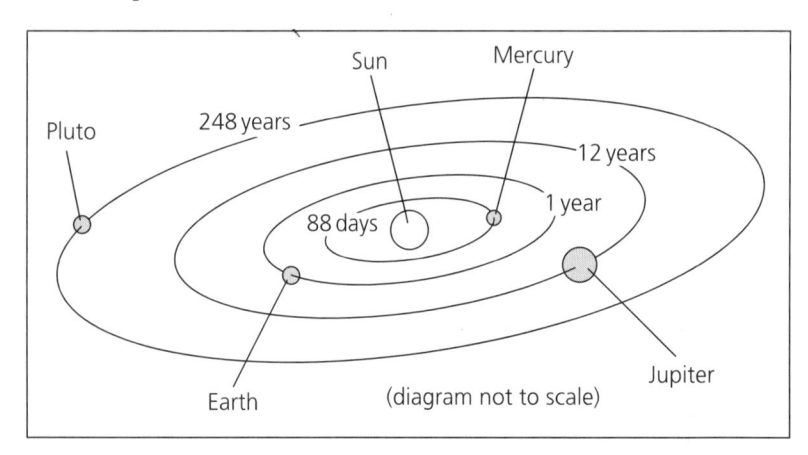

Planets orbit the Sun

Comets have orbits which are far from circular – sometimes they are much closer to the Sun than at other times. This is when we see them.

Satellites

Satellites are put into orbit . They have a number of uses:
- to send information between places a long way apart (e.g. TV)
- to look at weather conditions across the Earth
- to observe the Universe without the Earth's atmosphere getting in the way.

Communication satellites are usually put into orbit high above the equator and they move around the Earth at the same rate that the Earth is spinning. This means that they are always above the same place above the Earth's surface. This is known as **geostationary orbit**.

Monitoring satellites are usually put into a lower **polar orbit** above the Earth so that the Earth spins below them and they can scan whole of the Earth each day.

The origin of the Universe

Our Sun is one of many millions of stars in a group called the **Milky Way**. These stars are often many millions of times further away from us than the planets in our **solar system**.

The Universe is made up of at least a billion galaxies. **Galaxies** are often many millions of times further apart than stars within the galaxy.

The life history of a star

Stars, including the Sun, form when enough dust and gas from space is pulled together by gravitational attraction. Smaller masses also form and can be attracted by larger masses to become planets in orbit.

As stars are so massive:

- the force of gravity tends to draw the matter together
- the very high temperatures tend to make the star expand.

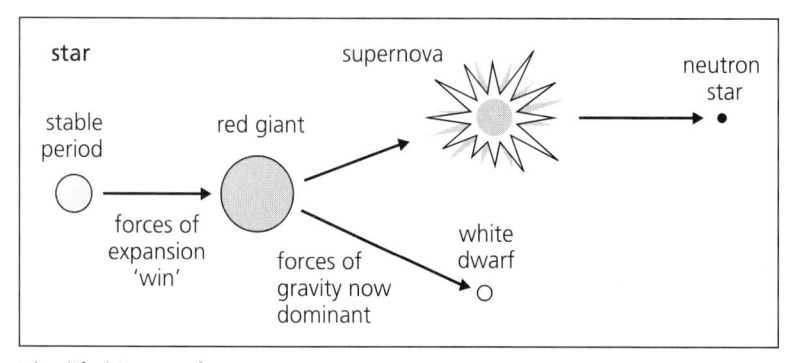

The life history of a star

During the **stable** period (which may last for billions of years) these forces are balanced. Our Sun is at this stage in its life. However, the forces of expansion then begin to 'win' and the star expands and becomes a **red giant**. It now becomes so big that the forces of expansion decrease and the force of gravity becomes the stronger force.

The star now contracts under its own gravity to become a **white dwarf** and its matter may be millions of times denser than that of Earth. If the red giant is massive enough it may rapidly contract and then explode to become a **supernova**. Dust and gas are thrown into space and a very dense **neutron star** remains.

Questions

1. State *three* uses of satellites.
2. How are satellites kept in geostationary orbit?
3. Why are monitoring satellites placed in a lower polar orbit?
4. Describe the life history of a star.

The chemistry of the stars

During a star's life the nuclei of lighter elements (mainly hydrogen and helium) gradually fuse together (nuclear fusion) to produce nuclei of a heavier element. These reactions release a lot of energy which is radiated by the stars.

Nuclei of the heaviest elements are present in the Sun and atoms of these elements are present in the inner planets of our solar system. This suggests that our solar system was formed from the material thrown out when earlier stars exploded.

The future of the Universe?

Scientists have observed that:

- light from other galaxies is shifted to the red end of the spectrum
- the further away the galaxy is, the greater this **'red shift'** becomes. This means that the wavelength of the light is becoming longer.

The current way of explaining this is that:

- other galaxies are moving away from us very quickly
- the further away a galaxy is, the faster it is moving away from us.

This suggests that the Universe is expanding and that it may have started with a huge explosion from one place. This is known as the **'big bang'** theory.

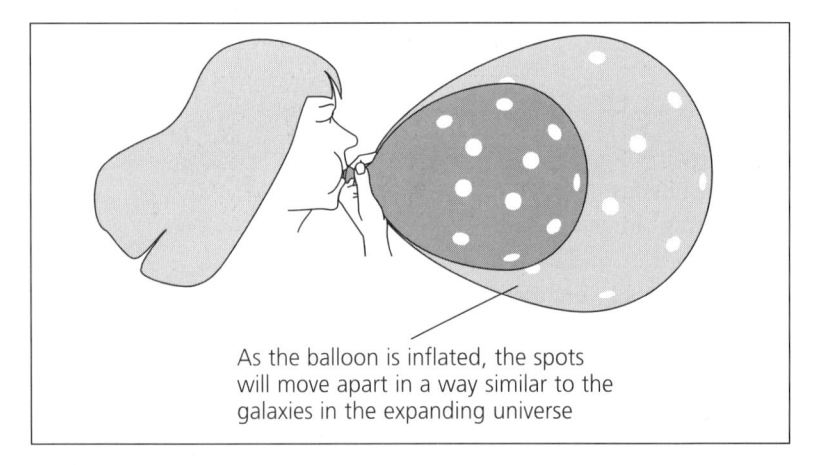

As the balloon is inflated, the spots will move apart in a way similar to the galaxies in the expanding universe

The 'big bang' theory

If the forces of expansion 'win' then the universe will continue to expand. If gravity eventually overcomes the forces of expansion, then the universe will crunch together again.

Questions

1. What evidence is there that the Universe is getting bigger?
2. What is meant by the 'red shift'?

Terminal exam questions

1 A crane is used to lift a concrete block on a building site.
When the crane lifts the block:
- the block accelerates from rest to a speed of 0.9 m/s in the first 3 seconds
- it then rises at a steady speed.

The block has a mass of 200 kg and it is lifted 25 m.

a Calculate the acceleration of the block. [3]

b i What is the weight of the block? [3]

ii What force is the crane exerting? [4]

10 marks

2 a i A satellite is orbiting the Earth. Explain how it stays in orbit. [2]

ii A different satellite is placed in geostationary orbit. Explain what this means and how it is achieved. [3]

b Describe the *two* different possibilities for the future of the Universe. Give reasons for your answers. [4]

9 marks

3 a This diagram is of an hydraulic system.

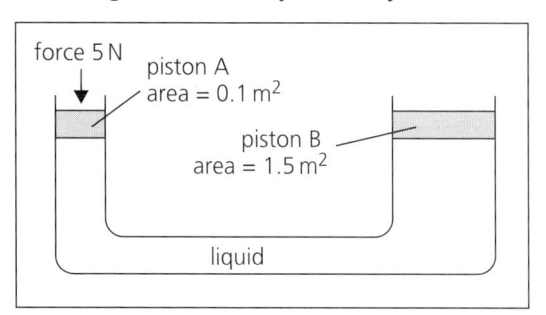

force 5 N
piston A area = 0.1 m^2
piston B area = 1.5 m^2
liquid

What force will be exerted on piston B? [6]

b Hydraulic systems rely on the fact that liquids are not compressed. Gases can be compressed.
700 cm^3 of a gas is kept at a pressure of 50 N/m^2. The pressure is altered to 25 N/m^2. What will be the new volume of the gas, assuming the temperature remains constant? [5]

11 marks

4 A car sets off on a journey.

a i It travels 1800 m in 80 s. What is its average speed? [3]

ii At one point the car accelerates from 30 m/s to 45 m/s. This takes the car 3 s. What is the car's acceleration (m/s^2)? [3]

b As the car slows down the negative acceleration of the car is 5 m/s^2. The force required to stop the car is 5500 N. What is the mass of the car? [3]

c Look at this diagram.

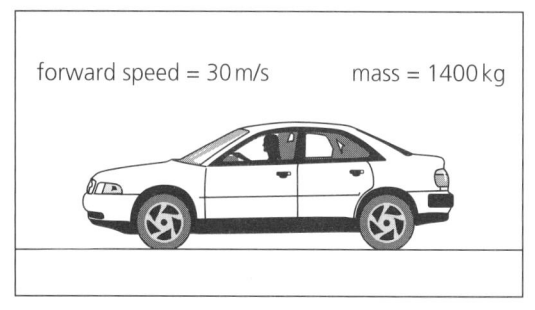

forward speed = 30 m/s   mass = 1400 kg

What is the kinetic energy of the car? [4]

d The parachutist below is falling at a steady speed towards the Earth.

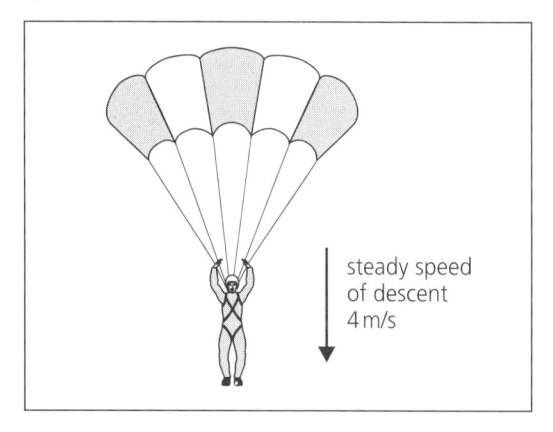

steady speed of descent 4 m/s

Describe the forces acting on the parachute. [4]

17 marks

Total for test: 47 marks

Waves

Light and sound behave like waves. When a ray of light is **reflected** from a flat, shiny surface (e.g. a plane mirror), the angle it leaves the surface is the same as the angle at which it hits the surface.

If a ray of light crosses from one transparent substance into another (e.g. from air into glass) then the ray usually changes direction – it **refracts**.

The only time it does not change direction is when it meets the boundary between the two substances at right angles, along a **normal** (that is, a line perpendicular to the boundary).

When a ray of light travels from glass, perspex or water into the air, some of the light is also reflected from the boundary.

Sound is also refracted in this way. Sound waves change direction when they cross the boundary between different substances at angles less than a right angle.

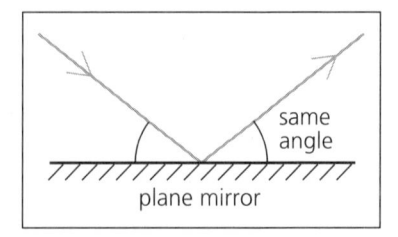

Reflection

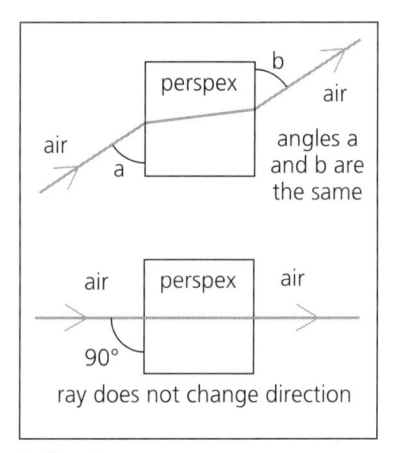

Refraction

Other types of wave

There are other sorts of waves. You can produce them in ropes and springs as well as ripples on the surface of a pond.

Waves travelling along a rope, along a spring or across water can be reflected. Waves travelling across water can also be refracted if the wave enters a deeper or a shallower area (unless their direction of travel is along the normal).

It is the change in speed of the waves of water (as they cross the boundary from deeper to shallower water) that causes the change in direction.

This behaviour shown by waves suggests that:

- light and sound also travel as waves
- light and sound waves are refracted, because they will travel at different speeds as they cross a boundary from one substance to another.

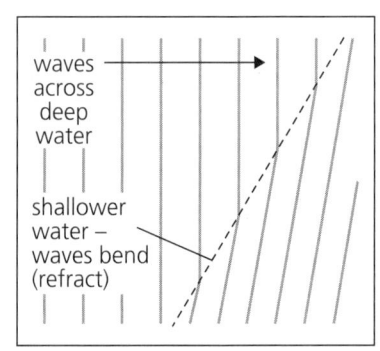

Waves refract

How waves travel

A wave is a regular pattern of disturbances, usually through a substance such as water, air, rope, a spring and so on. Only light waves are able to travel through a vacuum (that is, they do not need to be carried by any substance).

A wave moves energy from one place to another without transferring any matter. So, for example, a wave travelling through a spring does not carry the metal from the beginning to the end of the spring.

Types of wave movement

There are two types of wave movement.

Transverse waves
The disturbances in transverse waves travel at right angles to the direction that the wave is travelling. This is what you probably imagine when you think of a wave. Waves through water and rope travel this way. Light waves are also transverse waves.

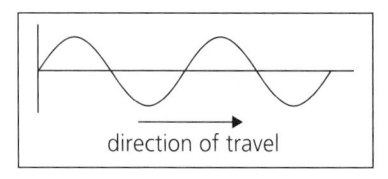

A transverse wave

Longitudinal waves
The disturbances are in the direction of travel. This is the way that waves travel through springs. It is also the way that sound waves travel through solids, liquids and gases.

A longitudinal wave

Measuring waves

You need to know three things about waves: their height, length and frequency. These can most easily be seen on a transverse wave.

- The height (maximum disturbance) of the wave is called its **amplitude.**
- The distance between a particular point on one 'peak' of the wave and the next is the **wavelength.**
- The number of waves passing a particular point each second (or produced by the source) is the **frequency**. This is measured in **hertz** (Hz).

All of these measures also apply to longitudinal waves.

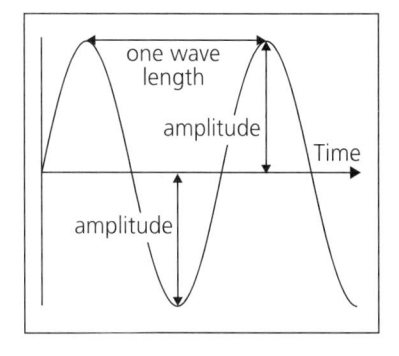

Wave speed

The speed at which a wave is travelling can be found by:

wave speed (m/s) **= frequency** (Hz) × **wavelength** (m)

> ### Worked example
>
> **Q** A wave has a speed of 50 m/s and a frequency of 10 hertz. What is the wavelength of the wave?
>
> **A** wavelength = $\dfrac{\text{wave speed}}{\text{frequency}}$
>
> $= \dfrac{50}{10} = 5\,\text{m}$

Questions

1. When you stand in water up to your knees, the lower half of your legs look shorter and 'bent'. Explain this.
2. Draw a transverse wave. Mark on your diagram the amplitude and wavelength of your wave.

Using reflection and refraction

Ultrasound

A vibrating object produces a sound. The greater the amplitude (size) of the vibrations, the louder the sound.

The number of complete vibrations per second is the frequency (hertz). The higher the frequency, the higher the **pitch** of the sound.

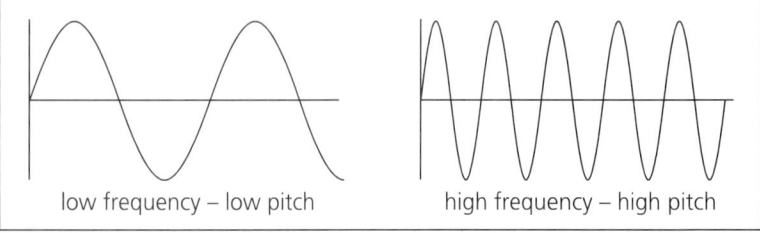

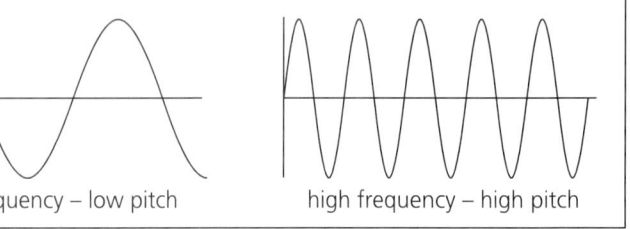

Help

The pitch of a sound is a measure of how high or low it sounds.

low frequency – low pitch

high frequency – high pitch

An electronic system can be used to produce electrical oscillations with any frequency, and these can be used to produce **ultrasonic waves**. Their frequency is higher than humans can hear.

Ultrasound is used:

- in industry – for cleaning and quality control (e.g. detecting flaws in metals, perhaps in bridges)
- in medicine – for pre-natal scanning (forming pictures of the baby in the womb)
- in liquids – for cleaning delicate instruments without having to take them apart.

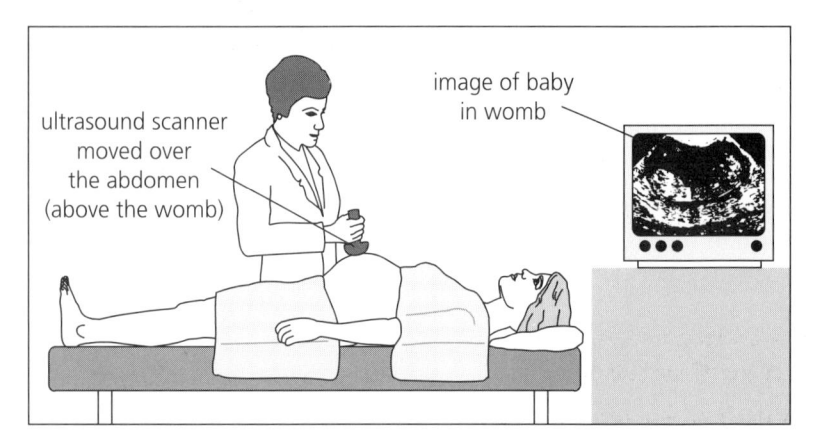

These scans work because the ultrasound waves are reflected when they meet a boundary between two different media (e.g. the growing baby and the fluid in the womb). The time taken for the reflections of ultrasonic pulses to reach a detector is a measure of how far away this boundary is. The detector is placed near to the source. Information about the time taken for reflections to travel is usually presented as a visual display of the body or the object being scanned.

Waves and Radiation

Earthquakes

An earthquake produces shock waves. These are seismic waves and have been used to study the structure of the Earth. Seismographs detect the waves.

There are two types of wave:

- P waves are fast, longitudinal and travel through liquids and solids
- S waves are slower, transverse and travel only through solids.

Both types travel faster through denser materials.

- If the density of the material changes gradually then the waves travel in a curved path.
- If the density changes quickly then the direction of the waves changes abruptly.

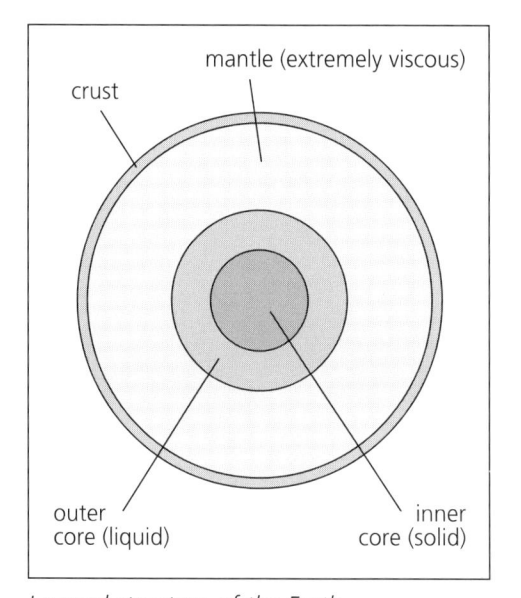

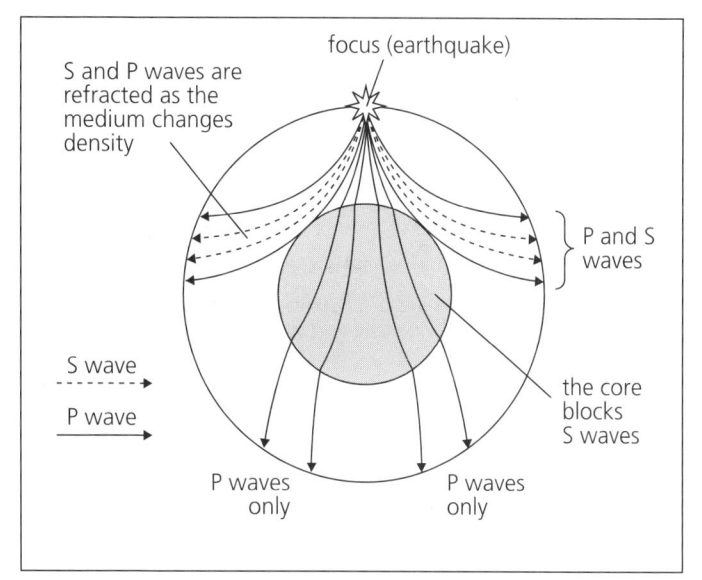

Layered structure of the Earth

P and S waves are used to determine the structure of the Earth

If the paths of these waves are observed, then the results suggest the Earth has a layered structure with:

- a thin crust
- an extremely viscous mantle (density increasing with depth) which goes almost half way to the centre of the Earth
- a core, just over half of the Earth's diameter – outer part liquid, inner part solid.

Questions

1. When engineers use ultrasonic waves to check bridges, what do you think they are checking?
2. How are both P and S waves used to determine the structure of the Earth? Explain your answer in terms of the nature of the waves and in terms of refraction.

Electromagnetic radiation

If you pass white light through a prism, the light splits into different colours because each colour is refracted to a different extent. This results in a spectrum of light which has the same colours (and in the same order) as a rainbow.

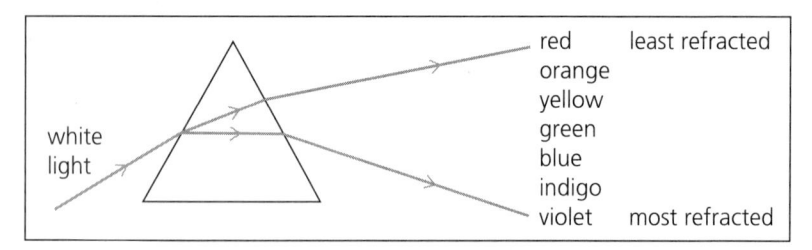

red — least refracted
orange
yellow
white light → green
blue
indigo
violet — most refracted

Help
Remember:
Richard **O**f **Y**ork **G**ained
Battles **I**n **V**ain

The colours are refracted at different angles because they have different wavelengths.

Light is only one type of **electromagnetic radiation**. There are other types which you cannot see. They form a continuous spectrum. All types of electromagnetic radiation travel at the same speed (the 'speed of light') through space (a vacuum).

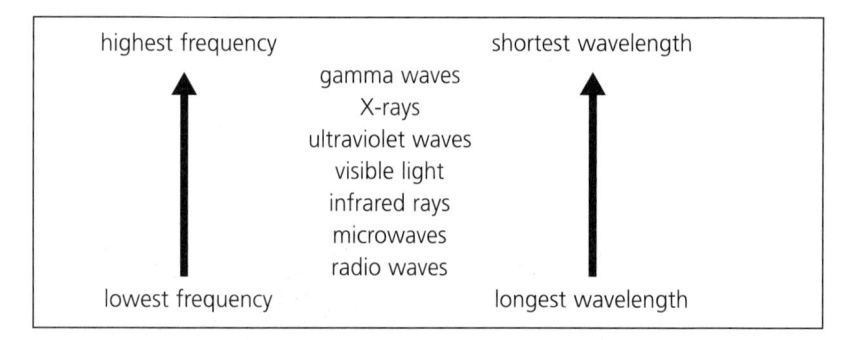

highest frequency ↑   shortest wavelength ↑
gamma waves
X-rays
ultraviolet waves
visible light
infrared rays
microwaves
radio waves
lowest frequency   longest wavelength

Uses of electromagnetic radiation

Different wavelengths are reflected, absorbed or transmitted in different ways, depending on the substance and the type of surface. When electromagnetic radiation is absorbed by an object or a surface:

- it makes the substance hotter
- it may create an alternating electric current with the same frequency as the radiation itself.

The uses and the effects of the different types of radiation depend on these properties as well as others.

Radio waves

Radio waves are used to transmit radio and television programmes across the Earth. The longer wavelength radio waves are reflected back down to Earth by an electrically charged layer in the upper atmosphere. It is therefore possible to send these waves long distances, despite the curvature of the Earth.

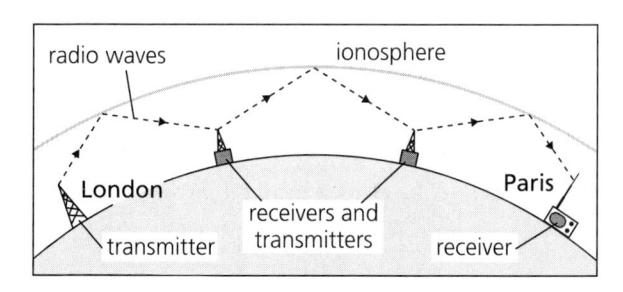

Waves and Radiation

Microwave radiation
Microwave radiation has wavelengths which can easily pass through the Earth's atmosphere. It is therefore used to send information to and from satellites in orbit. This type of radiation has wavelengths strongly absorbed by water molecules, so is used in microwave cooking.

source — microwaves strongly absorbed by water molecules, which vibrate more and cause the liquid or food to heat up and cook

Infrared radiation
Infrared radiation is used in grills, toasters and radiant heaters (e.g. electric fires). It is also used in optical fibre communications and for television and video remote controls.

infrared rays heat up the first object that is in their pathway

Ultraviolet radiation
Some people use ultraviolet radiation to get a sun tan on a sun bed. We can all get a natural tan from the Sun's UV radiation. Special coatings, which absorb UV radiation and then emit it as light, are used in fluorescent lamps and in security coding.

UV light

X radiation
X radiation is used in X-rays. These can be 'shadow' pictures of bones or metals. These pictures can be used to identify broken bones or problems in metal structures.

X-rays pass through flesh to produce a dark image

X-rays do not pass through bone – a white 'shadow' is produced / photographic plate (developed)

Gamma radiation
Gamma radiation has several uses:
- to kill harmful bacteria in food and make it sterile
- to sterilise surgical instruments
- to kill cancer cells.

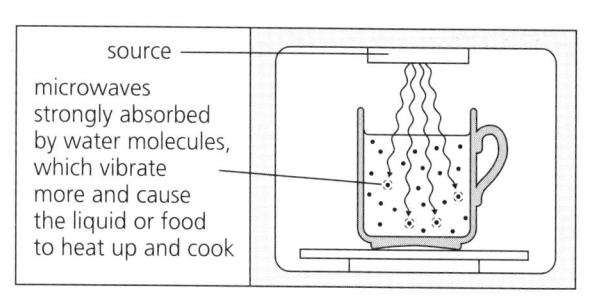

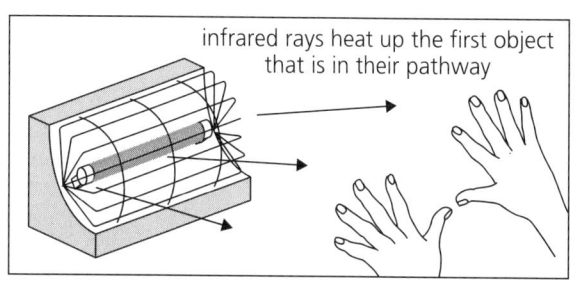

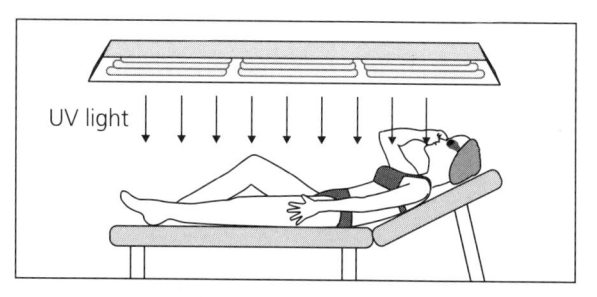

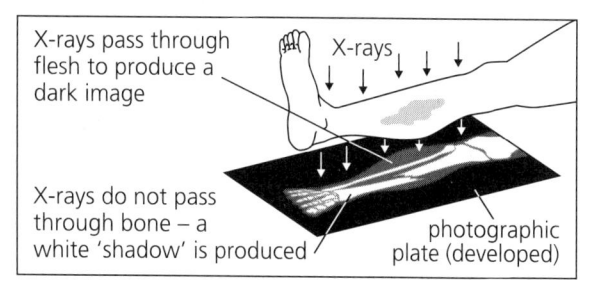

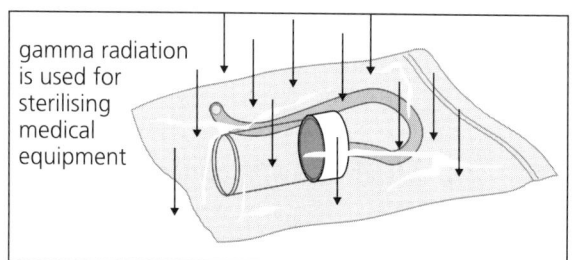

gamma radiation is used for sterilising medical equipment

Questions

1. List the following types of electromagnetic radiation from that with the shortest wavelength to that with the longest: UV, X-rays, microwaves and radio waves.
2. Give *two* uses of infrared radiation.
3. Suggest an explanation for how a rainbow is formed.

More uses of waves

Diffraction

When a wave moves through a gap or spreads out as it passes an obstacle, the wave spreads out from the edges. This is called **diffraction.**

Electromagnetic radiation and sound can be diffracted. This supports the idea that they travel as waves.

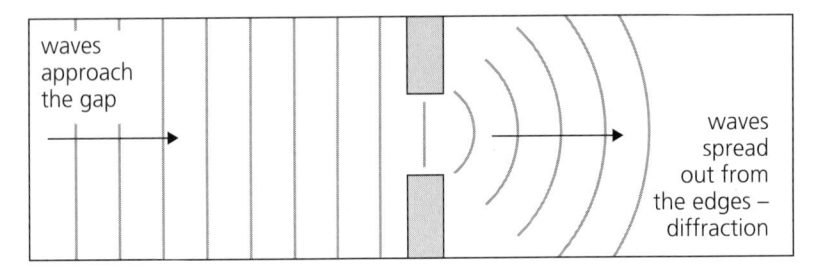

It is because of diffraction that:

- sounds may be heard in the shadow of buildings (around corners)

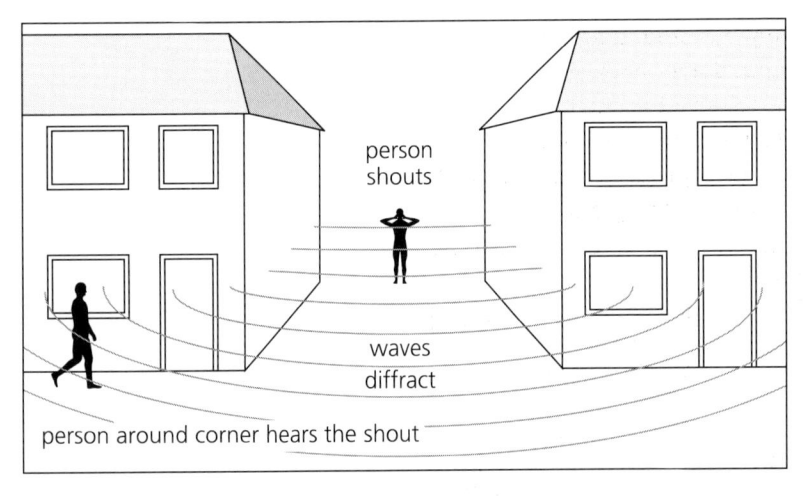

- radio signals can sometimes be picked up in the shadow of hills.

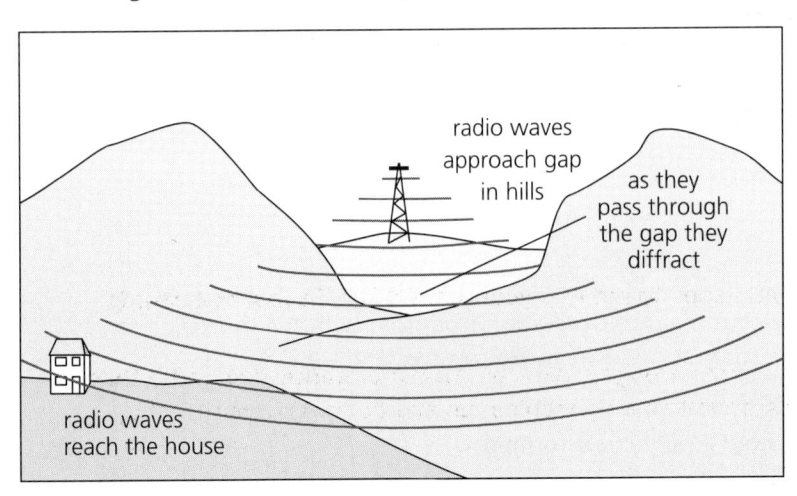

Waves and Radiation

Total internal reflection

If the angle between the light ray and the normal is greater than a certain **critical angle** (different for different substances), then **total internal reflection** occurs.

This is the how optical fibres work. For example, endoscopes containing optical fibres are used by doctors to see into parts of patients' bodies such as the gut and blood vessels. Light stays in the optical fibre until it comes out of the other end.

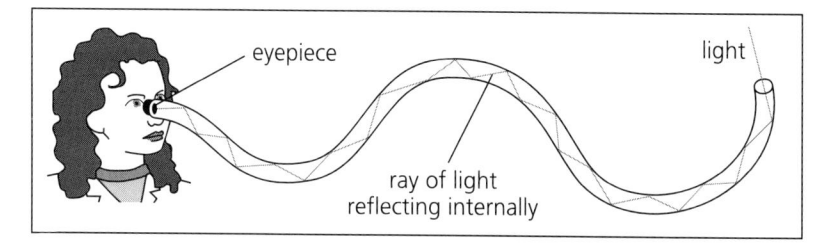

An endoscope

Another important use of total internal reflection is in communications. Optical fibres can carry more electrical signals than cables of the same diameter. The signal also weakens less on its journey than in cables.

A mirage on a hot day is another example of total internal reflection. As heat rises from the ground, the air above forms layers of different densities. Some sunlight is refracted through these layers until it reaches the critical angle when the rays totally internally reflect back up through the layers, producing an image of the sky superimposed over the normal view of the ground.

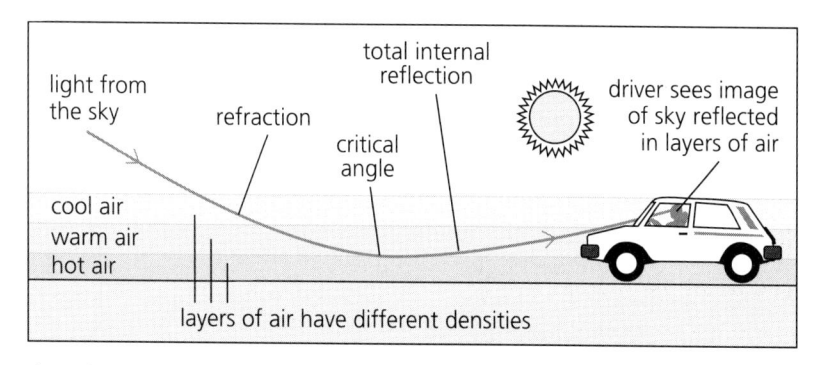

A mirage

Another use of total internal reflection involves the lighting of dials on a car dashboard, without the need for light bulbs.

Questions

1. A doctor is able to use an endoscope to see into your gut. Explain, in your own words, how this is possible.

2. You are watching the waves come through a narrow harbour entrance. You notice that the small boats inside the harbour wall are 'bobbing' up and down. Explain why they are doing this.

The effects of radiation

Electromagnetic radiation

The effect on living cells depends on the type of radiation:

- **microwaves** – the energy is absorbed by the water of living cells and may kill them
- **infrared** radiation is absorbed by the skin and we get hot
- **ultraviolet** radiation can pass through the skin to deeper tissues – the darker the skin, the more UV radiation it absorbs and the less reaches deeper tissues
- **X-rays and gamma rays** mostly pass through the soft tissues but some is absorbed by cells.

High doses of UV, X or gamma radiation can kill normal cells.

Lower doses can cause normal cells to become abnormal, which may result in cancer cells.

Radioactive substances

Some substances give out radiation all of the time. There are three types of radiation emitted by these radioactive substances:

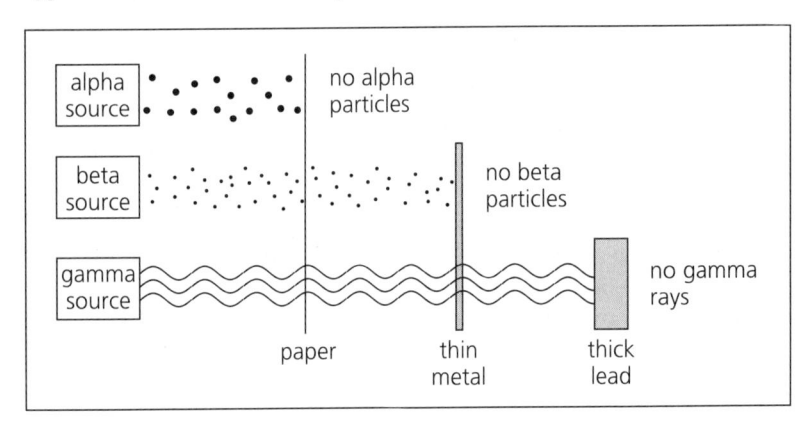

- **alpha radiation** – easily absorbed by a few centimetres of air or a thin sheet of paper
- **beta radiation** – passes through paper but will be absorbed by a few millimetres of metal
- **gamma radiation** – very penetrating and requires many centimetres of lead or several metres of concrete to stop it.

How do we explain this? The three types of radiation are all different:

- **alpha (α) particles** are the same as a helium nucleus – they consist of 2 protons and 2 neutrons
- **beta (β) particles** are very fast-moving electrons – for each beta particle emitted by a radioactive substance, one proton becomes one neutron
- **gamma (γ) rays** are very short wavelength electromagnetic radiation – no particles are emitted.

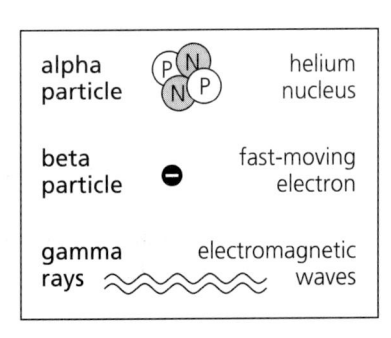

When a radioactive substance emits alpha or beta particles, its atoms change from one element to another (because the number of protons changes). For example:

- radium $^{226}_{88}$Ra loses an alpha particle ($^{4}_{2}$He) and becomes radon $^{222}_{86}$Rn
- polonium $^{218}_{84}$Po loses a beta particle ($^{0}_{-1}$e) and becomes astatine $^{218}_{85}$At.

There are radioactive substances all around us. They are in the ground, the air, building materials and food. We also receive radiation from space. All of this we call **background radiation**.

When radiation collides with neutral atoms or molecules then these may become **ionised** (charged). If this happens in living cells cancers may result. Alpha particles are strongly ionising. The larger the dose or radiation, the greater the risk. Even higher doses of radiation can be used to kill cancer cells or harmful micro-organisms.

The **dangers of radiation** to humans depend on where the source is:

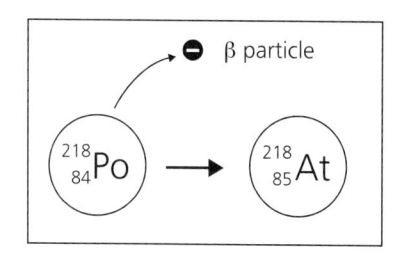

Source outside the body	Source inside the body
beta and gamma radiation are the most dangerous as they can pass into the body and be absorbed by cells and therefore damage them	alpha radiation becomes the most dangerous as it is strongly absorbed by cells and is strongly ionising
alpha radiation is unlikely to reach the cells	beta and gamma radiation are less dangerous as they are less strongly absorbed

Using radiation

Certain substances will absorb different forms of radiation. This means that a radioactive source can be used to monitor or control the thickness of materials manufactured in industry (e.g. paper).

- If the paper is too thick, not enough alpha particles will pass through to the detector so the rollers are adjusted to make the paper thinner.
- If the paper is too thin, too many alpha particles are detected so the rollers are adjusted to make the paper thicker.

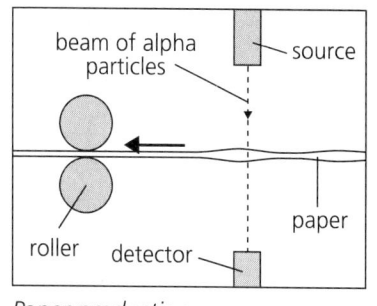

Paper production

Questions

1. Some people use sun beds to get a tan. What sort of radiation do sun beds emit? Describe some of the possible advantages and some disadvantages of their use.
2. Alpha radiation is used to check the thickness of paper. Why are gamma or beta radiation sources not used?
3. The following sequence shows the radioactive decay of plutonium 242 to uranium 234:
$^{242}_{94}$Pu → $^{238}_{92}$U → $^{234}_{90}$Th → $^{234}_{91}$Pa → $^{234}_{92}$U
How does uranium decay to thorium?
How does thorium decay to protactinium?

Radioactive decay

Decay is a result of changes in the nucleus of an atom.

Atoms are made up of protons and neutrons in the nucleus with electrons orbiting the nucleus.

An atom has no charge. It has the same number of protons as electrons.

The number of protons in an atom determines what element it is (e.g. carbon always has 6, sodium always has 11).

The mass number of an element equals the number of protons and neutrons in the nucleus.

	Mass	Charge
proton	1	+
neutron	1	0
electron	negligible	−

Theories of the atom

One early theory was the 'plum pudding model'. This described the atom as a positively charged sphere with negative electrons studded throughout, like raisins in a pudding.

In 1911 Ernest Rutherford carried out an experiment in which he fired alpha particles at a very thin piece of gold foil. Most of the alpha particles went straight through, but a few were scattered at wide angles by the foil. He worked out that this could only be explained if all the positive charge was concentrated in the nucleus of the atom, not throughout the atom as in the plum pudding model. He calculated the size of the nucleus from the scatter patterns and found that it was a minute part of the atom. If an atom was the size of a school hall, its nucleus would be the size of a full stop! This work led to our current view of the atom.

Isotopes

Some atoms have different numbers of neutrons. Chlorine has always got 17 protons. However some forms have 18 neutrons and some have 20 neutrons. These are **isotopes** of chlorine.

Help

Two isotopes of chlorine are $^{35}_{17}Cl$ and $^{37}_{17}Cl$.

Radioactive isotopes (radionuclides)

These have atoms with unstable nuclei. When an unstable nucleus breaks down (disintegrates):

- it emits radiation
- a different atom, with a different number of protons, results.

The older the material, the less radiation it emits. It will have passed through several half-lives.

Half-life

The **half-life** of a radioactive source is the time taken for the number of radioactive atoms to half. In other words, for the substance to become half as radioactive.

For example, the half-life of substance X = 100 years:
- after 50 years it is half as radioactive
- after another 50 years it has lost another half of its radioactivity and is only 25% as radioactive as when it was formed.

The graph shows this.

Uranium atoms have a very long half-life. They decay through a series of isotopes with short half-lives. Eventually they produce stable isotopes of lead.

If you want to date an igneous rock you can do this by working out the relative proportions of uranium and lead in the rock.

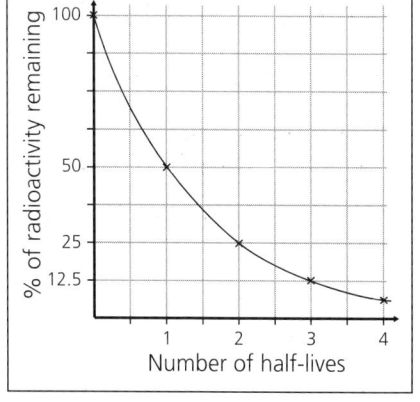

You can also use a radioisotope of potassium (potassium 40) to date rocks. It breaks down to argon. If the argon remains trapped in the igneous rock, then again you can work out the proportions and date the rock.

The nuclear process

This involves splitting atoms – a process known as **nuclear fission**.

An atom with a very large nucleus is bombarded with neutrons. This results in:

- the nucleus splitting into two smaller nuclei
- further neutrons being released – these may cause further nuclear fission and could lead to a 'chain' reaction (rods can be placed between the nuclear material to stop the chain reaction 'getting out of hand')
- new atoms being formed which are also radioactive.

The energy released during nuclear fission is very large compared to that released when a chemical bond is made between two atoms.

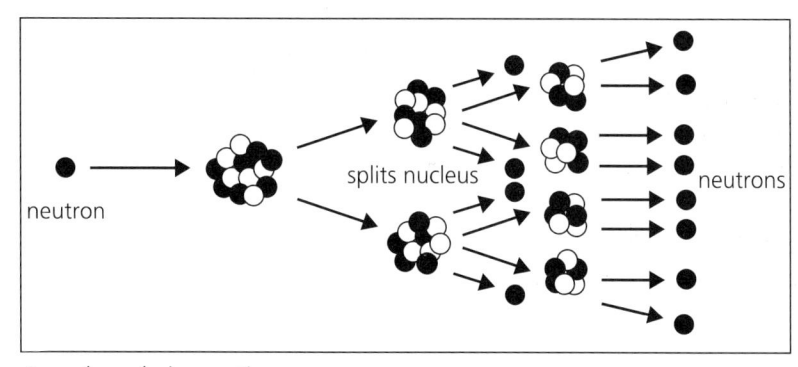

A nuclear chain reaction

Questions

1. A substance has a half-life is 100 years. How long will it be before three quarters of its radioactivity has been lost?
2. How many protons, neutrons and electrons does uranium $^{238}_{92}U$ have?
3. The nuclear process releases a great deal of energy. How do nuclear scientists prevent a chain reaction occurring and the power station blowing up?

Terminal exam questions

1. Wave ripples are crossing a pond as shown in the diagram.

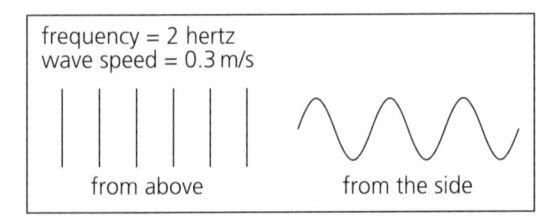

   frequency = 2 hertz
   wave speed = 0.3 m/s
   from above — from the side

   a. Are the waves transverse or longitudinal? Explain your answer. [3]

   b i What is the wavelength of the waves? [4]

   ii Copy this diagram. Mark one wavelength. [1]

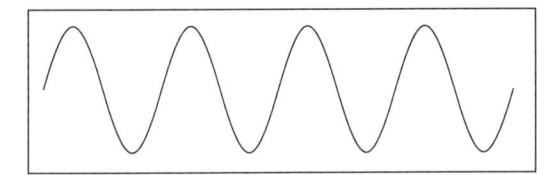

   c. The waves pass through a gap between two wooden blocks as shown in this diagram.

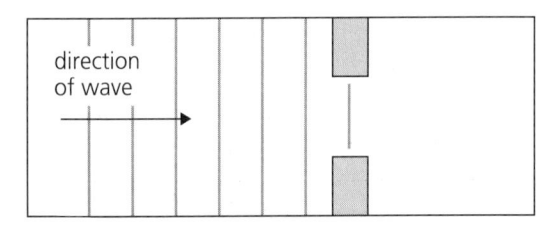

   direction of wave

   i Copy and complete the diagram to show what would happen to the waves. [1]

   ii Why would the direction of the waves change if the water suddenly became deeper? [2]

   11 marks

2. a Radioactive substances can emit three different types of radiation. The following diagrams represent two investigations of radioactive sources.

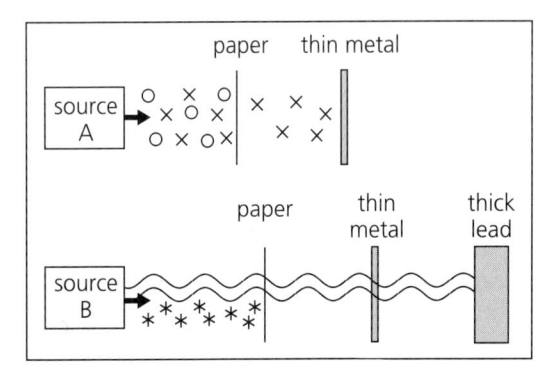

   source A — paper — thin metal
   source B — paper — thin metal — thick lead

   i What type(s) of radiation is source A emitting? [2]

   ii What type(s) of radiation is source B emitting? [2]

   b i Under what conditions is alpha radiation the most dangerous to the body? Explain your answer. [3]

   ii What are alpha particles? [3]

   c Suggest *two* uses of radiation in a hospital. [2]

   d The following table illustrates the radioactivity of a source.

Seconds	Particles emitted per minute
0	1000
50	750
100	500
150	375
200	250

   i What is the half-life of the substance? [1]

   ii After what period of time will the emissions have reduced to 125 per minute? [1]

   iii How many half-lives does this represent? [1]

   15 marks

3. Earthquakes produce shock waves.

   a How are these shock waves detected? [1]

   Use this diagram and labels X, Y and Z to help answer the questions which follow.

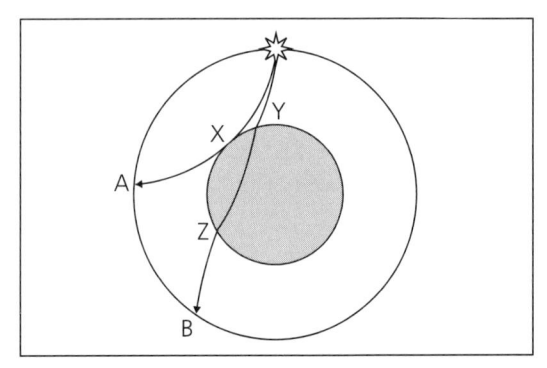

   b i Describe and explain the path of wave A. [4]

   ii Describe and explain the path of wave B. [2]

   iii What type of wave are waves A and B? [2]

   9 marks

Waves and Radiation

4 a A ray of light passes into a perspex block from the air.

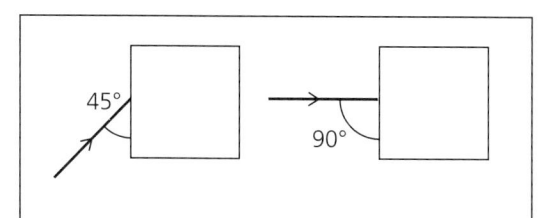

Copy and complete the diagrams to show the path of the rays as they pass through the blocks and back into the air. [3]

b You can use a prism to split up the colours in white light.
Why do the colours separate as they pass through the prism? [2]

c i What is an endoscope used for? [2]

ii How does the endoscope work? [4]

d Light is part of the electromagnetic spectrum.

i What is meant by electromagnetic radiation? [2]

ii Copy and complete the following diagrams by placing the types of electromagnetic radiation listed in sequence **1–4** against the arrows.

gamma rays   **microwaves**
light rays   **UV rays**

Highest frequency   ↑ 1
                      2
                      3
Lowest frequency   4   [3]

light rays   **X-rays**
radio waves   **infrared waves**

Shortest wavelength ↑ 1
                      2
                      3
Longest wavelength   4   [3]

19 marks

5 Study the graph which shows the radioactive decay of a substance.

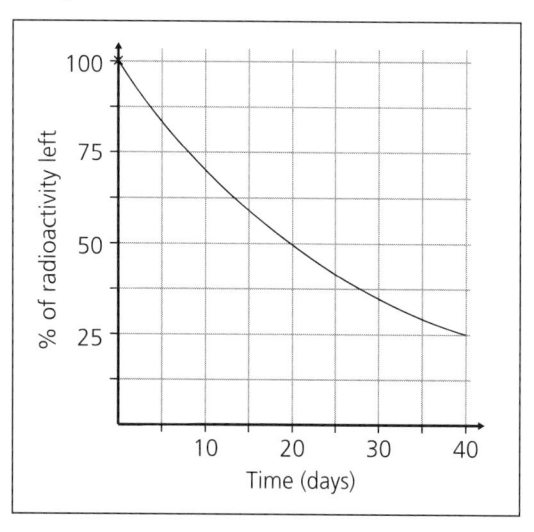

a i How much radioactivity is left after 30 days? [1]

ii After how many days will $\frac{1}{32}$ of its initial radioactivity be left? [1]

b How are radioisotopes used to date rocks? [3]

c Gamma radiation has a number of uses. State *three* of them. [3]

d Microwaves are a different form of electromagnetic radiation.

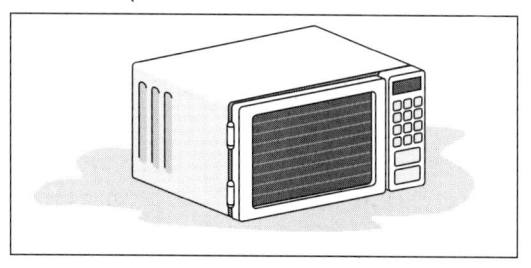

How do microwaves heat up food? [3]

11 marks

Total for test: 65 marks

Answers to module tests and terminal exam questions

Humans as Organisms

Question	Answer	Marks	Total
1	1 red cells 2 plasma 3 platelets 4 white cells	1 1 1 1	4
2	1 flattens 2 contracts 3 increases 4 decreases	1 1 1 1	4
3	1 stomach 2 liver 3 large intestine 4 pancreas	1 1 1 1	4
4	**B** and **C**	2	2
5	**A** and **D**	2	2

Question	Answer	Marks	Total
6	1. **A** 2. **D** 3. **C** 4. **C**	1 1 1 1	4
7	1. **B** 2. **C** 3. **C** 4. **C**	1 1 1 1	4
8	1. **D** 2. **B** 3. **A** 4. **D**	1 1 1 1	4

Total for test: 28 marks

Maintenance of Life

Question	Answer	Marks	Total
1	1 chloroplast 2 nucleus 3 cell wall 4 cytoplasm	1 1 1 1	4
2	1 carbon dioxide 2 nitrate 3 sugars 4 potassium	1 1 1 1	4
3	1 effector 2 receptor 3 sensory neurone 4 relay neurone	1 1 1 1	4
4	**D** and **E**	2	2
5	**B** and **E** *many pupils confuse glycogen and glucagon*	2	2

Question	Answer	Marks	Total
6	1. **A** 2. **C** 3. **A** 4. **B**	1 1 1 1	4
7	1. **A** 2. **C** 3. **D** 4. **A**	1 1 1 1	4
8	1. **C** 2. **A** 3. **A** 4. **D**	1 1 1 1	4

Total for test: 28 marks

Answers to module tests and terminal exam questions

Environment

Question			Answer	Marks	Total
1	a	i	Vole/small bird/beetle.	1	
		ii	There are small numbers of trees compared to the animals	1	
			but the trees' mass is very much greater	1	
			one tree can support many animals.	1	
	b		*Any eight points from*: • made into sugars/carbohydrates • made into fats • made into proteins • makes plant structures • eaten by animal • made into animal structures • lost from animal through respiration • as carbon dioxide • animal may die • decomposed • by microbes • microbes respire • release carbon dioxide. *These are the general ideas – you do not have to use the exact words.*	8	
	c		*Any five points from*: • plant dies • decomposed • by microbes/bacteria/fungi • nitrogen in plant converted to ammonia/ammonium compounds • ammonium compounds converted to nitrates • by nitrifying bacteria • taken up by another plant. *The ideas would have to be in a logical sequence to obtain full marks.*	5	
	d		Some energy is transferred to the production of waste	1	
			chemical energy in respiration	1	
			heat energy and	1	
			kinetic (movement) energy.	1	**21 marks**
2	a		*Any six points (in a reasonably logical sequence) from*: • plants continue to grow • many die • due to competition/not enough light • decompose • microbes use up oxygen • to respire • fish die • through suffocation. *Alternative answers referring to the drying out of the pond would receive marks – although this is not on the syllabus, it is correct. For example:* • plants die • they sink to the bottom • the layer of dead plants builds up • eventually wetland/marsh-loving plants may grow • these take up water and further dry out the pond • meadowland plants and then trees may establish.	6	**6 marks**

Answers to module tests and terminal exam questions

3	a	i	Carbon dioxide and methane.	2	
		ii	*Any three correct points (max. of 2 marks for each gas) from:* • methane – more cattle • methane – more rice fields • carbon dioxide – more people • carbon dioxide – more industry • carbon dioxide – more cars/burning of fossil fuel.	3	
		iii	More carbon dioxide in the air absorbs more of the Sun's energy less is reflected back into space the Earth warms up.	1 1 1	
	b	i	*Any two from:* • sulphur dioxide • nitrogen oxide(s) • carbon dioxide.	2	
		ii	*Any four points from:* • may damage buildings • will damage trees/other plants • will get into lakes/ponds/rivers • makes the water acidic • kills animals/plants in the water.	4	**14 marks**
4	a		Vegetation → snail → partridge → humans *Note: there are several other examples but the example must come from this food web.*	1	
	b	i	Vegetation.	1	
		ii	It will increase as there is more food so more young can be reared.	1 1 1	
		iii	They might increase as there is more vegetation to eat or they might decrease as thrushes may eat them instead of snails.	1 1 1 1	
	c		Total amount of food available competition for food predation disease.	1 1 1 1	**13 marks**
5	a	i	Photosynthesis.	1	
		ii	*Any three from:* • oxygen • fats • proteins • carbohydrates *or* sugar *or* starch.	3	
	b	i	Respiration.	1	
		ii	Water.	1	
	c		Bacteria and fungi *(or microbes for 1 mark)* decay *or* break down mouse during respiration.	1 1 1 1	
	d		Climate changes sea level rises.	1 1	**12 marks**

Total for test: 66 marks

Answers to module tests and terminal exam questions

Inheritance and Selection

Question			Answer	Marks	Total
1	a		Mitosis results in two cells and meiosis four cells.	1	
			Mitosis cells genetically the same, meiosis they are different.	1	
	b		Chromosomes all the same as parent's	1	
			so genetically identical.	1	
	c	i	You choose the male and female	1	
			with the best characteristics	1	
			so the offspring inherit these characteristics.	1	
		ii	Reduction in the number of gene types in the population	1	
			if a change in circumstances/environment	1	
			e.g. temperature drops, new disease	1	
			and species can't adapt.	1	**11 marks**
2	a	i	Artificially altering the genetic make-up of an organism.	1	
		ii	Cut the gene	1	
			from the chromosome	1	
			and place in other species.	1	
		iii	Place genes in bacteria	1	
			which produce the protein	1	
			insulin.	1	
	b		Two alleles/genes	1	
			controlling the same characteristic	1	
			are different.	1	
	c	i	The nervous system.	1	
		ii	[Genetic diagram: Hh × Hh → HH, Hh, hH, hh; hh at risk; 75% chance]	4	**15 marks**
3	a	i	Tissue culture	1	
			embryo transplant.	1	
		ii	Tissue culture:		
			small group of cells from an organism	1	
			grown into a new organism.	1	
			Embryo transplant – *any two from*:		
			• cells from a developing embryo		
			• transplanted into host organism		
			• before the cells have become specialised.	2	
	b		[Genetic diagram: Cc × CC → CC, CC, cC, cC; no children cc; 0% chance] *Note: it is better to draw a genetic diagram*	4	**10 marks**

Answers to module tests and terminal exam questions

4			Wide variation in a species	1	
			weakest do not survive	1	
			e.g. caught and eaten/easily catch disease	1	
			best adapted left to breed	1	
			so the species evolves.	1	**5 marks**
5	a	i	A gene which masks the affect of another.	1	
		ii	Pairs of genes	1	
			controlling the same characteristic.	1	
	b	i	At **A** the chromosomes replicate (are copied).	1	
			At **B** four new cells are produced each with:		
			half the original number of chromosomes	1	
			one chromosome from each original pair.	1	
		ii	To produce sex cells.	1	
	c	i	Ss × SS [1] No chance of sickle cell anaemia	1	
			S s S S [1] 50% chance of being a carrier.	1	
			SS sS sS SS [1]	3	
		ii	Helps prevent malaria.	1	
	d		*Any four points from*:		
			• made of DNA		
			• genes are short lengths of DNA		
			• DNA codes for amino acids		
			• proteins give us our characteristics.	4	**17 marks**
6	a	i	**A** FSH	1	
			stimulates egg production	1	
			B oestrogen	1	
			now stops FSH production	1	
			C LH	1	
			causes the release of the egg.	1	
		ii	Pituitary gland.	1	
	b	i	FSH.	1	
		ii	Oestrogen (*progesterone is also correct*).	1	**9 marks**

Total for test: 67 marks

Answers to module tests and terminal exam questions

Metals

Question	Answer	Marks	Total
1	1 aluminium 2 carbon 3 iron 4 gold	1 1 1 1	4
2	1 NaCl 2 Na_2O 3 $NaNO_3$ 4 Na_2SO_4	1 1 1 1	4
3	1 neutralisation 2 reduction 3 oxidation 4 displacement	1 1 1 1	4
4	A and C	2	2
5	A and E	2	2

Question	Answer	Marks	Total
6	1. C 2. C 3. A 4. C	1 1 1 1	4
7	1. C 2. B 3. B 4. D	1 1 1 1	4
8	1. A 2. D 3. C 4. B	1 1 1 1	4

Total for test: 28 marks

Earth Materials

Question	Answer	Marks	Total
1	1 sedimentary 2 metamorphic 3 magma 4 igneous	1 1 1 1	4
2	1 non-porous rock 2 oil 3 porous rock 4 gas	1 1 1 1	4
3	1 carbon dioxide 2 ammonia 3 nitrogen 4 ozone	1 1 1 1	4
4	A and E	2	2
5	C and E	2	2

Question	Answer	Marks	Total
6	1. A 2. B 3. D 4. B	1 1 1 1	4
7	1. B 2. D 3. B 4. C	1 1 1 1	4
8	1. C 2. C 3. D 4. C	1 1 1 1	4

Total for test: 28 marks

Patterns of Chemical Change

Question			Answer	Marks	Total
1	a	i	$3H_2$	1	
			$2NH_3$	1	
		ii	200 atmospheres pressure	1	
			450°C	1	
			Iron catalyst.	1	
		iii	Reaction is reversible	1	
			so ammonia formed could break down.	1	
			These conditions ensure maximum ammonia production.	1	
	b	i	$2 \times N = 28 +$		
			$4 \times H = 4 +$		
			$3 \times O = 48$ answer = 80	1	
		ii	M_r of ammonia is 17 and M_r of ammonium nitrate is 80	1	
			therefore 17 tonnes of ammonia will produce 80 tonnes of ammonium nitrate.	1	
			85 tonnes of ammonia is five times this amount	1	
			so 5×80 tonnes will be produced = 400 tonnes	1	**13 marks**
2	a	i	Bonds broken:		
			4 C—H bonds at 413 = 1652 +		
			1 C=C bond at 612 = 612 +		
			3 O=O bonds at 498 = $\underline{1494}$		
			total for bonds broken 3758 kJ	2	
			You would lose a mark for each error, up to 2 marks.		
			Bonds made:		
			4 C=O bonds at 805 = 3220		
			4 H—O bonds at 464 = $\underline{1856}$		
			total for bonds made = 5076 kJ	2	
			The difference between bonds broken and bonds made is 1318.	1	
		ii	The reaction is exothermic as energy is released.	1	
	b		*Any three from:*		
			• increase the pressure (if a gas is involved)		
			• change the temperature		
			• increase the concentration		
			• lower the activation energy/use a catalyst.	3	**9 marks**
3	a		M_r of sodium chloride is 58	1	
			116 g represents two moles	1	
			1 mole of chlorine is released ($2NaCl \rightarrow 2Na + Cl_2$)	1	
			1 mole occupies 24 litres at room temperature and pressure.	1	
	b		Calcium Chlorine		
			40 35 atomic mass	1	
			20 35 mass reacting	1	
			0.5 1 moles reacting		
			1 2 converted to whole numbers	1	
			The formula is $CaCl_2$.	1	**8 marks**

Total for test: 30 marks

Answers to module tests and terminal exam questions

Structures and Bonding

Question			Answer	Marks	Total
1	a	i	39	1	
		ii	19	1	
		iii	20	1	
	b		*1 mark each for showing:*		
			2 electrons in inner shell	1	
			8 electrons in next shell and	1	
			1 electron in outer shell.	1	
	c	i	Lithium as 2,1 (electronic structure)	1	
			chlorine as 2, 8, 7 (electronic structure)	1	
			outer electron of lithium joins outer shell of chlorine.	1	
		ii	Ionic.	1	
		iii	An ion is an atom	1	
			with a charge.	1	
			It loses	1	
			one electron.	1	**14 marks**
2	a		Atoms	1	
			held together	1	
			by bonds.	1	
	b		1N 3H [1]		
			H∶N∶H with H below (dot-cross diagram) ×× [1] 3(×•) [1]	3	
	c		The bonds holding them together	1	
			are weaker/more easily broken.	1	**8 marks**
3	a	i	$2K + 2H_2O \rightarrow 2KOH + H_2$	1	
		ii	Outer electron is closer to nucleus	1	
			so is less easily lost	1	
			as greater attraction to nucleus.	1	
	b		Chlorine more reactive	1	
			so displaces the iodine.	1	**6 marks**
4	a		So that the ions	1	
			are free to move.	1	
	b		Sodium ions are attracted	1	
			each gains an electron	1	
			to become a sodium atom.	1	
	c	i	*Any two from*:		
			• kill bacteria (water/swimming pools)		
			• bleach		
			• disinfectant		
			• polymers (e.g. PVC).	2	
		ii	Bleaches	1	
			damp	1	
			litmus paper.	1	**10 marks**

Answers to module tests and terminal exam questions

5	a	i	1 atom of hydrogen	1	
			1 atom of chlorine	1	
			they share outer electrons.	1	
		ii	1 proton	1	
			0 neutrons	1	
			1 electron.	1	
	b	i	2 atoms bonded together to form the molecule (e.g. O_2).	1	
		ii	*Marks for showing in the diagram*:		
			2 oxygen atoms	1	
			each with 6 electrons in outer shell	1	
			they each share 2 electrons with the other atom.	1	
	c		When heated new covalent bonds form	1	
			between the chains	1	
			these are strong cross-linkages.	1	
	d		*Any four points from*:		
			• each carbon atom		
			• is covalently bonded		
			• to four others		
			• the structure is rigid		
			• it is a giant structure.	4	**17 marks**

Total for test: 55 marks

Energy

Question	Answer	Marks	Total
1	1 solar	1	
	2 nuclear	1	
	3 wind	1	
	4 coal	1	4
2	1 joule	1	
	2 metre	1	
	3 newton	1	
	4 watt	1	4
3	1 radiation	1	
	2 waves	1	
	3 vacuum	1	
	4 conduction	1	4
4	B and E	2	2
5	A and D	2	2

Question	Answer	Marks	Total
6	1. B	1	
	2. C	1	
	3. B	1	
	4. A	1	4
7	1. D	1	
	2. A	1	
	3. C	1	
	4. D	1	4
8	1. B	1	
	2. C	1	
	3. A	1	
	4. D	1	4

Total for test: 28 marks

Answers to module tests and terminal exam questions

Electricity

Question	Answer	Marks	Total
1	1 diode	1	
	2 fuse	1	
	3 resistor	1	
	4 thermistor	1	4
2	1 diode	1	
	2 LDR	1	
	3 thermistor	1	
	4 resistor	1	4
3	1 battery	1	
	2 force field	1	
	3 split ring	1	
	4 current	1	4
4	**B** and **D**	2	2
5	**A** and **C**	2	2

Question	Answer	Marks	Total
6	1. **C**	1	
	2. **B**	1	
	3. **D**	1	
	4. **B**	1	4
7	1. **D**	1	
	2. **B**	1	
	3. **A**	1	
	4. **D**	1	4
8	1. **C**	1	
	2. **C**	1	
	3. **A**	1	
	4. **D**	1	4

Total for test: 28 marks

Forces

Question			Answer	Marks	Total
1	a		acceleration = $\dfrac{\text{change in speed}}{\text{time}}$	1	
			$= \dfrac{0.9}{3}$		
			$= 0.3$	1	
			m/s^2	1	
	b	i	weight = mass × force of gravity	1	
			= 200 × 10		
			= 2000	1	
			N	1	
		ii	force = mass × acceleration	1	
			= 200 × 0.3	1	
			= 60	1	
			N	1	
			Note: it is common in the higher level questions to have to work the answer to one question and use this answer to solve a second problem.		**10 marks**
2	a	i	A combination of:		
			high speed and	1	
			gravity.	1	
		ii	The satellite is:		
			stationary above one point on the planet	1	
			placed in orbit high above the equator	1	
			travelling at same speed as Earth spins.	1	
	b		It may get bigger	1	
			if forces of expansion continue.	1	
			It may collapse (crunch together)	1	
			if forces of gravity take control.	1	**9 marks**
			Note: in questions like this you may only get the first mark if a correct explanation is given, it may otherwise be assumed that you have guessed.		

Answers to module tests and terminal exam questions

3	a	For piston A: $$\text{pressure} = \frac{\text{force}}{\text{area}}$$ $$= \frac{5}{0.1}$$ $$= 50$$ $$\text{N/m}^2$$ For piston B: $$\text{force} = \text{pressure} \times \text{area}$$ $$= 50 \times 1.5$$ $$= 75$$ $$\text{N}$$	1 1 1 1 1 1	
	b	initial volume × initial pressure = final volume × final pressure 700 × 50 = ? × 25 $$\text{final volume} = \frac{35\,000}{25}$$ $$= 1400$$ $$\text{cm}^3$$ *Note: many calculations will be worth 3 marks. This is worth 1 extra mark because you have to re-arrange the formula.*	1 1 1 1 1	**11 marks**
4	a i	$$\text{speed} = \frac{\text{distance}}{\text{time}}$$ $$\text{speed} = \frac{1800}{80}$$ $$= 22.5\,\text{m/s}$$	1 1 1	
	ii	$$\text{acceleration} = \frac{\text{change in speed}}{\text{time}}$$ $$\text{acceleration} = \frac{45 - 30}{3}$$ $$= 15\,\text{m/s}^2$$	1 1 1	
	b	force = mass × acceleration *(but you must rearrange the equation)*: $$\text{mass} = \frac{\text{force}}{\text{acceleration}}$$ $$\text{mass} = \frac{5500}{5}$$ $$= 1100\,\text{kg}$$	1 1 1	
	c	kinetic energy = $\frac{1}{2}mv^2$ kinetic energy = $(\frac{1}{2} \times 1400) \times (30^2)$ kinetic energy = 700 × 900 = 630 000 J or 630 kJ	1 1 1 1	
	d	The force of gravity is accelerating the parachute and the parachutist downwards air pressure (friction) is balancing these downward forces.	1 1 1 1	**17 marks**

Total for test: 47 marks

Answers to module tests and terminal exam questions

Waves and Radiation

Question			Answer	Marks	Total
1	a		Transverse *(but mark only given if explanation given)*	1	
			because disturbances	1	
			at right angles to direction of travel.	1	
	b	i	wave speed = frequency × wavelength	1	
			therefore: wavelength = $\dfrac{\text{wave speed}}{\text{frequency}}$	1	
			= $\dfrac{0.3}{2}$		
			= 0.15	1	
			m(etres)	1	
		ii	(wave diagram with wavelength marked as 1)	1	
	c		(diagram of waves passing through gap)	1	
		ii	Change in speed	1	
			as it crosses the boundary.	1	**11 marks**
2	a	i	Alpha and beta.	2	
		ii	Alpha and gamma.	2	
	b	i	*Any three points from*:		
			• inside the body		
			• they can't pass through skin		
			• strongly absorbed by cells		
			• ionising.	3	
		ii	Two neutrons	1	
			two protons	1	
			a helium nucleus.	1	
	c		*Any two from*:		
			• X-rays for broken bones		
			• killing cancer cells		
			• sterilising equipment.	2	
	d	i	100 s	1	
		ii	300 s	1	
			3 half-lives	1	**15 marks**
3	a		Seismographs.	1	
	b	i	Curves because it refracts	1	
			gentle curve as density changing gradually	1	
			won't pass through liquid	1	
			so changes direction abruptly at point X.	1	
		ii	Will pass through liquids	1	
			changes abruptly at points Y and Z as density changes abruptly.	1	
		iii	Wave A is an S wave	1	
			wave B is a P wave.	1	**9 marks**

Answers to module tests and terminal exam questions

4	a	Refracts back towards normal	1	
		leaves block at 45 degrees.	1	
		In second diagram ray passes straight through, no change in direction.	1	
	b	Different colours have different wavelengths	1	
		so they refract to different extents.	1	
	c i	Seeing	1	
		into people's bodies/gut/blood vessels.	1	
	ii	Light down an optical fibre	1	
		totally internally reflected	1	
		angle between light and normal greater than critical angle	1	
		light rays emerge at the end.	1	
	d i	Radiation that can pass through space/a vacuum	1	
		no particles involved.	1	

	ii	*1 mark deducted for each mistake (maximum loss of 3 marks):*
		  1 gamma rays
		  2 UV rays
		  3 light rays
		  4 microwaves.
			3	

		1 mark deducted for each mistake (maximum loss of 3 marks):
		  1 X-rays
		  2 light rays
		  3 infrared rays
		  4 radio waves.
			3	**19 marks**

5	a i	35% ± 1%	1	
	ii	100 days (5 half-lives).	1	
	b	Work out the proportion of the radioactive substance compared to the substance it decays to.	1	
		Find out the half-life of the radioactive substance.	1	
		Work out how many half-lives have passed and multiply this figure by the number of years for one half-life.	1	
	c	Sterilise food	1	
		sterilise surgical instruments	1	
		kill cancer cells.	1	
	d	*Any three points from:* • waves strongly absorbed • by water • causes increased vibration of particles • the friction caused results in heat.	3	**11 marks**

Total for test: 65 marks

ns to end of spread questions

Answers to end of spread questions

These notes accompany the questions which are to be found at the end of each double-page spread. They are not mark schemes as these questions are not the same as those you will find in your final examination. Where candidates have common misconceptions, these are added to the notes.

Humans as Organisms

Page 3

1.

Enzyme	Where made	What does it do?
carbohydrase	salivary gland pancreas small intestine	digests starch to sugars
protease	stomach pancreas small intestine	digests protein to amino acids
lipase	pancreas small intestine	digests fats to fatty acids and glycerol

2. Acid conditions.
3. Increases the surface area for enzymes to work on. *Pupils frequently do not know this.*

Page 5

1. Glucose: in blood from small intestine from food you eat. *In a later chapter you will find that some may be converted to glycogen in the liver to be stored if there is already too much sugar in the blood.*
   Oxygen: absorbed into blood through alveoli, picked up by haemoglobin and transported to respiring cells in body where it is released. *This is dealt with in detail on the next spread.*
2. It is carried in capillaries away from the cells. Eventually the capillaries form veins. It is transported through the heart and on to the lungs where it diffuses through the alveoli and is breathed out.
3. There is a greater surface area for the gas to diffuse through which prevents any build up (rather like preventing a traffic jam).
   You will find this idea of surface area very important in biology.
4. Diffusion is the movement of particles from an area of higher concentration to an area of lower concentration. There is a greater concentration of oxygen in the lungs than in the blood returning from the body so oxygen diffuses into the blood. The exact opposite is true for carbon dioxide.
5. When we breathe out the ribs move down and in, the diaphragm moves up, this causes an increase in pressure on the air in the lungs – so we breathe out.

Page 7

1. Plasma transports a great many things. Those you need to know are: carbon dioxide, digested food and urea.
2. Veins have thinner walls with less muscle and elastic tissue. They also have valves to prevent backflow of blood. *Remember there are also valves in the heart to prevent backflow of blood.*
3. There are many substances exchanged. Those you need to know are: oxygen, carbon dioxide and glucose.
4. White cells help defend the body against microbes (they ingest or eat them). Red cells transport oxygen (in the haemoglobin as oxy-haemoglobin). Platelets help form scabs over cuts.
5. The red cell passes into the ventricle then the main artery. It then passes into the capillaries which form the blood supply to an organ (e.g. the liver). It will then pass into a vein leading away from the organ. It will eventually find its way into the main vein taking blood back to the right atrium of the heart.

Page 9

1. Viruses have a protein coat surrounding a few genes. There is no cell membrane or nucleus.
2. Toxins are poisons (often produced by invading microbes). White cells produce anti-toxins to neutralise them.
3. White cells will attack the microbes. White cells may produce antibodies and antitoxins to help destroy particular microbes.
4. By having a complete skin (i.e. a skin without any cuts in it). By having the air passages covered in a sticky mucus which helps trap any microbes being breathed in. Also the stomach is acidic.
5. People in much closer contact allowing microbes to transfer from one person to another either by touch or in droplets (e.g. sneezing).

Maintenance of Life

Page 13

1. Your spider diagram should include: cell wall, chlorophyll (chloroplasts) and vacuole.
2. Too cold and less light; enzymes controlling photosynthesis only working very slowly.
3. Diffuses in from air, through stomata, then diffuses through large air spaces to all cells, it then diffuses through the cell walls.
   Note: a question like this could well be worth 4 marks in an exam. Make sure you write in the necessary detail.
4. Starch for storage, cellulose for cell walls, combined with other nutrients to produce proteins for growth.

Answers to end of spread questions

5. It would have poorly formed roots and the younger leaves would have a purple colour.
6. carbon dioxide + water $\xrightarrow[\text{chlorophyll}]{\text{light}}$ glucose + oxygen

Page 15
1. Large surface area.
2. Movement of water from an area where there is a higher concentration of water molecules to one where the concentration is lower.
3. Your diagram should include: to help new cuttings grow roots, to help ripen fruit, and as weedkillers.

Page 17
1. When watching the television the lens was its natural shape (quite thick). This is necessary to bend light rays, which are diverging quickly, to a focus. When looking at your friend the rays of light are not diverging quickly so do not need to be bent as much. The ciliary muscles relax, ligaments attached to the lens pull on the lens, the lens becomes thinner.
2. The hot kettle is the stimulus, sensory nerve endings in the fingers are triggered, a message passes along the sensory nerve to the spinal chord. A relay nerve is triggered and this passes the message on to the correct motor nerve. This nerve takes the message to an effector – in this case a muscle which contracts pulling your hand away from the kettle.
3. The impulse is an electrical message sent through the nerves. Then chemicals are released across the synapses.

Page 19
1. You are respiring quickly to release energy. Some energy is released as heat so you need to cool down. Blood vessels near the skin's surface dilate to allow more blood to flow near the surface. The blood radiates heat. The skin looks red.
2. You have lost a lot of water in sweating. The blood contains less water – it is concentrated. The pituitary gland releases ADH. The kidney tubule walls become more permeable and reabsorb more water. The urine is therefore more concentrated.
3. Your diagram should include: lung cancer, lung disease (emphysema), heart disease and disease of blood vessels.

Environment

Page 23
1. The kestrel is the predator and the mice are prey.
2. The kestrel population would rise as there would be more food to feed their young. The mouse population would, as a result, decrease.
3. Your diagram should refer to: the amount of food available, the number of predators, disease, competition with other animals for the food available.
4. Your food web should show the two producers – seeds and berries. Birds are eating the seeds and berries, mice are eating the seeds only. The mice and birds are being eaten by the kestrels.

Page 25
1. Because a pyramid of numbers does not take account of the fact that some organisms are much larger than others (e.g. a tree and a caterpillar).
2. There are many ways including: excretion, movement, radiated as heat, all of the food is not digested in the first place.
3. There are thousands of examples. You would normally start with a producer much larger than the next stage organism (e.g. rose bush, greenfly and then ladybirds eating the greenfly).

Page 27
1. Photosynthesising, respiring, decomposing, respiring.
2. Carbohydrates, fats and proteins.
3. The dead bodies are decomposed by bacteria, the protein is broken down into ammonium compounds, the ammonium compounds are converted to nitrates by nitrifying bacteria.

Page 29
1. Sulphur dioxide given off, dissolves in rain, this makes the rain acidic as it falls on the lake. The lake water becomes acidic. Enzymes in organisms are very pH dependant. If the enzymes denature because of the acidity the organism dies. *Note: this last point on enzymes is frequently forgotten but is the most important point.*
2. The plants grow quickly, the surface of the pond will quickly become covered by plants. Many plants die. They may fall to the bottom where bacteria will decompose them. Bacteria use up oxygen in this decomposition as they are respiring. There is too little oxygen left for other animals. The process is called eutrophication.
3. You should mention: fewer trees to take it up, alongside this more is being produced by combustion (e.g. cars, power stations, burning trees).
4. The carbon dioxide in the atmosphere absorbs some radiation from the Sun which enters the atmosphere. As less is radiated back out into space the atmosphere warms up.

Inheritance and Selection

Page 33
1. Environmental and genetic.
2. A copy of each chromosome is made so that there are now four of each type of chromosome in the cell. The cell divides twice so that each new cell has only one chromosome from each original pair.
3. Because they have exactly the same genetic make up.
4. 41 chromosomes, one from each original pair.

{width=0}

Answers to end of spread questions

Page 35

1. They have become trapped in the amber where there is no oxygen present. Bacteria cannot decompose them as they cannot respire due to the lack of oxygen. *Note: it must be apparent to you that a number of examination answers rely on the fact that bacteria respire and use up oxygen when they decompose dead organisms.*
2. Any three of: X-rays, UV light, radiation, some chemicals.
3. Pale moths are camouflaged against predators where tree trunks are grey. They therefore survive to breed and dark ones are eaten. The opposite applies in industrial areas.
4. Your diagram should include: environmental change, predators wipe them out, disease wipes them out, a new species evolves which competes successfully with the species.

Page 37

1. Bacteria producing insulin. *Note: if you know a well known example try to use it, some examiners may not have heard of more unusual ones.*
2. The programme only used a certain type of the species – the most attractive ones! The gene pool of the species was therefore reduced (there was less variety of genes present in the population). When disease struck, the gene which helped the animals fight off the disease was no longer present in the population.
3. Taking part of an organism (e.g. a cutting or a cell) and growing a new member of the species from it. The cell division is mitosis.

Page 39

1. One parent is SS the other is Ss. The possible combinations of the genes in the offspring are SS SS Ss or Ss. There is therefore a 50% chance of a child being a carrier (Ss).
2. If the parents do not have the disorder the parents must both be hh as the allele which results in the disorder is dominant (H). There is no chance of any of their children having the disorder.

Metals

Page 43

1. Copper will be displaced by the zinc as zinc is more reactive. Zinc chloride will result.
2. Your diagram should include four of: solid at room temperature, high melting points, shiny, form alloys, mostly strong and tough, good conductors of heat and electricity.
3. It is liquid at room temperature.
4. Burns with a 'squeaky' pop.

Page 45

1. To react with impurities and form molten slag.
2. It is less reactive than aluminium so nothing would happen.
3. It is melted so that electricity will be conducted. It is dissolved in molten cryolite to reduce its melting point and save the manufacturer money. *Note: if there is an economic point to make in the answer to a question then it is always advisable to mention it.*

Page 47

1. A reaction where one reactant is reduced whilst another reactant is oxidised.
2. A reaction where hydrogen ions are reacted with hydroxide ions.
3. potassium chloride   potassium sulphate
   calcium chloride   calcium sulphate
4. potassium hydroxide + hydrochloric acid → potassium chloride + water
   or KOH + HCl → KCl + H_2O
5. $SO_2 + H_2O \rightarrow H_2SO_3$ (sulphurous acid)

Earth Materials

Page 51

1. Their shapes seem to fit together and they seem to have similar rocks and fossils.
2. Tectonic plates sliding past each other. It is only movements of the plates that causes earthquakes. If there are no mountains then the plates cannot be moving towards each other. If they were moving apart there would be no earthquake.
3. The iron stripes are basically iron rich magma. The iron lines up in the direction of the Earth's magnetic field. This field changes. There is therefore an indication of when the magma erupted showing that the sea floor is spreading.

Page 53

1. The sedimentary rock could be forced deep below the Earth's crust. It would melt and become magma.
2. It is intrusive igneous rock usually cooling beneath the Earth's surface. The crystals are likely to be large as the rock is likely to cool quite slowly below the Earth's surface.
3. Metamorphic rocks are formed from other rocks which are put under great pressure and heat at the same time. This is most likely to occur where mountains are forming.

Page 55

1. If the igneous rock is worn away (eroded) it may eventually become sedimentary rock. If the sedimentary rock is placed under great heat and pressure then it may become metamorphic rock.
2. Sedimentary rock is continually being worn away exposing more fossils. Movements of the sedimentary rocks (e.g. folding) may result in more fossils being exposed.
3. These are formed by processes far beneath the Earth's surface. Organisms did not live there.

Answers to end of spread questions

Page 57

1. Porous rock is likely to contain water. Oil floats on water. It cannot rise any further as non-porous rock will not let liquids through it.
2. Oil is a mixture.
3. Short-chain hydrocarbons burn easily, evaporate quite quickly and are generally gases or liquids – no use for roads! Long-chain hydrocarbons are thick (very viscous) and do not burn easily – no use for fuels!

Page 59

1. One of the bonds in the carbon–carbon double bond can break leaving the two carbon atoms free to react with another element.
2. Not all long-chain hydrocarbons can be used. There may be too much of them. They can be broken ('cracked') into short-chain hydrocarbons which may be useful as fuels, etc. Essentially they are 'cracked' so that oil companies can make more money! Alkenes also result, which can be used to make plastics.
3. They may give off chemicals which are harmful to the environment.

Page 61

1. It is increasing as more and more fuels are burned (e.g. there are more cars in the world). Therefore more gases are given off (e.g. sulphur dioxide and nitrogen oxides) which cause acid rain.
2. Partly due to the reaction between ammonia and oxygen and partly due to organisms evolving which subsequently died and decomposed releasing nitrogen. Denitrifying bacteria are involved in this nitrogen release.
3. Less carbon dioxide as it became locked up in sedimentary rocks and fossil fuels as well as being used by plants in photosynthesis. Less ammonia and methane because they reacted with oxygen (given off by plants). More oxygen due to photosynthesising plants. The oxygen also helped develop an ozone layer protecting us from the Sun's radiation (UV rays). *Note: these changes in the atmosphere questions are nearly always poorly answered, even by the best of candidates.*

Pattern of Chemical Change

Page 65

1. Any three of: increase temperature – particles bump into each other more often with more energy; increase concentration – particles bump into each other more often; increase pressure (gases only) – particles bump into each other more often; increase surface area of reactants – particles bump into each other more often; use a catalyst – lowers the amount of 'activation' energy required.
2. Chemicals which speed up reactions – they are used to lower costs.
3. Make more product or make more profit.

Page 67

1. A reaction which releases heat.
2. One atom of nitrogen reacts with two atoms of oxygen, you must 'add' energy to make them react, the product is nitrogen dioxide and it is at a higher energy level than the reactants. Therefore the reaction is endothermic.
3. Endothermic (the nett energy transfer is positive).

Page 69

1. Your diagram should include: bacteria used to make yoghurt, yeast used to make alcohol and cause bread to rise.
2. A reaction which, depending on the conditions, will go either way.
3. It would be expensive to create temperatures of 350°C and equally expensive to create reaction vessels capable of withstanding pressures of 400 atmospheres.

Page 71

1. $2 \times H = 2 \times 1 = 2$
   $1 \times S = 32$
   $4 \times O = 4 \times 16 = 64$ Answer = 98
2. $1 \times Ca = 40$
   $1 \times C = 12$
   $3 \times 16 = 48$ Total = 100
   of which oxygen = $\frac{48}{100}$
   or 48%

Page 72

1. $2H_2O_2$ and $2H_2O$. *Note: you will almost certainly have to balance at least one equation in the examination.*
2. M_r ammonia is 17. M_r ammonium hydroxide is 35. Therefore 34 g of ammonia will produce 2×35 g of ammonium hydroxide, or 70 g.
3. A_r magnesium is 24. Therefore 24 g of magnesium will evolve 24 litres of hydrogen. However there are 48 g of magnesium reacting. The volume of hydrogen evolved would be 2×24 litres or 48 litres.

Structures and Bonding

Page 75

1. When ice melts the bonds between the water molecules have become weaker. The molecules are able to move over one another.
2. 2, 8, 7.
3. Four.
4. Magnesium 2, 8, 2; silicon 2, 8, 4; argon 2, 8, 8; oxygen 2, 6.

Page 77

1. Your diagram of calcium should have 2 electrons in the first and fourth shells with eight electrons in the second and third shells.
2. Calcium needs to lose two electrons, chlorine can gain only one electron. Therefore calcium needs two chlorine atoms to react with. The formula of calcium chloride must be $CaCl_2$.

Answers to end of spread questions

3 You should draw the structure 2, 8, 8 within a bracket. Outside of the bracket should be two positive charges.

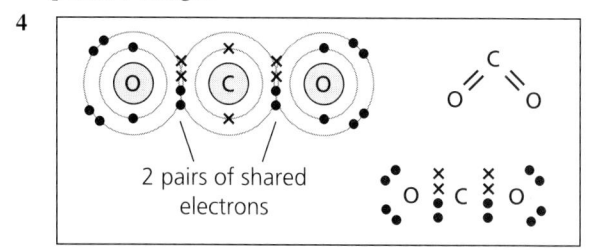

4

Page 79

1 The bonds between molecules are generally weak and easily broken.
2 Each carbon atom is covalently bonded to four other carbon atoms. The structure is a giant structure which is rigid owing to the strong bonds between the atoms.

Page 81

1 The one outer electron in potassium is at a higher energy level than that of the outer electron in sodium, as it is further from the nucleus. The electron is therefore more easily 'lost'.
2 When they react with water an alkaline solution is left (e.g. sodium reacts with water to produce sodium hydroxide with hydrogen gas evolving).
3 They have a complete outer shell of electrons.
4 Xenon is present simply as single atoms. In chlorine two atoms bond together, covalently, to form a molecule of the gas (hence diatomic).

Page 83

1 Your diagram should include: chlorine used for killing bacteria, it is also used in disinfectants, bleaches and to produce plastics (e.g. PVC or polyvinyl chloride); hydrogen is used in the production of ammonia and margarine; sodium hydroxide is used in the production of soap, paper and ceramics.
2 Chloride ions are attracted, they lose electrons to become atoms, pairs covalently bond together to form chlorine gas molecules which evolve. *Note: in an examination a question like this could be worth 4 marks – it would be insufficient to state simply that chlorine gas evolves.*
3 They only need to gain one electron as they are only one electron 'short' in the outer shell.
4 Chlorine would displace bromine from hydrogen bromide. *Remember that reactivity decreases as you go down the group – the opposite to the alkali metals in group 1.*

Energy

Page 87

1 Radiation.
2 The air above the radiator warms up. It becomes less dense. The air rises. It spreads across the ceiling and cools a little. It becomes denser and so falls in other parts of the room. It is still quite warm and therefore the person feels the warmer air. Some heat will also be radiated from the radiator.
3 Air between the bricks is still likely to warm slightly – the insulation prevents convection of this air. Such convection would draw cooler air into the bottom of the wall.

Page 89

1 $\frac{1500}{60(s)} = 25\,\text{W}$
2 $500 \times 2300 = 1\,150\,000\,\text{J}$ or $1150\,\text{kJ}$

Page 91

1 Hair drier as movement (the fan) and heat; toaster as heat; television as sound and light; vacuum cleaner as movement.
2 It would still save money over a long period of time. It also cuts down any noise pollution.

Page 93

1 Examples might include:

Energy source	Advantage	Disadvantage
coal	fairly cheap	will eventually run out
hydroelectric	renewable	only useful in certain areas
nuclear	much energy from a small amount of fuel	non-renewable
wind turbine	renewable	spoils the landscape
tidal	renewable	expensive to set up

2 Hydroelectric, wind turbine, tidal.
3 Hilltops as they are exposed to the wind, coastal areas as there is more likelihood of wind, off-shore as this is less unsightly.

Electricity

Page 97

1 You can show how power can be calculated using this series of equations:

$$\frac{\text{power}}{\text{(watts)}} = \frac{\text{energy transferred (joules)}}{\text{time (seconds)}}$$

energy transferred = potential difference × charge
(joules)   (volts)   (coulombs)

charge (coulombs) = current (amps) × time

$$\frac{\text{power}}{\text{(watts)}} = \frac{\text{potential difference} \times \text{current} \times \cancel{\text{time}}}{\cancel{\text{time}}}$$

power = potential difference × current
(watts)   (volts)   (amps)

Answers to end of spread questions

2 The electricity passes through a filament which offers resistance. As well as the filament becoming hot some energy is emitted as light.

Page 99

1 In the first graph: the current is directly proportional to the voltage (this means it increases at the same rate). If you reverse the voltage you reverse the current.
   In the second graph: at first the current increases rapidly as you increase the voltage, however as you further increase the voltage the current increases more and more slowly. If you reverse the voltage you reverse the current.
   In the third graph: the current is directly proportional to the voltage. However if you reverse the voltage you get very little current flowing at all. This component offers great resistance to current flowing in the 'wrong' direction.

2 Static electricity builds up in the clouds. If the charge becomes large enough it will jump the gap to an earthed conductor – the umbrella!

Page 101

1 The current is continually changing direction.
2 They can be reset quickly and work more quickly than a fuse.
3 Increase the current, or the number of turns in the coil, or place a soft iron core in the coil.

Page 103

1 There should be reference to: when you switch the current on the coil becomes an electromagnet; it reacts with the force fields of the magnets present and moves; when it becomes vertical momentum takes it past the position; the split ring keeps reversing the current so that the coil keeps spinning.
2 There should be reference to: when you switch the current on the coil becomes an electromagnet; it interacts with the magnetic field of the magnets; the coil moves in and out as a result of these interactions.
3 The current required to start a car is very high. Such a high current would require very thick, expensive wires. You would want these to be as short as possible. Therefore long, thin wires are attached to the ignition on the dashboard and when a current flows they trigger a much larger current in the short, thick wires.

Page 105

1 The secondary coil has 50 times as many turns as the primary coil. The voltage induced will, therefore, be 50 times greater than the input voltage. $50 \times 200 = 10\,000$ V.
2 You want the output voltage to be $\frac{1}{25}$ of the input voltage $\frac{5000}{200}$. The ratio of primary coils to secondary coils is therefore 25:1.

Forces

Page 109

1 Average velocity = distance/time = $\frac{60}{4}$ = 15 m/s
   Acceleration = change in velocity/time = $\frac{(60 - 0)}{4} = \frac{60}{4} = 15$ m/s^2

2 Your graph should have these features:

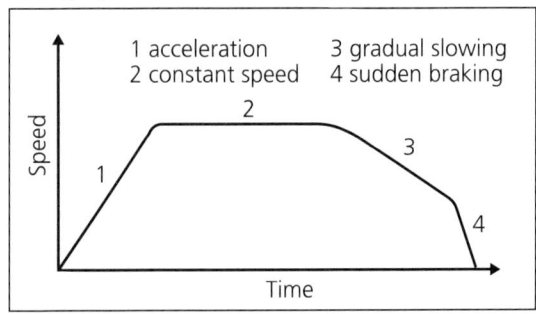

   1 acceleration   3 gradual slowing
   2 constant speed 4 sudden braking

   (Speed vs Time graph showing phases 1, 2, 3, 4)

3 Velocity is speed in a straight line (velocity is a vector).

Page 111

1 For example, if your mass is 57 kg then your weight is 57×10 N or 570 N.
2 The downward force due to the weight of the boat (due to gravity) is balanced by the upward force of the water.
3 There is a backward force exerted by the car engine. There is a force resisting this caused by both air resistance and the friction of the tyres on the ground. The forces are unbalanced so the car moves backwards.
4 Kinetic energy = $\frac{1}{2}mv^2$
   Therefore ($\frac{1}{2} \times 100) \times 30^2$.
   This equals 50×900 or $45\,000$ J or 45 kJ.

Page 113

1 Force = mass × acceleration.
   Therefore force = $1000 \times 6 = 6000$ N. *Note: the weight of the car was 10 000 N therefore its mass is 1000 kg.*
2 Work done = force × distance. The force is therefore $10\,000$ N × 50 m or $500\,000$ J or 500 kJ.
3 The force of gravity causes the stone to accelerate as it falls. At a certain speed the pressure of the air prevents the stone falling any faster. The forces are now balanced and the stone falls at steady speed. This steady speed is known as the terminal velocity. *Note: never answer this question just by stating 'terminal velocity'. The question asks what has happened not what is it called.*

Answers to end of spread questions

Page 115

1. The master cylinder: pressure = force/area so the pressure is $\frac{20}{0.1}$ or $200\,\text{N/m}^2$.
   The slave cylinder: force = pressure × area so the force = 200×0.4 or $80\,\text{N}$.
   Note: the calculation can be done using simple ratios. The slave cylinder has an area 4 times that of the slave cylinder. The force it exerts will be 4 times greater: $4 \times 20 = 80\,N$.

2. The pressure is so great and there is no light.

Page 117

1. Weather, communication, to see the Universe without atmospheric interference.

2. Placed in orbit high above the equator, at the same speed as the Earth is spinning.

3. So that the Earth spins below; the whole of the Earth can be scanned in a day.

4. In the stable period the star stays the same size as the forces of attraction (between all of the particles, due to gravity) and repulsion (due to the very high temperatures) are balanced. The forces of repulsion will start to 'win' and the star will become a red giant. These forces then begin to decrease and so the force of gravity becomes the larger force. The star contracts to become a white dwarf. If the star was large enough and contraction takes place quickly then it may explode and become a supernova. A very dense neutron star remains.
   Note: a question about this may be worth about 5 marks – do not waffle make sure that you write down five correct facts in the right order.

Page 118

1. As galaxies are moving apart quickly the wavelength of light is increasing. As it increases red light moves into the far red part of the spectrum. This is known as the 'red shift'.

2. As galaxies move away light is shifted to the red end of the spectrum.

Waves and Radiation

Page 121

1. As the light passes from one substance into a substance of a different density it changes speed. This change of speed results in the light bending. This is known as refraction.

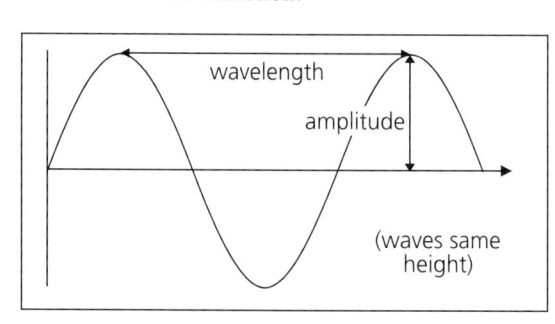

2. [Diagram showing a wave with labels "wavelength", "amplitude" and note "(waves same height)"]

Page 123

1. They are checking for structural defects (e.g. cracks).

2. P waves travel through solids and liquids. S waves only pass through liquids. They both refract as they pass into substances of a different density. *(Note: liquids will also change in density.)* If you know the point of the Earth the shock wave starts from and where it can be detected as it is felt at a different point of the Earth's surface, then you can work out the densities of the substances it has passed through to result in the refraction the wave has experienced.

Page 125

1. X-rays (shortest), UV, microwave, radio waves (longest).

2. Any two of: electric grills, toasters, heaters, optical fibres and video remote controls.

3. The white light from the Sun passes through water droplets. The light is refracted to different extents and therefore the colours are seen.

Page 127

1. A light is shone down the endoscope. The light totally internally reflects so emerges only at the end of the endoscope. It internally reflects because the angle at which the light 'hits' the side of the endoscope is greater than the critical angle.

2. As the water enters the harbour entrance the waves spread out from the edges and cause the boat to 'bob'. This is known as diffraction.

Page 129

1. UV radiation. Advantages might include giving people a sun tan and making them feel better within themselves. Disadvantages might include burns and possible skin cancer.

2. Beta and gamma radiation will pass through very thick paper.

3. Uranium loses an alpha particle (two protons and two electrons). Thorium loses a beta particle (and one proton becomes a neutron).

Page 131

1. 200 years (two half-lives).

2. Uranium has 92 protons and 92 electrons (so as an atom is electrically neutral). It has 146 neutrons.

3. They use control rods to absorb the neutrons (these are generally made of boron or cadmium).

Index

A

absorption, and surface area 2, 3
acceleration
 formulae 109, 113
 speed and velocity 108–11
acid rain 28, 60
acids
 acid-alkali reactions 46
 pH scale 47
activation energy 67
active transport 4, 15
aerobic respiration 4
alcohol 19
alkali metals 81
alkalinity, pH scale 47
alkanes/alkenes 58
alleles 32, 38
alpha particles 128, 130
alternating current 104
aluminium
 extraction by electrolysis 45
 reactivity 42–3
alveoli 5
amino acids 2, 3
ammeter 96
ammonia, structure 76
ammonium compounds 27
ammonium nitrate, Haber process 68–9
anaemia, sickle cell 38–9
anaerobic respiration 5
anode 44–6
antibodies 9
antitoxins 9
argon (noble gas) 60, 75, 81, 131
arteries 7
asexual reproduction 33
atmosphere, and green plant evolution 60–1
atomic mass 70
atomic number 80
atomic structure 74–5
atom(s)
 mass number 74
 theories 130
atria 6

B

background radiation 129
bacteria 6, 8–9, 27
 see also microbes
basaltic rock 50, 52
beta particles 128
big bang theory 118
bile 3
biomass pyramid 24
birth control 37
blast furnace 44
blood cells
 red 6
 white 6, 9
blood sugar 19
blood vessels, types 7
body temperature, thermoregulatory centre 19
boiling point 74
bonds
 bond energy 66
 covalent 76–7
 double 77
 ionic 76
brakes, force multipliers 114
braking distance 112
breathing and respiration 4–5
bronze 42
burning see combustion

C

calcium carbonate 52, 54, 70–1
calcium hydroxide 42, 54
calcium oxide 54
cancer 34, 129
capillaries 7
 thermoregulation 19
car
 acceleration 110
 stopping distance 112
carbohydrases 2
carbohydrates 2
carbon cycle 26, 61
carbon dioxide
 absorption by plants 12, 13
 carbon cycle 26, 60–1
 carbonates 52, 54, 61
 carbonic acid 47
 greenhouse effect 29, 60
 from respiration 4, 18
 transport 7
carbon monoxide, blast furnace 44
carbonates 52, 54, 61
catalysts/catalysis 2, 64–5, 81
cathode 44–6
cell division 32–3
cell membrane 2, 8, 12
cell wall 12
cells 2
 bacterial 8
 plant and animal 12–13
cellulose 13
cement 55
charge (electric current) 96
chemical equations 72, 77
chemical formulae 71
chemical quantities 70–1
chemical reactions
 see reactions
chemical structures, and bonding 74–83, 84
chlorides 46, 76
chlorine 77, 83
 isotopes 130
chlorophyll/chloroplasts 12
chromosomes 32, 36
 definition 39
circuit breakers 101
circuits 97
 symbols 97
circulatory system 6
cloning, and clones 33, 36
combustion 60
community
 definition 22
 stability 27
competition and survival 22–3
compounds 76–80
 chemical formulae 71
 covalent 78
 formation 46–7
 ionic 78, 99
 metal-halogen 82
 properties 47
 reactions see reactions
 relative formula mass 70–1
 structure and properties 78–83
concentration 64
concentration gradient 14
concrete 55
conduction 86
continental drift 50
contraception 36–7
convection 86
copper, uses 42
copper purification, by electrolysis 45
covalent bonds/compounds 76–8
current
 alternating (a.c.) 100, 104
 direct (d.c.) 102
current-voltage graphs 98
cystic fibrosis 38
cytoplasm 2, 8, 12

D

Dalton, John 80
decomposition processes 26–8, 61
deforestation 29
diabetes 19
diamond, structure 78–9
diaphragm 3, 4
diffraction 126
diffusion 3, 74
digestion 2–3
digestive system 3
disease
 defence against 8–9
disorders
 inherited 38
distillation, fractional 56–7
DNA 39
dominant gene 38
door bell 102
drugs, effects 19

E

Earth
 materials 50–63
 structure 50–1, 123
 tectonic plates 50
earthing (appliances) 100
earthquakes 51, 123
effectors 17
electric plug, wiring 100
electrical appliances 88, 90–1
electricity 96–107
 generation 92–3
 manufacture 104–5
 measurement 96–7
 safety 100
 static 98–9
 use 88–9, 100–1
electrode 44
electrolysis 44–5, 82–3, 99
electromagnetic radiation 124–5
electromagnets 101–3
electrons 75, 81
elements 80–3
 percentage 70
embryo transplant 36
emulsification 3
endoscope 127
endothermic reaction 66
energy
 activation energy 67
 changes 67
 costs 89
 efficiency 90–1
 geothermal 93
 gravitational potential 89
 kinetic 111
 loss from buildings 87
 release, chemical reactions 66–7
 renewable/non-renewable 92
 solar 23, 29, 93
 sources 92–3
 tidal/wind 92
energy levels, electrons 75
energy transfer 60, 90–1
 amount (formulae) 96
 in appliances 90
 radiation 86
 rate 96
 types 86–7
environment 22–9
enzymes 2, 28, 68
equations, balancing 72
equilibrium 69
ethane/ethene 58
eutrophication 28

Index

evaporation 14, 74
evolution 34
exothermic reaction 66
extinction 35
extraction of metals 44–5
eye 16

F

fat, emulsification 3
fermentation 68
fertilisers 28
   ammonium nitrate 68
   production 68–9
fertility 36–7
follicle stimulating hormone (FSH) 37
food, digestion 2–3
food chains and webs 23–5
force multipliers 114
force(s) 108–18, 119
   balanced/unbalanced 110
   formula 113
   stretching 114
formula mass 70, 111
fossil fuels 29
fossils 35, 55
fractional distillation 57
friction, and work 112
fuses 100

G

galaxies 117
gall bladder 3
gametes 32
gamma radiation 125, 128
gases 60–1, 83, 115
   diatomic 77
   greenhouse 60
   noble 60, 75, 81
   polluting 60
   pressure/volume 115
   properties 74–5, 86–7
   volume of 71
generator, a.c. 104–5
genes 8
   alleles 32
   gene transfer 36
   in inheritance 38–9
   mutation 34
genetic engineering 36
geothermal energy 93
glands 2
glass 55
glucagon 19
granitic rock 50
graphite 78–9
gravitational potential energy 89
gravity 111, 116
greenhouse effect 29, 60
growth, mitosis 33

H

Haber process 68–9
haemoglobin 6
half-life 130
halides, uses 83
halogens 82
heart 6–7
heat loss, from buildings 87, 91
heat transfer 86–7
helium see noble gases
hertz (Hz) 121
heterozygous/homozygous 38–9
hormones 15, 18
   fertility 36–7
   menstrual cycle 37
   plant, effects on seedling 15
human biology 2–9, 16–19
   inheritance 38–9
human effects on environment 28–9
Huntington's chorea 37–8
hydraulic systems 114
hydrocarbons 56–9
   saturated/unsaturated 58
hydrochloric acid, stomach 3
hydroelectric power 93
hydrogen
   metal reactivity 47
   uses 83
hydrogen chloride 76
hydrogen test 42

I

igneous rock 52, 54
   intrusive and extrusive 52
immunity 9
infrared radiation 86, 125, 128
inheritance, and selection 32–9
insulation, heat 91
insulators 86
insulin 19, 36
intestine 3
ionic bonds 76
ionic compounds 78, 99
ionisation 129
ions 18, 44
iron
   extraction 44
   uses 42
iron oxide 71
isotopes 75, 130

J

joule, kilojoule 66, 88

K

kidney, function 18
kilowatt 88
kinetic energy, and formula 111

L

lactic acid 5
large intestine 3
lattices 78–9
leaf structure 13
lens, of eye 16
light
   critical angle 127
   for photosynthesis 12
limestone 52, 54
lipases 2
lipids 2
liquids 74–5
lithium atom 81
liver 3, 19
loudspeaker 103
lungs, gas exchange 5
luteinising hormone 37

M

magma 51–2
magnesium atom 75
magnesium oxide 42
malaria 39
marble 53
mass(es)
   atomic 70
   formula 70, 111
   reactants and products 70–1
materials see compounds
matter, states of 74
meiosis 32, 33
melting point 74
membrane 2
Mendeléev's Periodic Table 80
menstrual cycle, hormone control 37
metals 42–9, 78
   alkali metals 80–1
   extraction from ore 44–5
   metal-halogen compounds 82
   non-metals 43
   properties 42
   reactivity series 42–3
   transition metals 81
   uses 42–3
metamorphic rock 53–4
methane gas 29, 61, 66
microbes 6, 8–9, 68–9
   decomposition 26–8, 61
microwave radiation 125, 128
Milky Way 117
mirage 127
mitosis 33
mole, defined 71
monomers 58
Moon, gravity 116
motor, d.c. 102
motor neurone 17

muscles 2
mutation 34

N

natural selection 34–5
neon see noble gases
neurone, motor/sensory/relay 17
neutral wire 100
neutralisation reaction 46
neutron star 117
neutron(s), number 74
newton (unit) 111
nitrates 13, 27, 46
   Haber process 68–9
nitrifying bacteria 27
nitrogen 60–1
nitrogen cycle 27
noble gases 60, 75, 81, 131
non-metals 43
normal, definition 120
nuclear fission 131
nucleus
   atomic 75
   cell 2, 12

O

oestrogens 37
oil and products 56–7
optical fibres 127
orbit
   geostationary 116
   polar 116
organs and systems 2, 12
osmosis 14
oxidation 46, 60
oxygen
   release by plants 12
   structure 77
   transport 6, 7
oxygen debt 5
oxyhaemoglobin 6

P

pancreas 3, 19
paper production 129
periodic table 80–3
pH scale 47
phloem vessels 14
phosphate 13
photosynthesis 12–13
pituitary gland 18, 36–7
planets 116
plants
   cells 12–13
   and food production 12
   hormones 15
   nutrient deficiency 13
   responses 15
   water loss 14–15
plasma 6
plastics 58, 79
   thermosetting 79
   thermosoftening 79

Index

plate tectonics and polarity 50
platelets 6
polluting gases 60
polymers 58–9, 79
   addition polymerisation 58
   alkanes and alkenes 58–9
polythene, formation 59
population
   animal 22
   control 22, 28
porous rock 56
potassium
   in plants 13
   radioisotope 131
   reactivity 43
   structure 81
potassium hydroxide 47
potential difference (p.d.) 96
potential energy 89
power
   hydroelectric 93
   measurement 88
   solar 93
   steam 93
   tidal/wind 92
power supplies 97
predators/prey 22
pressure
   formula 114
   reaction rate 64
proteases 2
proteins 2, 13, 27
proton(s) 80
   number 74
PVC (polychloroethene), formation 59
pyramids (number/biomass) 24–5

Q
quartz (silicon dioxide) 78
quicklime 54

R
radiation 23, 86, 120–32
   alpha/beta/gamma 128
   background 129
   electromagnetic 124–5
   energy transfer 86
   gamma 125, 128
   infrared 86, 125, 128
   microwave 125, 128
   and mutation 34
   sources 129
   ultraviolet 34, 125, 128
   use in industry 129
   X rays 125, 128
radio waves 124
radioactive decay 129–31
   half-life 130–1
radioactive substances 128–9
radionuclides 130–1
radium 129
radon 129

reactions
   displacement 82–3
   endothermic/exothermic 66
   energy changes 67
   energy release 66–7
   rate and surface area 64–5
   redox 46–7
   reversible 69
reactivity series 43
receptors 17, 19
recessive genes 38
red giant 117
red shift 118
reduction 44, 46
reflection 120, 122–3
   total internal 127
reflex actions 17
refraction 120
relay, (electricity) 103
relay neurone 17
reproduction
   asexual 33
   control of 36–7
   sexual 32
resistance, electrical 96, 98–9
resistors
   defined 96
   light and temperature dependent 98–9
respiration
   aerobic 4
   anaerobic 5
   in plants 13
retina 16
right atrium/ventricle 6
rock
   basaltic/granitic 50
   dating 131
   formation/transformation 54
   fossils 35
   igneous 52, 54
   intrusive/extrusive 52
   metamorphic 53–4
   molten 51–2
   porous 56
   sedimentary 52–4
rock cycle 54
root hair cell 14
roots, active transport 15
Rutherford, Ernest 130

S
safety symbols 64
salivary gland 3
salts 46
sandstone 52
satellites 116
schists 53
sea-floor spreading, magnetic stripes 51
sedimentary rock
   fossils 55
   movement 53–4

seismograph 123
selection and inheritance 32–9
selective breeding 36
sensory neurone 17
sewage 28
sex determination 38
sexual reproduction 32–3
shale 53
sickle cell anaemia 38–9
silica/silicon dioxide 78
silver halides, uses 83
slag 44
slaked lime 54
small intestine 3
smoking 19
sodium
   atom, structure 75, 81
   chlorine, reaction 76
   reactivity 43
sodium chloride 82, 99
   giant lattice 78
sodium hydroxide 77, 83
solar energy 23, 29, 93
solar power 93
solar system 116–17
solids 74–5
solvents 19
space, movement in 116–17
species 32
speed, velocity 108–9
spinal cord 17
starch 13
stars 117–18
state symbols 77
steam 93
stomach 3
stomata, transpiration 13, 14
stretching force 114
sugar 18
sulphuric acid/sulphates 46, 70
supernova 117
surface area
   absorption 2, 3
   leaf 13
   lungs 5
   reaction rate 64
   root hairs 14
   villi 3
sweat glands 19
symbols
   safety 64
   state 77
synapse 17
systems and organs 2, 12

T
tectonic plates 50
temperature, reaction rate 18, 64
thermoregulation 19
thermosoftening (plastic) 79
tidal power 92
tissue culture 36

tissues 2, 12
toxins 8
transformers 105
transition metals 81
transpiration, stomata 13, 14–15
transport
   active 4, 15
   in plants 15
turgidity 14

U
ultrasonic waves 122
ultraviolet radiation 125, 128
   mutation 34
Universe, origin and future 117–18
uranium, half-life 130–1
urea 18
ureter 18
uterus 36

V
vacuole (cell) 12
veins 7
velocity
   acceleration and speed 108–9
   terminal 112
velocity–time graphs 109
ventricles 6
villi 3
viruses 8
volcanic emissions 52, 60
voltage, voltmeter 96

W
water
   chemical structure 76
   control in body 18
   in plants 14
wavelength 121
waves
   diffraction 126
   measurement 121
   movement 120–1
   radio waves 124
   refraction 120
   total internal reflection 127
   transverse/longitudinal 121
   ultrasonic 122
white dwarf 117
wilting 14
wind farms 92
work, formula 113

X
X-rays 125, 128
   mutations 34
xylem vessels 12, 14

Z
zinc, reactions 42